THE HISTORY OF
LOGIC

THE HISTORY OF LOGIC

EDITED BY
JOHN H. PIET
AND
AYODHYA PRASAD

COSMO PUBLICATIONS
2000 INDIA

THE HISTORY OF LOGIC

First COSMO Print 2000

ISBN 81-7755-007-1

*This indipendent and complete volume has been derived from the set - **Encyclopaedia of ETHICS AND LOGIC***

Published by

MRS. RANI KAPOOR
for COSMO PUBLICATIONS Div. of
GENESIS PUBLISHING PVT. LTD.
24-B, Ansari Road,
Darya Ganj,
New Delhi-110 002, INDIA

Composed at

Cosmo Publications

Printed at

Mehra Offset Press

CONTENTS

Chapter-1

Sketch of the History of Logic

Chapter 1

1. One of the latest speculative discoveries at which the civilised man arrives is the high expedience of drawing as sharp and distinct a line as possible around each several science[1] (the word "science" being here taken in its highest sense, as any kind or quantum of knowledge that has been reduced to rules).

2(a). The naturalists have in modern times at least set the example and furnish us with an illustration.[2] It is not indeed improbable that Aristotle himself, who in his logical and metaphysical works has devoted so large a space to the principles of definition, distinction, and distribution, was led to the subject by the experience required in his *physical* researches.[3] Impressed with the necessity of method to the successful cultivation of *natural philosophy,* and sensible that a method, which should be suited to all understandings, must be drawn from the laws and constitution of the understanding itself, he invented *logic* as a supplement to mathematics and the other organ (οργανον δευτερον)[4] of the *real* sciences. To this view of the art, compared with which its uses as a groundwork of rhetoric and a training for forensic debate are but accessory and of equivocal worth, we may, I repeat, not improbably attribute the noticeable fact that in one and the same great mind we venerate the inventor of logic and the father of natural philosophy. Equally singular, through calculated to excite very different emotions, in the fact, for fact it is, that he defect for the prevention of which logic was invented is perhaps nowhere more strikingly exemplified than in the most popular modern books, French and English, professing to *teach* logic and having its name as their title. In some of these (as in Dr. Watts' *logic,*[5] for instance) the essentials of common logic, which have remained without change from their first pr-omulgation by Aristotle and which are indeed as little sus-ceptible of change as the rules of common arithmetic, are to be found, but so blended with metaphysics, theology, psychology, grammar, and in short what not, that had it been the professed object of these writers to teach the art of comparison instead of the science of method they could scarcely have adopted a more successful plan.[6] In the far-famed *Logic* of Condillac, on the other hand, the student may find the whole theory of materialism (borrowed without acknowledgment from David Hartley) only not one syllable concerning logic itself.[7] How different has been the course pursued by the great naturalists of this and the preceding century,[8] who, rather than hazard co-nfusion by coordinating heterogeneous subjects, have chosen to create a new class-genus or species as the occasion appeared to warrant—and who at all times have preferred the inco-nvenience of a newly minted or obsolete term to the evil of a loose and equivocal designation, however the latter had been familiarised by usage or sanctioned by authority.[9]

2(b). If this insight into the distinct import of terms as well as into the necessity of new or newly defined terms for the expression of different objects be of high importance in science, the extension of the process to words in general as the exponents of all our thoughts and notices is no less fruitful and expedient in our practical concerns and in the intercourse of ordinary life. We may even assert that it is this power and habit which above all others marks and constitutes the int-ellectual superiority of one man over another. It need scarcely be observed that this approximate use of words canot exist without a proportionably indistinct knowledge of things.[10] The rules, however, by the knowledge of which the process is faci-litated, and by the acquirement of which the mind is led to the perception of its necessity, belong to logic.

2(c). But here arises a question of no mean importance. In what state do we suppose or require the mind of the individual to be to whom these rules are to be presented? The scheme of arranging the communication of knowledge scientifically, so as to begin with that knowledge which requires or supposes no other previous knowledge in order to its intelligibility, and much more the notion of teaching the sciences in a predetermined series on the same principle, such a scheme, I say, were it even feasible in itself (which in relation to the human intellect is more than doubtful) must at all events be impracticable in that state of society in which alone the sciences can be imagined to exist.

3. In the infancy and childhood of individuals (and something analogous may be traced in the history of communities) the first knowledges are acquired promiscuously.- Say rather that the plan is not formed by the selection of the objects presented to the notice of the pupils, but by the impulses and dispositions suited to their age, by the limits of their comprehension, by the volatile and desultory activity of their attention, and by the relative predominance or the earlier devel-opment of one or more faculties over the rest. This is the happy delirium, the healthful fever, of the physical, moral, and intellectual being, Nature's kind and providential gift to childhood.[11]

4. In the best good sense of the words, it is the light-headedness and light-heartedness of human life! There is indeed "method in't",[12] but it is the method of Nature, which thus stores the mind with all the materials for after use, promiscuously indeed, and as it might seem without purpose, while the supplies a gay and motley chaos of facts, and forms, and thousandfold experiences, the origin of which lies beyond memory, traceless as life itself and finally passing into a part of our life more rapidly than would have been compatible with distinct consciousness and with a security beyond the power of choice! Or shall we call this genial impulse a will *within* the will,[13] that forms the basis of choice and the succedaneum of instinct, which the conscious choice will perfect into knowledge? Promiscuously we have said, and seemingly without design,and yet by this seeming confusion alone could Nature (by which we would be always understood to mean the Divine Providence in the creation) have effected her wise purpose, without encr-

oachment on the native freedom of the soul and without either precluding, superseding, or overlaying, the inventive, the experimentative, combinatory, and judicial powers.[14]

5. But not alone this storing of the mind with the common notices of things, together with those expressions for the same which we acquire by imitation as our mother-tongue, not this alone is necessarily antecedent to all systematic study. The same holds good with regard to the rules and the habits of orderliness or arrangement, regulated by purposes of use and expedience relatively to time and place, to the object and the individuals immediately concerned. And for these likewise ample provision have been made by the necessities that continue the human animal for so long a time under care and governance; in short by the domestic state, and by the social, which is the extension of the domestic; both which, conjointly, are as truly the *natural* state of man, as the wilderness is that of the tiger, and the sea that of the solitary shark.

6. As far as concerns facts, or the knowledge of things derived immediately from the individual's own observation, enough and even more than the child has distinct places for in its memory, or powers of perception to distinguish, come of their own accord. Man's first effort in his behoof is to render him a *social* being; capable of communication and consequently capable of understanding and being understood.

7. The Latin word from which our "educate" is taken is itself a derivative.[15] *Educare ab educere:* "educate" from "educe", that is, "draw forth", "bring out". In its primary sense it is applied to plants and expresses the process by which man imitates, carries on, and adapts to a determined human purpose, the work of *education* (evolution, development) performed by Nature.[16] What Nature has *educed,* man *educates* or trains up. In the next step, by an obvious extension of the meaning, the term is made to include all the preparatory and auxiliary labours and contrivances by which the eductive powers and tendencies of Nature are protected, invigorated, or even called into act by adjustment of circumstances (= *surrounding* influe-

nces *quotquot* STANT CIRCUM).[17] Hence the vernal shower, as standing in a similar relation to the educible and eductive nature in the seed or plantule, and bringing to it at once excitement and nurture, is happily said by the Roman poet[18] to *educate* the flower: and in the response, that follows, by a still bolder metaphor he applies the word to the eductive or educing Nature itself, poetically contemplated as an *active* power distinct from the *educibility* and from the product *educed.*

Up flos in saeptis secretus nascitur hortis,
Ignotus pecori, nullo convulsus aratro,
Quem mulcent aurae, firmat sol, *educat* imber,-

. . . .

Ut vidua in nudo vitis quae nascitur arvo
Numquam se extollit, numquam mitem *educat* uvam ...

CATULLI LX.40-50[19]

8. Lastly, the word in its most comprehensive acceptation was applied to the householder man in relation to the young of his own species, and made to express the collective process in which the educator is himself (instead of) the dews and showers, the sun and the breeze, to the congenerous plant; and the home and its indwelling pieties are the protecting, warming and predisposing soil natal to both, which yet the trainer, like the enriching olive-tree, *forms* by continuing to *fill,* and by having gives to that which, as he helps and bends it to grow up beneath and around him, he at once *trains* and *supports.* It could not be otherwise therefore than that the simple and the metaphorical uses should at length change places, and the secondary or applied sense become the proper and ordinary acceptation of the term. Still, however, its correspondence to the primary import remains unaltered, and the analogy is kept up throughout. The process of *educing* from without is correlative to the *evolving* nature from within, to the intensity of the *power* and the *quid, quale et quantum*[20] of the possible *product.* In other words, the process of *eduction,* or bringing out, is determined by the forms and faculties developing or seeking to develop themselves from within. Still,

likewise, education consists of *two* parts, the process of *educing,* and that of *training*: and in the *human* education as in the education of plants, the educing must come first: and as this must be conducted with a constant view to the natural evolution, which it is to accompany and assist, so must the *training* likewise be regulated in part by its office as carrying on, and of course adapting itself to, the process of education, and in part by the particular purposes intended in each particular case.

9. If then eduction be the first stage of education, what is the first step in the eduction? In what way do we first draw or bring out the faculties of the nascent mind? We may reply without hesitation that *in substance* this is found in the question—"What is the *word* for such or such a thing?" Though *formally,* and as a direct *question,* it takes place more frequently in the teaching of a *foreign* language.[21] And what is the form or law in the mind to which this first act of education corresponds? Evidently, that by which we remember things in consequence of their co-presence. The word "table" is sounded at the same time that the eye and the touch are directed to the thing, table. We begin δεικτικιως that is, *demonstrando.*[22]

10. This, however, would barely lead us beyond the precincts of the powers common to men and the higher animals. Not only memory, but even perception, beyond a very limited extent, is impossible otherwise than by the sense of likeness. And here again, we see the beneficent effects of that promiscuous presentation of objects, of which we have before spoken, and which, like a puzzle invented for the purpose of evoking the faculties, at once sustains and relieves the attention by the charms of novelty and continual change, and at the same time by a gentle compulsion[23] solicits the mind to make for itself from the *like* effects of different objects on its own sensibility the links which it *then* seems to *find,* unconscious that both the form, and the light by which it is beheld, are of its own eradication and but *reflected* from external nature. We may confidently affirm that this catenary curve of likeness is the

line in which all the senses evolve themselves and commence their communion with the world, and their *purveyorship* for the understanding.

11. It cannot, indeed, be denied that in all *likeness* a *difference* is involved (*nil simile est idem*);[24] but it needs little observation of children to be convinced that they are attracted by the one without any conscious attention to the other. The child will select the harebell, the violet, the sweet-briar, the crocus, or the myrtle, because they are all alike *sweet;* or fill his lap with the gaudier flowers of summer, because they are all alike gaily *coloured,* long before he has adverted even to the most obvious differences. And even when he has begun to *distinguish,* it is by comparative intensity of impression, by difference of *degree* in the same *sort,* rather than by differences in the sorts themselves, that the child makes its earliest distinctions. "I *like* this, better than that", or "The violet is far sweeter than the primrose", are forms of comparison that precede the remark that the smell of the rose is a much sweeter sort than the smell of the jonquil. The latter comparison not only follows the former, but follows it with an interval, being indeed subsequent to the perception of difference by contrast. To illustrate this by a familiar instance—the perception, white, will awaken the recollection of black, and vice versa, before either of the two will be found to recall its own different *shades.*

12. It is a truth of no mean interest or pregnancy, and which requires only to be reflected on to be found such, though to many minds from want of reflection it will, at the first hearing, sound like a paradox, that of all the *material* elements of knowledge, all that external Nature can furnish as the *stuff* of which our knowledge is composed, the far greater part has been furnished by the time that the child passes into the boy or even at a yet earlier period. Nature has done her part. The needful notices (*notitiae rerum*)[25] have been given; the *tracing* is finished, and she but goes on to refresh and deepen the etching.

13(a). Here then the process of artificial education, that is, relative to the *intellectual* powers (and in this relation only it is here spoken of), may be said to commence: so far at least, that at this point the agency of *man,* the scheme of *human schooling,* may be singly and severally contemplated. What it *should* be, and what is the main it *is* and ever has been, among the cultivated portions of mankind, may be easily known from its aim and object: which can be no other than to render the mind of the scholar a fit organ for the continued reception and reproduction, for the elaboration, and finally for the application, of these *notices* supplied by sensation and perception, gradually superinducing those which the mind obtains, or may be taught and occasioned to obtain, by reflection on its own acts, and which, when formed and matured into distinct thoughts, constitute (and in a distinction from the former may be *called*) the mind's "notions"—the word being taken in its best and most proper sense. We take for granted that in order to a full and distinct attention the object to be attended to must be distinctly presented. The contrary position would indeed involve a contradiction in terms.

13(b). If then we have rightly stated the *aim* of human education, in its main divisions; and if the latter and that which is more especially the *end* or *final* aim, be the formation of right *notions,* or the mind's knowledge of its own constitution and constituent faculties as far as it is obtained by *reflection;* it is obvious that in order to its realisation the several faculties of the mind should be specially disciplined, and as(if I may be allowed the illustration) the muscles of the leg and thigh are brought out and made prominent in the exercises of the riding school,[26] that *so* should the intellectual powers be called forth from *their* dormant state, so as to become the possible and probable object of conscious reflection in and for themselves, apart from the particular and contingent *subject matters,* on which they are successively exerted—but, again, in order to this (at least as the best way of securing and facilitating this result) that the *subjects* themselves, on which the faculties are employed, should be in the first instance and as much as is possible the work and (if I may so say) the *reflection* of these faculties, such as owe their own existence to the functions of the human intelligence, and to the laws by which the exercise and application of these functions are governed and determined. But a subject perfectly answering this character is provided for us in the privilege and high instinct of language.[27]

13 (c) Now the law that first discloses itself is, as we have seen, the law of *connection or association* of different objects by perception of likeness—a process that will be found to involve the exercise of an *abstracting* power. For the likeness of A. B. C. (say, a rose, a peony, and a *camelia japonica*) consists of one or more marks *common* to all three: and the perception of the likeness supposes the act of attending to this common mark apart from the qualities and appearances with which in the *real* objects it is inseparably united. But though even the child on the lap both professes and exercises the power of abstraction, it does not follow that he abstracts *consciously*. In order to this, the act itself must be made an object of *reflection*.[28] The boy must not only abstract, but must be induced to *reflect* on what he is doing. This therefore is the second power that is to be exercised (dating from the supposed commencement of artificial and systematic education): it is to [be] called forth at the same time and in union with the law of likeness, and the simplest and more especially *human* products of that law, considered in its influences on the intellectual faculties of man.

14. It is clear that abstraction is an imaginary process;[29] that no form can really be presented, separated from some particular thing or reality, or that any law or rule can be made known, but by means of something which acts or is acted upon, under that law or according to those rules. Even the rule or ruler itself (to take a trivial instance) must be of some particular wood or metal, though when we are employing or considering it, merely as a *rule,* this becomes indifferent and we abstract from the particular concrete, that is, we draw away our attention

(*abstrahimus*) from the accidental fact that the ruler is of wood, or of iron, of oak, or of mahogany.

15. Everything in nature, is the inanimate no less than in the animate world, takes place according to *rules;* though we may not in all cases know them. These rules, again, must be all reducible to certain laws, though we may not hitherto have discovered them. The water falls according to law, to the law of gravity; and this law, modified in its application by the nature of the subject, gives the rules by which the water moves under all conceivable circumstances. The fish in the water, the bird in the air, move each according to pre-established rules; and the discovery and communication of these rules are the object of comparative anatomy and physiology. In short, universal nature is nothing more than a connected aggregate or chain of phenomena according to rules; and only in relation to human purposes can any appearance or natural incident be said to have taken place irregularly.[30]

16. To recall then and bring together the result of the preceding paragraphs, in order to call forth, to strengthen, and discipline the powers of the intellect, we have found it necessary to consider them apart from all particular occasions and subjects. Common sense would condemn the teacher of geometry who should present his circles, triangles, etc to the scholar in gaudy and variegated colours.[31] From this error, however, the child is preserved by Nature in that first period of his education which Nature herself begins as school-mistress and continues as guide. Here the choice of the subject has been made for us and the vehicle provided, as we have already observed. Words "were from the beginning",[32] nor would it have been possible, had the matter been left to our own invention, to have discovered or invented a medium possessed of advantages so many, so peculiar, and so appropriate, to all its various and numerous purposes.

17(a). But as words are, themselves, the earliest products of the abstracting power, so do they naturally become the first subject matter of abstraction; and consequently the commencement of human education. Hence it is that civilisation, and the conditions under which a people have become progressive and historical, commences with an alphabet, or with some equivalent discovery imperfectly answering the same purpose.[33]

17(b). Amid all the variety of sounds, of which any given language avails itself, those that most resemble each other will be the first noticed, the most easily imitated, and the longest retained. The fondness of children for rhymes will have struck every observer.In a following stage, the difference between likeness and sameness will have been noticed, and the first effort of art will consist in directing the attention to the mental elements or *factors* of likeness (viz. The same and the different) to effect which, one of the two must be presented to the attention separately, and this will of course be the one first mentioned (the *same*), as being the *radical* element, as it were, or the *positive* factor of the *conception* "likeness", "like", and that too which corresponds to the faculty earliest developed in the mind, namely, the sense of a like that differs from the same only by a difference of *degree,* or even (in the first instances) only numerically.

18. Consistently with this the first implement of artificial education are an alphabet and an accidence; that is, first, a catalogue of the letters, or articulate sounds, in which all the *differences* of language are comprised, and which of course, therefore, are the *positive* elements of the likeness of any two series of words, that contains each the whole number. They are that in respect to which the two series or sentences are the *same*, the relative *positions* of the letters constituting the difference, and supplying the negative element of likeness.

19. And secondly, a catalogue of the significant syllables, or that portion of language by which a *same* meaning is found in combination with a *different* meaning in any number of different words—a combination possible only under one condition, that the difference is in the object, the sameness in the *relation.* Thus in the alphabet, under which I include the process of reading and spelling, the letters themselves give the

positive element of the like = the same; and the relative *positions* of the letters form the negative element = the different: while in the accidence, as the process of parsing and construing, the *radical* portions of the words import the difference, and the positions in respect of space (cases) or of time (the tenses) or of subjective relations (the moods) express the sameness. Hence in [the]respect [that] their abstract and universal characters are concerned (and of these alone we are now speaking) [this community and intersimilitude of the parts of speech] is a necessary consequence of their common derivation or rather *production* from the verb substantive. For all words express either being or action, or the predominance of the one over the other. In philosophical grammar, they are either substantives, or verbs, or as adnouns and adverbs express the modification of the one by the other. But the verb substantive ("am", *sum*,ειμι) expresses the identity or coinherence of being and act. It is the act of being.[34] All other words therefore may be considered as tending from this point, or more truly from the mid-point of the line, the *punctum indifferentiae* representing the *punctum identitatis*,[35] even as the whole line represents the same point as produced or polarised.

20. In this simple diagram *A* (= the point of identity) is supposed to generate by perpetual eradiation the line *BC*, the pole *B* representing being in its greatest predominance, and the pole *C* action in like manner: while the point *a*, expressing the indifference of being and action, of substantive and verb, is the more especial representative or analog on of the *point A*, as a point. *A*, the point of identity, is verb and substantive in one and as one; *a*, the point of indifference, is *either* verb

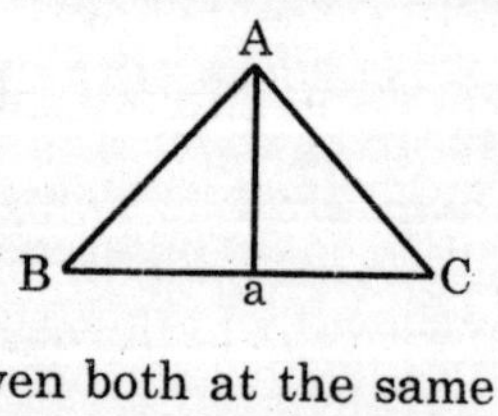

or substantive, or even both at the same time, but *not* in the same *relation*. Such in grammar is the *infinitive*: and though instances of its functions as indifferently verb or substantive are far more frequent and idiomatic in the Greek, Italian, French, and German languages, they are not wanting in our own. Take, for example, the two following lines from Spenser:

> For not to dip the hero in the lake
> Could save the son of Thetis from *to die*.[36]

Here the infinitive, "to dip", is a substantive as the nominative case of the verb, "could save", and at the *same* time but in a different relation, it is a verb active, governing "the hero" as its accusative case or object. So too the verb neuter is governed as a substantive in "from to die"; and in Greek the preceding article would have been declined in the case required by the preposition.

21. Before I proceed, however, I must request the reader to bear in mind that I am not speaking of language *historically* or pretending to narrate etymological *facts*. There have been men and of no mean rank in the republic of letters who have strenuously contended for the *bona fide* derivation of the whole Greek language from εω as the oldest form of the Greek verb substantive: and if this could be *proved* true of any one language, it would be irrational not to concede the high probability of a similar orgination in all.[37] But with this theory I am in no wise concerned, as opponent or advocate. Indeed, with *any* scheme of etymology the present subject is as little connected, as the doctrine of determinate proportions in the science of chemistry, or an enquiry into the generation or evolution of numbers according to Pythagoras, with the question whether the cyphers in use were originally Arabic, or Indian, or mere corruptions and gradual transformations of the Greek letters, used for the same purpose. It is to the elements of grammar that we are now directing our attention; and of grammar as a purely abstract and *formal* science, that therefore takes the lead in the scheme of artificial education because it reflects the forms of the human mind, and gradually familiarises the half-conscious boy with the frame and constitution of his own intellect, as the polished glass does the unconscious infant

with the features of its own countenance.

22(a). *Grammatically* considered then, I say, that all words may be classed under one or other, or (to take up my former metaphor) they may be described as tending to one or other of the two poles of the verb substantive, and as represented by the points between the mid-point and the two extremes of the line. But as they are all *like* to the verb substantive, they are for that reason at once like and yet opposite to (contra-distinguished from) each other, every substantive a verb, and every verb a substantive, in order to its own significance (the two sexes, their derivation from the *homo androgynus,* and the retiring of the latter from the world of the senses into the invisible world of self-consciousness, in the fable of Plato and of the rabbinical writers, may furnish an amusing illustration of the preceding ideas.[38] It is not indeed impossible that this mythic tale may have been originally intended as agrammatical allegory.)

22(b). It is sufficient, however, if I have succeeded in unfolding the true character of the education sanctioned by the experience of ages, and its perfect correspondence to the provisions and designs of Nature; if I have shown in what manner its first lessons come in aid of that power of abstraction by which, as the condition and the means of self-knowledge, the reasoning intellect of man is distinguished in *kind* from the mechanical understanding of the dog, the elephant, the bee, the ant, and whatever other animals display an intelligence that we cannot satisfactorily reduce to mere instinct; if, in short, against the caprice of fashion and the pretexts of its pandars and flatterers I have vindicated the old schooling as a scheme eminently entitled to the name of education, inasmuch as by means admirably adapted to the present faculties and the future purposes of the scholar it gradually raises into acts and objects of distinct consciousness what Nature and the alone true *natural* state of man had previously called forth as *instincts* of humanity.[39]

23. The charters and other records of our oldest schools,

both of those exclusively intended for the instruction of the more numerous class in and for their own rank (e.g. Sir Roger Cholmley's school at Highgate, founded in Elizabeth's reign)[40] and those of a mixed character, in which provisions were made for raising a certain number of the more promising scholars into a higher rank, and qualifying them for the learned professions (among which Christ's Hospital, never by me to be named without reverence, stands prominent).[41] furnish striking proofs, how highly our great ancestors, the fathers of our Church and the lights and pillars of Protestantism throughout the world, appreciated the advantages of learning, *in conjunction with common arithemetic,* the A B C, and the rudiments of grammar, independent of any further progress in the learned languages and without the remotest view to the study of the books therein written, or to what we now call *classical* scholarship. If our own experience on English ground permitted a doubt to remain as to the truth and justice of their conclusion, a moment's comparison of the Scottish with the Irish peasantry would remove it forever.[42]

24(a). Greatly then do those persons mistake the purpose, and [?unjustly] do they detract from the merit, of the invention, who suppose that the accidence (syntax included) was exclusively contrived for *the looking out for words* in a dictionary, that was itself contrived with a view to the accidence. Were this all, the object might be obtained in a much easier and more efficacious way by the use of a dictionary, which contains the significant, though indetachable, syllables; hence considered as *parts of speech,* or in respect of their abstract characters, according to which they are severally classed as verbs or nouns, adverbs or adnouns, etc, all words have a ground of *likeness* to each other: the most different are akin. (Abstractly considered, I mean: and of *abstracts* alone we are now speaking. The act and faculty of *abstraction* it is which through the medium of its earliest and most universal *proceeds* we are now endeavouring to elucidate.)

24(b). This community and intersimilitude of the parts of

speech is a necessary consequence of their common derivation, or rather *production*, from the verb substantive. For all words express either being or act, or the predominance of the one or the other.[43] We cannot conceive even the merest *thing*, a stone for instance, as simply and exclusively *being*, as absolutely passive and *actionless*. Were it but the act of reflecting the light by which it is seen, or as the sum of the acts of attraction by which its particles cohere, and the stone *is*. And as little, on the other hand, can we conceive or imagine the purest act, a flash of lightning of instance, as *merely* an act, or without an abiding or continuing somewhat, as the inseparable ground, subject, and substance of the action.

25. As soon as the pupil has been sufficiently familiarised with words and their import, to possess a somewhat to which the rules could apply; from thence to the doctrine of arranging words and sentences perspicuously; an art which has hitherto had no appropriate title, having been confounded with one or all of the others, and which I therefore propose to distinguish by the term "rhematic",[44] for reasons the importance of which will be seen in another place when we have to speak on the syllogistic figures.[45]

26. Thence rhetoric, or the art of declaming persuasively; and lastly logic, as the art and science of discoursing conclusively. In the following table the reader will find these four with their several definitions.

27. A table of the formal sciences, or systematised arts, of which words are the subject and medium.

1 *Grammatice*—Συναρτνσις γραμματων
2 *Rhematice*—Συνταξιξ ρηματωυ
[3] *Rhetorice*—Συνθεαις πεισματων
[4] *Logic*—[?Συνδησις] λογισμων[46]

28. How valuable, how desirable in all cases, and how indispensable, the formal sciences of figure, number, and motion are, and fully disposed as I am to prefix over the portal of schools of higher philosophy ονδεις[αγεωμετρητος εισιτω][47] still

the four presented in this table assuredly contain all the preparation for the study of realities, scientific, historic, or technical and are adapted to awaken and discipline all the powers to be exerted in the acquirement and exercise of them, which the concerns of life and society require, whether for the bar, the pulpit, or the senate.[48]

29. These, however, in substance at least, are indispensable for all men whose object supposes knowledge and the development of the intellect.

Footnotes

1. A characteristic theme. In *Friend* (*CC*)I 94, C stresses the need to distinguish between what is science and what is not; here he refers to the importance of distinguishing between one science and another; as the *Logic* proceeds he turns to distinctions between the different branches of philosophy. In this paragraph and the next, C seems to be expanding on material in N 29 f 46*V*, which is in turn based on Kant "Ueber den Gebrauch teleologischer Principien in der Philosophie" *VS* III 107, C himself providing the reference. Ff33*V* and 47-47*V* also anticipate the *Logic;* see below, pp 21-3.

2. In N 29 f 46*V*, C uses botanists as his example. For his views on the contribution of botanists in the eighteenth century, see *Friend* (*CC*) I 466-9.

3. C is probably drawing on Tennemann here (III 31). Cf *P Lects* Lect 5 (1949) 184, where Aristotle's progress through the stages of observation, discrimination, and abstraction is referred to.

4. I.e. the "second instrument" or "other organ" of the sciences concerned with physical reality.

5. Isaac Watts *Logick: or, the Right Use of Reason in the Enquiry after Truth* . . . (1725). This Lockean book passed through seven editions by 1740 and was still being reprinted in 1822. In Nov 1799, C was reading selections from it in Vicesimus Knox *Elegant Extracts: or, Useful and Entertaining Passages in Prose* (1784) (*CN* I 531), and he quoted one of them in *The Friend in* 1818 (*Friend-CC*-I 484). For a detailed account of the nature and significance of Watts's *Logick,* see Wilbur Samuel

Howell *Eighteenth-Century British Logic and Rhetoric* (Princeton 1971) 331-45.

6. On the adequacy of Aristotle's logic and the wrongheaded interpolation of other materials into it by the moderns, see Kant *C d r V* pp viii-ix (17-18).

7. Étienne Bonnot de Condillac (1715-80) *La Logique, ou les premiers developpements de l'art de penser, ouvrage élémentaire* (Paris 1781). C claimed an acquaintance with Condillac's book as early as 13 Feb 1801 (*CL* II 675); he seems to have intended to take it to Malta with him in 1804 (*CL* II 1139) and may have done so; he proposed to attack Condillac's "Ψευδο-Logic" as alte as 8 Jan 1821 (*CL* v 133). C's charge that Condillac plagiarised from David Hartley (1705-57) appears in a letter to William Godwin on 4 Jun 1803 (*CL* II 947); it is repeated in the posthumously published *Theory of Life* (*TL*-1848-61n).

8. See above, p 5 n 2.

9. Cf *P Lects* Lect 5 (1949) 173-4 on the minting of new terms. C wrote the following note on the flyleaf of his copy of Kant's *Logik* (BM copy): "An advantage great beyond what a regular Scholar unacquainted with the English World as it now is & has been for the last century can easily appreciate, did the old Logicians, Philologists and Philosophers possess—in that they had either to *ground* the pupil's mind in the appropriate import & use of terms, or might safely presume on readers so grounded by others. The self-conceit of well-clothed Sciolism and the consequent only not universal abuse & laxity of words they had not to struggle with."

10. A conventional theme: cf Bacon *Novum Organum* "Aphorismi" bk I 43: *Works* (1740) I 367; Hobbes *Leviathan* pt I ch 4; Locke *Essay on Human Understanding* bk III ch 10; Berkeley *A Treatise Concerning the Principles of Human Knowledge* (*B Works* II 39-40); Leibniz *Nouveaux essais* bk III ch 10; and, in jest, Sterne *The Life and Opinions of Tristram Shandy* vol III ch 31.

11. C objected to what he regarded as underestimates of the importance of what children learn, in works such as Kant's *Anthropologie* and Eschenmayer's *Psychologie*. Cf *Destiny of Nations* lines 18ff: *PW* (EHC) I 132.

12. Shakespeare *Hamlet* II ii 204.

13. I.e. the conscience.

14. Paragraphs 2(c), 3, and 4 are almost identical with N 29 f 43*V*.

15. Cf the account in the *Bristol Gazette* of C's lecture of 18 Nov 1813 on "The New System of Education" (reprinted *Athenaeum* 13 Mar 1909 pp 316-17). For C's association of "educing" with Dr Bell's "eliciting the faculties of the human mind", see *Friend* (*CC*) I 540n and *SM* (*CC*) 40-1. C described James Boyer—his own teacher at Christ's Hospital—as "an admirable educer no less than Educator of the Intellect . . . ". *PW* (EHC) I 3n.

16. Cf *AR* (1825) 6n: "there are few modes of instruction more useful or more amusing than that of accustoming young people to seek for the etymology, or primary meaning, of the words they use". In the *Logic,* C often makes a point by considering the derivation of term. Cf *C&S* (*CC*) 13n.

17. "As many as stand about".

18. Catullus.

19. *Poems* 62.39-49. In C's ed, *Catulli Tibulli Propertii Opera* (1774), numbered 60. Tr. F. W. Cornish (LCL 1962) 89: "As a flower springs up secretly in a fenced garden, unknown to the cattle, torn up by no plough which the winds caress, the sun strengthens, the shower draws forth....As an unwedded vine which grows up in a bare field never raises itself aloft, never brings forth a mellow grape...".

20. Mediaeval Scholastic terms: "the what, what sort of, how much".

21. Cf C's own way of learning German in Ratzeburg in 1798. *BL* ch 10 (1907) I 137-8n.

22. I.e. we begin demonstratively, by pointing things out. On the part played by touch in our "first education", cf *P Lects* Lect 3 (1949) 115.

23. Cf *BL* ch 14 (1907) II 12: "gentle and unnoticed, controul" of the will and understanding.

24. One of C's favourite tags—"nothing like is the same", or, in another version, "no likeness goes on all fours". See below, e.g., pp 132 and 143.

25. Literally, "the notices of things".

26. The analogy between mental and physical exercise was a favourite one.See *CL* III 253,253-4, 255, and *Sh C* II 35-6.

27. C's ideas about the way in which children should be taught are exemplified in a fragmentary ms dialogue in which a teacher discusses the peculiarities of Greek, Latin, and English by catechising a child of ten. BM MS Egerton 2800 ff 175-7. The paper is watermarked 1825, and the dialogue is probably a by-product of C's tutoring of the young Henry Gillman in the winter of 1825-6. Cf *CL* VI 535. There is another similar ms dialogue in the BM: MS Egerton 2800 ff 179-80V.

28. Fichte makes the same remark. Johann Gottlieb Fichte *Uber den Begriff der Wissenschaftslehre order der sogenannten Philosophie* (Jena & Leipzig 1798) 46. C's annotated copy is in the BM.

29. Cf Berkeley *Alciphron: B Works* III 293.

30. This paragraph is a free translation of the opening paragraph of the Introduction of Kant *Logik* (1800) 1.

31. J.P. Collier's diary transcript of the second of C's 1811-12 series of lectures records that "Coleridge in the strongest manner censured the practice of teaching mathematics by making the illustrations obvious to the senses. We should think and not feel". R. A. Foakes, ed *Coleridge on Shakespeare* (1971) 58. C may have had in mind the suggestions of his friend Thomas Beddoes *Observations on the Nature of Demonstrative Evidence:with an Explanation of Certain Difficulties Occurring in the Elements of Geometry: and Reflections on Language* (1793) viiff, 63-5. Cf also the passing reference to "[*tangible*] geometry" in *P Lects* Lect 9 (1949) 281. Cf *CN* III 3455n.

32. John 1.1 (var).

33. Cf C's notion that "The whole of the progress of society might be expressed in a dictionary...". *P Lects* Lect 5 (1949) 173-4.

34. See Editor's Introduction, above, pp lxv-lxvii.

35. "Point of indifference", "point of identity".

36. *The Ruins of Time* lines 428-9 (var). The quotation and the application of it are taken from James Harris *Hermes: or a Philosophical Inquiry Concerning Universal Grammar* (1751): *The Works* ed Earl of Malmesbury (1801) I 305n; the variation

is C's own. He uses the same example in N 29 f 28 and in annotations to Edward Irving *Sermons* (3 vols 1828) and *The Quarterly Journal of Foreign Medicine and Surgery* I (1818-19) 331.

37. C seems to have been thinking of the theory that the "duads" "αω, εω, ιω, οω, υω", are the "roots of the [Greek] language . . .": Jame Burnet, Lord Monboddo *Of the Origin and Progress of Language* (6 vols Edinburgh 1773-92) II 193 and 522. Thomas Beddoes misrepresents this theory slightly as implying "that the verb is the parent word of the whole Greek language . . .". *Observations* 156. William Vincent (1739-1815), the headmaster of Westminster, was prominent among the men who argued that the verb "to be" was the original Greek verb. See his anonymous *The Origination of the Greek Verb. An Hypothesis* (1794) and *The Greek Verb Analysed. An Hypothesis. In Which the Source and Structure of the Greek Language, and of Language in General, Is Considered* (1795), esp pp 1-26. (C's annotated copy is in VCL.) C referred to Vincent's work in a disparaging tone in a letter to George Coleridge in 1802 (*CL* II 803). Vincent's views were given a spirited trouncing by the associationist Thomas Gunter Browne: *Hermes Unmasked* . . . (1795).

38. See Plato *Symposium* 189-93 and *Midrash Rabbah* ed H. Freedman and Maurice Simon (1939) I 54. See also Philo *De opificio mundi* 151. The allusion was commonplace. See, e.g., Isaac D'Israeli *Curiosities of Literature* 4th ed (1795) I 217-18. For C's interest in rabbinical materials, see *CL* IV 558-9 (?24 Mar 1815), *CL* IV 656-7 (16 Jul 1816), *CL* IV 681 (22 Sept 1816). He had included some "Specimens of Rabbinical Wisdom" in *The Friend,* derived from J.J. Engel *Schriften* (Berlin 1801) vol I. See *Friend (CC)* I 370-3 and II 170-1, 308-9.

39. For C's low opinion of the new schools, see *BL* ch 1 (1907) I 7-8.

40. The Highgate free grammar school was founded in 1562 and incorporated by letters patent in 1565 by Sir Roger Cholmley. For C's interest in the school see E.L. Griggs *CL* v 171-3n; it was particularly on his mind in the summer of 1822 and again in 1839 (*CL* v 235, 237, 241 242-3, and VI 833-5).

41. For accounts of C's connection with Christ's Hospital, see *BL* ch

1 (1907) I 4-11; Charles Lamb "Recollections of Christ's Hospital" and "Christ's Hospital Five and Thirty Years Ago" *L Works* I 139-49 and II 12-22.

42. Cf the similar comparison in *AR* (1825) 7-8n.

43. C repeats the botched passage of p 16, above.

44. C's use of word (*TT* 23 Sept 1830) is the first instance recorded in *OED*.

45. See below, pp 53ff.

46. "Grammar-fitting together of letters/ Rhematic-Arrangement of words/ Rhetoric-Putting together of persuasions/ Logic-[?Binding together] of reasonings". The missing word is supplied from a similar table in N 29 ff 46*V*-47*V*

47. The motto said to have been placed above the door of Plato's Academy: "Let no man enter . . . who has not previously disciplined his mind by Geometry" (C's paraphrase in *LS-CC*-173). He continues: "He considered this science as the first purification of the soul, by abstracting the attention form the accidents of the senses". C used the quotation in *Watchman* (*CC*) 34 and in a marginal note to Jakob Bohme *Works* 4 vols 1764-81) cited in *CN* II 2894n.

48. An indication of the audience *C* has in mind. Cf the outline in BM MS Egerton 2801 f 197, addressed to "Individuals. ...not younger than eighteen or nineteen. . ." who are preparing themselves for "the Bar, the Pulpit or the Senate...".

Chapter-2

Sketch of Greek Logic

Chapter-2

1. Logic from the Greek λεγω.[1] The absolute etymon of this word, by which I mean the particular visual image, or other sensuous impression, which is at the root of its proper constituent syllable, is far beyond historic research, though an equivalent of the particular root, if not the root itself, may perhaps be discovered by speculative combinations and analogy of roots certainly known.

2. The old Greek grammarians, or rather philologists, or men of letters (for either of these would be a more appropriate translation of the *grammatici*), assign to the initial λ the sense of additional force, whether in consequence of a single energy or of the same energy repeated.[2] The objections of Ruhnkenius are weak, and the very words on which he founds his own whimsical hypothesis, that the initial λ expresses ugliness or hatefulness, may readily be explained in conformity with the more simple and natural belief of the ancients themselves.[3] The feelings of disgust and hatred, we know by experience, either find or make some sound significant of additional effort, as the means of expressing their own intensity. It is probable that offences to the taste, as connected with food, form the first objects of hate, in other words, that hate was primarily *disgust*: (*disgustas*) thus—"eat", "ate", and "hate"; *essen* and *hassen;* while in the Latin, the same addition of strength is expressed by the change of the lower to a higher vowel and this probably in the earlier ages of the Latin language-aspirated—*edi—odi*—[4]

3. I have said that the words given by him in proof of his hypothesis might be brought under the rule to which he opposes them; but it would be far more consistent, both with analogy and probability, to consider them as purely accidental, and, by way of proof, to select an equal or greater number of words equally or more associated with dislike and aversion under

any one of half a dozen other initials.

4. Assuredly the sound of this liquid,[5] as it is now sounded, and doubtless was so by the Greeks, from the first periods of their literary history, must appear a strange choice for the expression of effort of any kind, painful or pleasurable. If it expressed any one act or image more than another, it would seem to be—continuity and the absence of resistance, as in the word "liquid"; thence, easy motion, and in this way, it might easily [?come to mean] motion rendered easy by repetition, as that of [a] pendulum or the motion in rocking;[6] and thus would maintain or justify its affinity, as well as its neighborhood, to the μ. But the λ as well as the soft σ, the *b*,[7] and the *v*—the *h* and the modern *w*—are frequently the softer, and more easily pronounced, representatives and substitutes of those harsh and difficult sounds that occur in the first and ruder states of all nations and of all languages spoken by a rude and imperfectly civilsed people. Such doubtless was the digamma of the Pelasgic Greeks,[8] for had it originally marked a sound similar to our *v* or *w*, I know not what reason could be assigned, or what cause imagined, for its having become obsolete and lost out of the alphabet; but if we suppose it to have resembled the Hebrew "again",[9] or the sound which, by the vowel prefixed, is still preserved in the double *g* as in αγγεγος[10] and in the Latin *angor*,[11] we need only attempt to pronounce it as an initial to convince ourselves that it requires organs of pronunciation which travellers have so often found occasion to wonder at in the language of barbarous tribes but which they have in vain attempted to imitate.

5. The gradual diminution of the effort and consequent gradual softening of the sound into others less distinct but more vocal will be an unfailing accompaniment of civilisation. Nor unfortunately does this process always stop at the desirable mean. A nation may rebarbarise into the opposite extreme of effeminacy, or mere paucity of conception and combinations, from the loss of ancient literature; may produce the same effect, even where positive feebleness cannot be justly asserted.

Thus the modern Italians have gradually dropped the aspirate and indeed as many other of the stronger and deeper sounds as the necessity of retaining the distinct meaning of their words would permit. A similar loss of all the gutturals and of most of the dipthongs is noticeable in the modern Greek; though an Italian effeminacy will be the last censure cast on the present natives of the Peloponnesus and its adjacent islands.[12]

6. I am far, however, from contending that this representation of a harsh by a softer sound is generally or even frequently instanced by the initial λ, though the transition of the Latin *clamare* into the Spanish *llamare*[13] might lead us to infer that the philologists who wrote while the Greek was yet a living tongue might have found reasons for supposing such a pronunciation of the initial λ in so large a number of words (in many perhaps the relics of the former sound)[14] as, taken in conjunction with the import of the words, appeared to sanction the supposition that the letter was characteristic of power, or what is called, technically, corroboration, generally in connection with motion in its easiest form—that of recurrency.

7. The original sense of the word λεγω appears to have been that of picking up, a taking up a something that had been sought after; hence a choosing, a determining; all in connection with the discursion, deliberation, or the going backward and forward, or the balancing of the mind, antecedent to, or accompanying, the act of picking up or selecting; hence by natural association, it became associated with the balance and signified to ponder, to weigh, which is found in the classical λογιζεσθαι[15] thence lastly, that which is the result of weighing or considering, λογοι[16].

8. In the early periods of the human race and at present, whatever a scanty population is spread over a large and uncultivated domain,whether in the pastoral or the hunting states, man is comparatively a silent animal.[17] Conversation is almost confined to affairs of moment. The conversations themselves are entitled "words", or some equivalent term, as

for instance the "palavers" or "palabras" of the Africans: we might therefore expect that the particular speeches, the harangues of the individual, should be distinguished from light or ordinary talk by some appropriate name. At all events, we may expect to find it so, whenever, as was the case in Greece, the race, climate, geographical circumstances, and above all the confluence of kindred tribes, were favorable to the formation of a copious language; thus it was that select, considerate,well-weighed, deliberate words were named λογοι in distinction from ρηματα, that is, fluents, *vocabula fluentia*: λογο[ιλογιζομενοι.[18]

9. That fables are likewise entitled λογοι, as λογοι [?Αισωπικοι],[19] will surprise those only who, misled by the unwise custom of putting books of fables in the hands of children, have forgotten that the original and, at all times, the most pertinent use of apologues was in speeches on delicate and hazardous subjects, addressed to kings or unruly popular assemblies. The fable of Jotham [is] the earliest on record;[20] that of Menippus[21] might be cited in proof, if indeed the subjects and purposes of all the ancient fables (those of Phaedrus are undoubtedly modern)[+] did not suffice of themselves to convince an intelligent reader. At a somewhat later period, those who collected the speeches or "words of weight", and with these (as was natural) the momentary events that were the occasion or result, were entitled λογιοι, and the writings themselves λογοι. As these were supposed to be the faithful reports of the speeches, they of course could not be metrical; this is the most probable origin of prose writing.

10. Thus λογοι acquired the sense of histories, which at first, like our oldest chronicles, included natural, as well as political, events, incidents, and phenomena-*voces natura*[e] *et mortalia verba;*[22] and hence the earliest Greek historians were the first prose writers.

11. A chronicle can of course have no closer connection than what the circumstances of time, place, and the identity of the agent, in a series of acts or fortunes, may supply; what is more than this must be given by the skill or the passion of the

narrator: thus the meaning of the word λογοι as histories was limited by επος[23] from επειν-επειν in the sense still preserved in επεσθαι, *sequi,* "to follow"—"to folow in close order".[24]

12. A skilful arrangement of events and harangues to an artful and harmonious whole was an επος, an epic poem; the poet, εποποιος[25] or simply ποιητης, the maker, to distinguish him from the historian, who received the form and sequency of his narration, no less than the contents, from the actual occurrences. He alone can be appropriately styled a poet who, whencesoever he may have derived the materials of his work, supplies the form, connection, and unity from his own mind, or, as both the piety and humility of the early poet dictated, from his genius, his muse, or special αγαθ [οδαιμων][26] That such works among the Greeks were all material follows from the process above given, and indeed flows out of the nature of the language itself.

13. It is, however, the επος, the ποιησις, the contexture, the original infusion of the poet's own shapings, that constitute the essential qualities, εποποιια, and distinguish the *Waverley* or *Guy Mannering,* with no less propriety, than the *Marmion* and *Lady of the Lake,* from the λογος or λογ [ι] οι of the chronicles.[27]

14. Soon, however, the happy genius of Greece inspired a portion of the same power into the works of her prose narrators, but working by different means. Intelligent research came in the stead of invention; thought and reflection supplied the links of causation and formed while they explained the connection of events and their common relation as parts of one comprehensive scheme; either general, or what we now call the ways of Providence, or for the manifestation and evidence of some particular purpose or moral as in Thucydides. Thus the λογογραφια, or record of weighty matters, or memorabilia, was elevated into history (ιστορια, ιστορησις, from ιστορειν, to search into, to make a diligent enquiry concerning) and the logograph into the historian. But in how extensive a sense the term "history" was received we learn

from the invaluable treatise of Hippocrates on Air, Water, and Situation; which he himself entitles ιστ[ορικη] αποδειξις, i.e. an experiential representation, a demonstration founded on enquiry, literally inquisitive demonstration, in the sense in which the word demonstration is still used, by the teachers of anatomy.[28]

15. Thus, the poet and the historian having obtained each a proper name, the derivatives from λογος, are now appropriated to men of superior knowledge, the highly informed, the men of understanding, e.g. the [λογιοι τωνΠερσεωνκαι Αιγυπτιων][29] in Herodotus, i.e. the intelligent class among the Persians of Egyptians, not the *learned*, which, as an honorary epithet, was not introduced till a later stage of the process. In the earlier time, yet still later than the Homeric period, the great men were entitled σοφοι and σοφιστα,[30] but in the sense of wise men-the wise. The latter term was afterwards appropriated by Plato and Aristotle to those adventurers who pretended to teach wisdom as an art or trade. But in Herodotus the two words σοφοι and [σοφισται] occur as perfect synonyms, signifying men distinguished as the lights and ornaments of society, whether as legislators, poets, or men of research. The name, however, as I have already hinted, is later than the epic period. The word σοφον first occurs in the hymns falsely attributed to the author or authors of the *Iliad,*[31] and of a later date even than the *Odyssey,* but still proceeding from the Homeric school[32]. Yet from the time of Lycurgus to that of Pindar, poets, philosophers, and lawgivers were comprised indifferently under this term as friends and familiars of the gods, the inspired, the enlightened from above, the formers and benefactors of mankind! What they knew, was regarded by their countrymen as a kind of loftier property, a power that belonged to the possessor by an especial gift or infusion, which no diligence could acquire, which no rules could teach, which no effort of volition could produce, but as an immediate presence of which it was not lawful to enquire whence it sprang, as if it were a thing subject to place and motion, nor to pursue it with a view of detecting its secret source; but they—the wise—watched

quietly till it suddenly shone upon them, preparing themselves for the same, as the eye waits patiently for the rising sun. Such was the conception which the Greeks, soon after their formation into constitutional states, had of all honourable eminence in intellect, of all genuine intellectual greatness; as Appollo, the god of conscious intelligence, manifested future events through the mouth of the Pythoness,[33] so, through the mouth of Pindar, he revealed the powers of song, and through Pythagoras he brought forth the hidden principles into light:—these were all alike inspired—all alike had a genius ([δαιμων]) and the influences and illapses of the god or genius were diffused through the whole man, his moral impulses no less than his intellectual perceptions.

16. Hence on the one hand it was supposed a contradiction to be vicious and yet a man of genius and on the other what was learnt or could be learnt was but little in extent, still less in value, and least of all in worth.

17 Learning was a servile attainment as opposed to the ingenuous or the distinctions suitable to free men or citizens, which in this point of view we might not inaptly render-gentlemen. We may refer to the well-known passage of Pindar: "He alone is the wise man who understandeth much out of himself—but they who have learnt—the learned—pour forth empty words as the crows clamour against the godlike bird of Jove."[34]

18. This state of feeling, as associated with learning and the learned, could not be permanent; though the substantial part of the distinction, that which discriminates immediate knowledge from such attainments as were communicable by words or other mere passive impressions, will forever retain its worth and full value. Pythagoras himself, who modestly substituted the title [φιλοσοφος] for the [σοφοϖ][35] had already prepared for this change by giving the name of [μαθησις], that is, the learning and [μαθηματα], things to be learnt, to the study and contents of the mathematics, in which he included music and rhythm as a preparatory discipline or προπαιδεια,

through which the pupils were to pass on their road to wisdom or the knowledge of the immediate.[36] The original sense of the term was still so far present that the [μαθησις] and the [μαθηματα], the acquisition and the acquirements, were still subordinate: but they acquired a reputability by being employed in the service of that which was excellent on its own account. A still greater influence was exerted by the writings of Herodotus and of Hippocrates, or rather of the accumulation of knowledges derived from experience, the fruits of research ([ιστορια]). It became evident that the man who depended wholly on his experience was poor and unprovided for the contingencies of life compared with those in whose memory, as in a storehouse, the fruits of many men's experiences were preserved; that with the same degree of natural understanding or mother wit, the man who had appropriated to himself the judgments, the ends proposed, the means adopted, the results confirmatory or dissuasive, of all those who from tradition, whether fixed or still oral, were known to have distinguished themselves in any given office or exigence, would enter on such an office better qualified for the performance of its functions, would meet with that or other equivalent exigence with less probability of being taken by surprise, than any merely self-taught man at the conclusion of his career. Henceforward learning could not but dignify the possessor, and the communication of the same advantage to others, by collecting records and by comments and verbal intepretation, removing or lessening the difficulties which the collector and communicator had himself struggled with, could not but become merit, increasing with the progression and increase of human experience.

19. Still, however, so numerous were the passages in the ancient poets and philosophers, in which what we should now entitle book-knowledge was held in contempt for its emptiness and even reprobated for its tendency to inflate the mind and thus unfit it for communion with immediate truths, that a certain macula lives still adhered to the term.[37] The [σοφος]

was a title that never appears to have been chosen, even by those men whose chief claim rested on their learning. They went back again to the earliest period, and resumed the term derived.[38] The period at present in our view must have its commencement dated from the formation of the Platonic and Aristotelian schools, under the immediate successors of Alexander and principally in Egypt, if we speak of the full formation of the terminology to which the historic etymology of λεγω and its derivatives now leads us. But the aim, the philosophic anticipation which lies at the ground of this terminology, had a much earlier date and appears more or less distinctly , even from the introduction of the term νους into the speculative researches of Greece by Anaxagoras.[39] But as far as the term now under consideration is concerned, it is displayed with particular force and is of noticeable recurrence in the small number of genuine and unsuspected fragments of Heraclitus.[40] The doctrine of Aristotle differed indeed materially from the principle of the Platonist, such as the latter is proved to have been, under the second master of the Academus, by an invaluable fragment of Speusippus, Plato's nephew and successor.[41] That Aristotle, however, did not differ from his great master and rival as to the existence of the distinction which I am now about to notice is evident from his own words: "there must be something transcending the λογος"[42] that is, logical faculty, viz. that which is the principle of this faculty to which numerous other passages of the same import might be added from his logical and metaphysical works. As in the present stage of the enquiry we are not concerned with the truth or philosophical validity of the conceptions, nor the right with which the terms were appropriated to them, nor discussing the rightfulness with which the terms in question were selected for their expression, but solely with the historical fact that such conceptions were entertained and that certain words acquired such and such meanings, and underwent such and such changes of sense in consequence; the reader will perceive that these prefatory notices are neither not of place nor without a pertinent end. We will therefore proceed, having first premised that we shall name this fore proceed, having first premised that we shall name this, this the νους or pure reason, but without any reference to the divers opinions concerning its nature.

20. At this time the substantive λογος, we have said, acquired a new sense, and was employed to express the intelligential faculty itself and this in a threefold relation: first it signified the logical faculty, the reasoning power, in short the understanding including the judgment, in distinction from the Anu or reason. Secondly it signified the understanding, as the discursive faculty, or that which employed itself on the conceptions of the mind and the general terms representing them, in distinction from the intuition, or intuitive power of the mind, as employed on the forms of perception in time and space, that is, number and figure; but in both instances, with abstraction of all that is furnished from without, of all that does not belong to the mind of its own right. Here the λογος is distinguished from θεωρια, as the understanding from the sense, and of course distinguished as from its equal and collateral. Thirdly the λογος was used in a somewhat larger sense, as the mind or intellective power abstractedly from the *νους*, or pure reason, as the supposed identity of the *intellectio* and the *intelligible,*[43] from the reason, I say, as at once the light of the mind and its highest object, and no less in abstraction from, the sensations and impressions, as far as the conditions, causes, and materials of these were found in the body or through its medium. The knowledge derived from the latter sources, as far as it was derived from them exclusively, was considered as fluctuating and below the formal sciences; in our present use of words, it was merely empirical (that word used *in sensu inferiori,*[44] though exclusively of all moral defect), but which, when reduced under the forms or inherent rules of the understanding, was capable of being elevated into experience and of becoming the substitute, and often the indispensable substitute, of the permanent truths of the pure reason, that is, in all those numberless cases of which the large portion of our active life consists, where we must accept the probable in all

its degrees, in lieu of the certain. In this third distinctive use of the term, the λογος may be rendered the understanding, considered not so much as either excluding or including the sense as without any conscious reference to it. Or perhaps I should be better understood, if I said it was the understanding including the faculty of the *pure sense* without reference to its peculiar objects. The last sense is in immediate connection with the former, or rather an application of it to a particular and correspondent science—that of logic; of which no other definition need be given than that it contains the rules or forms of the understanding,on whatever objects they are employed, in exclusive reference to the correspondence of these objects to its own forms; in other words, it is the science which affirms or denies the formal truth of our conceptions or of positions the value of which is derived from their dependence the one on the other.

21. It is probable, however, that the following diagram may assist in the impression, if not be comprehension, both of what logic properly means and likewise of the sense in which the terms "above" and "below" have been used in the preceding paragraph.

22. We will suppose that NΛΘ is the section of a circle, of which N is the centre: from which the radii NΛ and NΘ are drawn and which, in conjunction with the extracircumferential E, we may conceive as determining the chord connecting Λ and

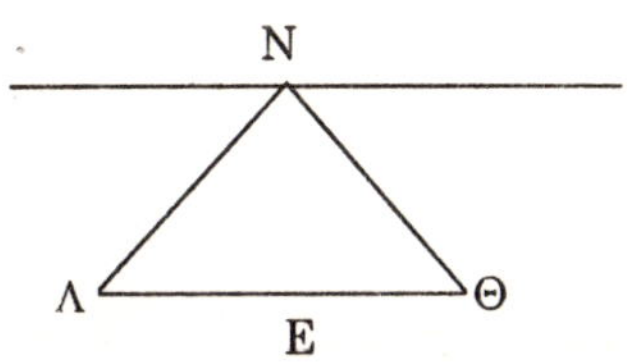

Θ, and we will also suppose that the eye is directed upward, from the chord to the centre.

23(a). Thus regarded, we should be allowed to speak of Λ as below N, = to Θ, and above E; or of N as above, and E as below, Λ. But it is equally evident that by imagining the figure in a different relation to the eye, instead of above we might with the same propriety use the word inward or more inward, central or deeper, and this commutation of terms exists in all cultivated languages; more especially when the subject spoken of [is] in reference to the mind or the feelings of man. Instances repeatedly occur in which the same truth may be indifferently extolled as sublime or profound: a high sense of honour, or a deep feeling of the right, etc. Now let the N signify the νους, or the reason, as the something transcendent of the understanding; the Λ and the Θ, the λογος and the θεωρια, represent the understanding and the sense as the two constituents of the mind; while the extracircumferential E, the power acting on or from without, and the chord ΛΘ, [serve] at once as the common boundary and medium of communication. Thus we have a view of the powers from which the sciences derive their name or character. To obtain a view of the latter we have only to consider the N as representing the indemonstrable, because the ground of all demonstration, or the absolute, that is, irrelative, because the ground of all relation (the consideration of which, as the primary truths—*aeternae veritates*[45]—independent of all time and place and in which the reason itself consists, gives rise to the science once called the first philosophy, then ontology, by others—but more laxly *et improprie*[46]—metaphysics, but for which the term "noetic", or the science corresponding to the νους, would be the most unpresuming and most appropriate exponent). The Λ would represent the science of the permanent relations in conceptions, as inferior to the absolute, but superior to the variably relative,or facts, which we find, but do not understand or conceive in and of themselves. And the Θ is the mathematics,as the science of number and measure, arithmetic and geometry, or the forms of perception inherent in the faculty itself, and which may be considered in itself as a collateral science with logic; which[47] in its use is fitly recommended by Plato as introductory to the other sciences in its elements and then their assiduous companion and ally, but which in no sense of the word can be admitted as a mode of logic or a substitute for it.[48]

23(b). These three sciences, [the] noetic, the logic, and the mathematic, are comprised in the term "metaphysics", as being all above, or transcendental to, the physics ([μετα φυσικα]), as having a higher evidence than that which the senses can afford, or which can belong to objects of the bodily sense considered as matters of fact, a phrase,[49] like many others which we shall have occasion to notice in the progress of the work, that has been vulgarised by its vulgar use, but [which,] in its origin and literal import, is strictly and beautifully expressive. Thus by the mathematic we have the immediate truth in all things numerable and mensurable; or the permanent relations of space and time. In the noetic, we have the immediate truth in all objects or subjects that are above space and time; and, by the logic, we determine the mediate truths by conception and conclusion, and by the application of all to the world of the senses, we form facts and maxims of experience which is one of the two provinces in and on which the formal sciences are to be employed and realised.

23(c). The reader is once more reminded that the truth and reality of the positions assumed in these distinctions is not here asserted; they would be wholly out of their place in this division of our work.

24. It is only necessary that such is the meaning of the words, and that such and no other are the appropriate objects of the sciences so called; for aught that we are here concerned with, thought may be the mere result of organisation; the brain may be an organ for the secretion of mind, according to the recent assertion of a medical philosopher;[50] or the aggregate of ideas, conceptions, and images may be founded in vibrations, either of strings, or of a tremulous fluid, permeating on strings.[51] With all this the logician has as little to do as common sense has; sufficient for him that thoughts are thoughts and that the laws by which they act are the laws of thought, for to these laws; and to these only as far as they contain the rules of reasoning conclusively, is his science confined. Finally, all truth,

and consequently all true knowledge, rests on the coincidence of the object with the subject. Even what is called fact merely expresses the result of this coincidence. On the other hand, the operations of the mind and the contemplation of nature, the act and power of contemplation itself, could not escape attention, and yet there was no evidence [that] *that* implied or [was] necessarily contained in the former.

25. This writing desk, for instance, would, it seems to us, exist though there were no subject, or sentient being, to look at it: nor should we expect any sentiency to arise out of it, or any power of contemplating itself to reside *within* it actually or potentially. As, then, the sum of the objective was entitled nature, as comprising all the phenomena by which other existence than our own is made known to us, *so was the sum of all the subjective comprehended in the name of mind* or intelligence. Both conceptions are in necessary antithesis. Intelligence is conceived as exclusively representative, nature as represented; the one as conscious, the other as without consciousness. From this state, there necessarily arise three distinct theories, each having its own value in its own proper province. In the act of perception, the object and subject are so instantly united that we cannot determine to which of the two the priority belongs.[52] In the tune produced on an Aeolian harp, it is perfectly indifferent whether we take the organic harp or the breeze as the first of its two efficient causes;[53] the quotient stands in the same relation to both the factors. There is here no first and no second, both are coinstantaneous, and the common product is indivisibly one. If then we would explain the one out of the other, we must of necessity begin by giving an arbitrary or hypothetical antecedence to one of the two. Take the following as an illustration. A person believing himself to be fully awake beholds the form of a well-known individual at the bedfoot. The figure remains the same in relation to the percipient whether we attribute the antecedence in its causation to a cause working outwardly or to the percipient himself. In the first instance we should explain the subjective, that is, the

state of the percipient, at that moment, out of the objective. We should conceive an object originating the production, and the subject as merely receiving the same, as the wax receives and retains the impression of the seal. In the latter case, we should begin with the state of the subjective, and from this explain the supposed object. And this object would in truth be no more unsubstantial in this instance than the subject is in the former, on the present supposition in which object and subject are taken separately for the purpose of explaining the one by the other. For what can the recipient or the subject be if it be not an object, after the object has been presumed as its efficient cause? In the thing all reality has been comprised, and there remains nothing for the subject but to be nothing, or a power or property of the former, or a result not separable from it, even as the cutting is a result not separable from the edge of the knife. In assuming the object as the antecedent of the subject, I make the subject objective; as when the beholder says, "it was a real man that I saw"; and, in like manner, the object becomes wholly subjective when we assume the subject as the proper antecedent of the object. "Nay", would the physician answer, "what you saw was a mere thought or fancy of your own."

26. Which then of these shall we choose, or by what means shall we evade the necessity of choosing between either, and what theory would result from this last division? We have asserted, however, that each of the three views has a value of its own, in its own province and for its own purposes. We will begin then as the philosopher of Greece began, with nature—here then the objective is taken as the first and we have to account for the subjective: it is evident then that we must jealously exclude whatever is confessdly subjective from our views, *our terms must be the pure exponents of the phenomena,* or, by generalisations, capable of being reduced to such phenomena, and, if this be impossible without presuming some power, this power must derive all its attributes from the phenomena in which it is manifested, and be assumed strictly

commensurate with its effects; a power thus taken is an empirical law in reality, and in severe accuracy of language, it is a fiction invented for the *generalisation of history,* and for the purpose of enabling the observer to reflect on the sum total of a successive series, collectively and abstracted from the succession. All interference of spirits, as existences, entities existing separately from the object, and of all final causes, in any way distinguished from the efficient cause and lastly of all cause, of cause itself, that can in any way be otherwise than verbally distinguished from the effect, is an inconsistency which, by removing all the force of the reasoning, not merely invalidates the conclusion, but by its inevitable action on the observer himself, and on the character of the images which he abstracts by means of his senses, renders the observations themselves insecure and places them in the list of things like garments mistaken in the dark for a person, or meteoric lights portion in which itself a task better suited to the fancy than to the philosophic judgment.

27. Yet a purity so austere, so stern and coercive a discipline of the mind, was not be expected in the first and youthful period of philosophy; and there was a craving withal which even the most strenuous exercise of the judgment could neither have explained nor gratified. The objects of sense are in continual flux, and the notices of them by the senses must, as far as they are true notices, change with them. The senses themselves are but particulars, subject to the same flux, and capable of communicating their own character to the notices of which they are the media; nay, the very understanding itself, even independent of the causes that always in each individual possessor render it, more or less turbid or uneven, does in the language of our immortal Verulam "ipsa sua natura radios ex figura et sectione propria immutat".[54] Our understanding not only reflects the objects subjectively; that is, substitutes the relations which the objects bear to its (the understanding's) own particular constitution for the inherent laws and properties of the objects themselves; but all its

presentations and reflexes; in other words, the understanding itself, as far as it expresses the aggregate of these, is itself but a phenomenon of the inner sense, and requires therefore the same corrections as the phenomena transmitted by the outward sense. Whence then arise the necessary, the permanent, the universal, or the truths having these attributes, and whence, if not from these, are we to derive the rules and principles by which our observations and reflections are to be corrected? The necessity therefore of a something prior to the objective, in the order of information, at least prior in order to a true knowledge of the objective itself, is strikingly exemplified in the fact that of all the observations or facts of nature collected in this first period, either in Greece or Egypt, nothing has survived but dreams and fancies, the hypotheses of children (see Stanley's history of philosophy before Anaxagoras).[55] and from which if our gratitude in other and higher respects did not influence our judgment, as far as natural history (physics) is concerned, Pythagoras himself is but an uncertain exception. Happy therefore was it for making when it occurred to try the alternative.

28. The subjective was assumed as the first, and previously to the attempt of directly explaining the objective out of it, it occurred to, might I not almost say it was inspired into, the greatest of philosophers,[56] if not the first who merited, as well as assumed, that name, to try first, by effectuating that rigid exclusion of the opposite, which ought to have been, but was not and indeed could not have been, persistently even attempted in the former case. The perception of a truth, permanent, necessary, raised above all accident and all change, had flashed upon him in a geometrical contemplation. He perceived at once that this truth had no respect either to the magnitude, the figure, or the tactual properties; to nothing, in short, into which phenomenal nature must be analysed, as into its ultimate elements; it was true, absolutely in and for the mind only; its proper being was in the mind, and in contemplating it, the intelligence was contemplating its own acts and their products,

as realised in its own imagination. Henceforward, then, it was to be inquired what the subjective could effect by its own powers, by reflection on its own acts and the products of those acts, for and within its own sphere. The mind was now considered as an island, unapproachable from without, or whatever importations were thrown on its shores from the unknown region were carefully distinguished from the indigenous growth. The result of this grand experiment was form knowledge—or science considered in its purity and prior to its application. Science then refracted itself, if I may use so bold a metaphor, into the sciences, as the pure light into its various rays, and these of two kinds, in accordance with the two different faculties of the mind. First the sciences that refer to the acts of sense, either to the sense which employs itself on ideal space or the sense which has time as the material of its contemplation. These are the sciences or, rather, twofold science of number and measure: arithmetic and geometry. The other division had for its subject the forms of thought, in their necessary dependencies, one on the other, and this, as we have before shown at large, is the science of logic. The third question which gives priority neither to the objective nor subjective, but subjects both, as co-ordinates, to a third, higher than either, belongs not to the present work. As the assumption in all natural enquiries (physics) is that of negative materialism, however remote the naturalist himself may be from a materialist, even so in the formal sciences there is no other assumption but that of negative idealism, however little faith may be attached to the latter as a system of philosophy. The logician, and in like manner the geometrician, will say, "I am no Berkeleyan, but while I am engaged in the science of logic I must reason as if I were." This is what is meant by the epithet "negative", that, namely, which abstracts from, without asserting the nonenity of, its opposite.[57] The logician, as far as he is treating of the forms of logic, abstracts his attention from the outward world without denying either its reality or the reality of its connection with the mind.

A synopsis of the main points contained in the preceding chapters, for the purpose of aiding a self-examination into the sum of our acquirements.

29. There are two questions which every student should put to himself, the one at each stage of his progress, the other at the end of the course. The former, "*Have I learnt, that is, made myself master of, that which has been taught, whether by oral or written instruction, and what are the main particulars?*" The second, "*Have I reason to believe that my faculties are improved and my means enlarged?*" For that alone is truly knowledge in relation to the individual acquirer which reappears as power,[58] and the improvement of the faculties, the only sure measure and criterion of the attainments.

30. In aid of the former question, I have thought it convenient to annex the following repetition. Let us suppose that on our ascent we have attained a convenient resting place, have agreed to pause, to turn round toward the road over which we had been passing, and employing ourselves in pointing out the principal objects and turns of the road, or, if I may be allowed the phrase, the several reaches which we had examined close at hand, and endeavoured to impress on our memory, as at once the landmarks of the road and the fruits of our journey. First, then, it has been required of me that I should consider the mind in and for itself, separately from the objects of the senses and sensations. All that belongs to the former we have for our present purposes agreed to comprise under the name of "subjective", or intelligence, and all the latter under the term "objective" or nature. By this, however, we are not bound, nor undertstood, to deny the existence of either the one or the other, nor to establish any real chasm or interspace between the two, any more than (to take a rude and sufficient illustration) we do in having the boundaries that divide Prussia from Saxony for the purpose of confining our a tention to the former. We may indeed assert the exclusive reality of either and we know, from the history of philosophy, that the assertion has been made seriously and in good faith

in both instances. But this belongs to philosophy and constitutes and philosphic system: in the one case the system of idealism, more commonly known to the English reader under the name of Berkeleyanism, and in the other the system of materialism. These, I say belong to philosophy, and we are engaged in the consideration of science, and moreover in relation to a particular science, that of logic. Next in importance is the distinction which I have been called upon to observe and make between real and formal knowledges, and the real and formal sciences in consequence. I need only ask myself, what are the matters treated of the will, the soul, the conscience, to see at once that, although I acquire my convictions otherwise than by my senses, and even without relation to the forms of sense, such as extension, motion, partibility, and the like yet I attribute as much reality to the former class as to the latter. Whether I speak of a man's soul or his body, I speak of a something which I suppose to subsist of itself and not contained in the act of my contemplation. But when I say that what is true of all must be true of each, or *quae de generica notione statuuntur omnibus inferioribus sub eadem complexis competere* , or simply affirm that *ominis cujuslibet notio est vel generalis vel individualis,*[59] I am not speaking of any thing, but of the acts of my own mind and the law or form according to which it acts or ought to act. Now the sciences which teach these forms are hence contradistinguished as formal sciences, and, in this acceptation of the word, logic, geometry, and arithmetic are all alike formal sciences. Thirdly, as we proceeded, we were led to consider the mind in the threefold relation. First in reference to those permanent and universal truths which in the peculiar sense are entitled truths of reason, and mind contemplated as the source of these is designated the reason, or, using the Greek term for the after-convenience of its derivation, the νους. These we characterised neither as object nor as subject exclusively, but as the identity of both as at once formal and real; or in other words, forms that implied their own reality. We will take mind itself; not this man's mind, nor yours, individually, nor even the human mind generally, but *mind* absolutely. Now of this we assert that the form or act of contemplating, which it will be found convenient to call the "position" of it, implies the reality. *Ponitur mens: ergo est,nam mentem ponere ipsa mens est.*[60] These truths (conceived as a system) form the science of noetics, more frequently, but less appropriately, entitled metaphysics. In subordination to these, and as more properly constituting the mind in its specific sense as the *human* mind, we found the λογος (the understanding) and the [θεωρια], the sense. Below these we have to add the senses which we may consider as the common boundaries of intelligence and nature: and the following table will place the whole before us in one view.[61]

31. The sciences pure and mixed and in the order of their senses.

Μετα Φνσικα

A—Noetics=the evidence of reason

B—Logic=the evidence of the understanding

C—Mathematics = the evidence of sense

Φνσικα

D—Empiric = evidence of the senses

Scholium. The senses = sense + sensation + impressions.

32. Now with none of these have we at present any immediate concern, B only excepted. We are now exclusively seeking that evidence which arises from the perfect coincidence of a conception or proposition (that is, words intended to express conception) with the laws of the understanding, or the rules that result from the constitution of the understanding itself considered abstractedly from its objects, even as the mechanist would examine an engine previously to its use, or an astronomer a quadrant or telescope.

33. It is the same whether we say the constitution of the understanding or the constituent forms of the understanding, the understanding being considered as the band or copula of

these. Thus a steam engine, of course, comprises all the component parts; but these parts, considered in themselves as individual things, do not involve or constitute the idea of the steam engine: it is the steam engine = the parts+the copula of the parts.

34. We have learnt that the proper subject of logic, in the strict and simple sense of the term, is not *what* we understand nor *how much,* but simply *how* we understand. Not *quid* nor *quantum*; but *quomodo.* This therefore is equivalent to the form or mode in which we understand: and a moment's reflection will convince us that a mode or form or scheme implies certain relations; either the relation A to the realtion B to the same subject, e.g., the relation of the length to the breadth in the same table: or of one subject to another subject having the same or different relations. But this, again, by pursuing the act of reflection we shall find to imply a plurality, or alterity,[62] in some sense or other; though it be a plurality which involves no breach of unity, that is, does not prevent us from asserting the unity of the same subject, in some other point of view. Try to represent space without inclosing the same in some figure, here you would have a subject perfectly arid of pluralrity and alterity, and in the same moment you will experience the impossibility of attaching any form thereto: in other words, you will see that to say the form of any subj-ect, or the mode, supposes at least certain distinctions in that subject, or, as in the present instance, certain distinct acts of the mind called forth in the treatment thereof.

35. Let not the student be either surprised or offended by these technical terms. If he have been previously a student in anatomy, in botany, or in chemistry, he must have learnt from his own experience that the feeling of uncouthness in technical terms will diminish as the sense of their convenience increases, and as the meaning expressed by each becomes more familiar both in itself and in its association with the given terms. At least, it would be difficult to discover why "identity", "unity", "plurality", or even "haecceity"[63] and "alterity" (*haec et altera*

sive res sive forma)[64] as abstract terms, expressing certain acts of the mind, should stand a worse chance than "hydrogenation" and "oxygenation" or "protoxides", "deutoxides", "tritoxides", and "preoxides" in chemistry, as generic terms for sundry acts of nature or for the forms and phenomena resulting. In both cases the words are employed as marks for recollection or marks of security—means by which we bring a train of equivalent or similar particulars into one group before the memory, or by which we refer to a past ascertainment with a conviction that we have ascertained the same, and have it in our power to renew our distinct insight into the grounds and process whenever we please. In another division of the present treatise, the student will find this subject treated of more at large, under the heads of abstraction and generalisation, and wherein they differ.[65] The bracketed sentences[66] therefore must be regarded as *anticipations,* the entire rejection of which we have already shown to be impracticable (see chapter first)[67] and, were it not so, yet obstructive and occasioning unnecessary difficulties in the acquisition of knowledge.

Footnotes

1. "I speak".
2. I.e. the lexicographers Hesychius and Suidas, quoted by Ruhnken; see next note, below.
3. David Ruhnken "Epistola critica I" in *Homeri hymnus in Cererem . . . acceduni duae epistolae criticae* (Leyden 1782) 86-9.
4. Cf *CN* I 1293 (Dec 1802): "cat-hate-cssen-hassen odi-edi".
5. I.e. the letter λ.
6. Cf Plato *Cratylus* 427B.
7. Cf *CN* I 4 for C's early theorising about labials. N 29 ff 28*V*-29 contains a discussion parallel to the *Logic.*
8. On whom see e.g. the long note in Lord Monboddo *Of the Origin and Progress of Language* I 414-16n.
9. In C's time, a current spelling of "ayin"-e.g. "the sixteenth letter of the Hebrew alphabet, Oin, as it is called by some, and Air or

Gnain by others . . ." *The Classical Journal* VIII (1813) 97. A parallel passage in N 29 f 43 has "Naing". For the difficult pronunciation of the letter, see *Gesenius' Hebrew Grammar* ed F. Kautzsch and A.E. Cowley (Oxford 1910) 32-3. In Wilhelm Gesenius *Ausführliches grammatisch-kritisches Lehrgebäude der hebäischen Sparache. . .* (Leipzig 1817) 12, "ayin" is used as an example of a Hebrew sound that is almost impossible for Western Europeans to imitate. C had access to Gesenius in J.H. Green's library (see *Green SC* item 214), and the topic is one he could have talked over with his learned frieng Hyman Hurwitz.

10. Pronounced "angelos", tr "messenger". Cf below, p 92.
11. "Anguish" or "torment".
12. C acknowledges the reputation popularised by Lord Byron's stirring characterisation of them in *Childe Harold's Pilgrimage* Canto II (1812), and confirmed by the outbreak of the Greek war of independence in 1821.
13. " To call". The verso of the preceding page of MS Logic has the word "dipthong" at this point.
14. The verso of the preceding page of the manuscript of the Logic has the word "stronger" at this point.
15. "To calculate".
16. "Words", "language".
17. C would have found a long exposition of this view in Monboddo *Of the Origin* . . . i bk 2. For C's awareness of a much discussed contemporary instance of man in a savage state, see *CN* i 1348.
18. Sentence ends with λογος (no full stop): "Flowing utterances [in distinction from] [considerate] word[s]". Cf below, pp 89, 96, and 120. Cf also the more elaborate discussion in N 29 f 60 of the distinction between λογος and *ρημα* which is based on Georg Friedrich Creuzer *Symbolik und Mythologie der alten Völker* (2nd ed 4 vols Leipzig & Darmstadt 1819-21) I 45-7.
19. "[Aesopian] fables". Cf "Μυθοι Αισωπικοι" in the parallel discussion in N 29 f 60.
20. Judges 9.7-15.
21. Menippus seems to have been substituted by mistake for the more obviously apt Menenius Agrippa with his fable of the belly

and the members—see *Coriolanus* I i 101-61.

22. "Voices of nature and human words".

23. Word speech, tale, saying" etc, and in the plural, "epic poetry".

24. A false etymology from Creuzer *Symbolik* I 46. According to him, επειν means "to fasten together".

25. "Epic poet"; by derivation, "word-maker".

26. "Good spirit".

27. Sir Walter Scott *Waverley; or, 'Tis Sixty Years Since* (1814), *Guy Mannering* (1815)-which C thought of going to see in the theathre (*CL* IV 625) in 1816-*Marmion; a Tale of Flodden Field* (1808), and *The Lady of the Lake; a Poem* (1810). Although Scott did not acknowledge his authorship of the Waverley novels until 1827 (in *Chronicles of the Canongate*—Edinburgh—i xxi-xxviii), C had guessed it in Mar 1820 (*C Life*—G—227; cf *CL* VI 602).

28. Περι αεπων υδατων τοπων. The passage that C attributes to Hippocrates does not appear in the course of the work. Is C thinking of the opening of Herodotus; "Ηροδοτου Αλικαρνησσεος ιστοριης αποδεξις ηδε..."? ("What Herodotus the Halicarnassian has learnt by inquiry is here set fort . . .". Tr A. D. Godley LCL 1960.)

29. Herodotus 1.1.

30. E.g. the Seven Wise Men are called σοφισται. Herodotus 1.29 C is perhaps using the discussion of the early meanings of σοφος Christoph Meiners *Geschichte des Ursprungs Fortgangs und Verfalls der Wissenschaften* . . . (2 vols Lemgo 1781-2) i 112-17. Tennemann (i 345n) would have drawn his attention to it.

31. C seems to have substituted the *Hymns* for the *Margites*. See the fragment preserved in Aristotle's discussion of Anu in *Nicomachean Ethics* VI (1141a).

32. For C's views on the multiple authorship of Homer's works, see *P Lects* Lects 2, 3 (1949) 87-8, 120. Cf *TT* 12 May 1830 (HNC's note) and *CRB* i 320-1.

33. The priestess of Apollo at Delphi.

34. *Olympian Odes* 2.85-8: "They who have learnt" is μαθοντες. Cf

μαθησις, μαθημα, below.

35. Cf *Friend* (*CC*) I 436. This tradition is recorded in Stanley 352.

36. Cf Stanley 377.

37. E.g. Plato *Phaedrus* 274E-278A.

38. I.e. "philosopher".

39. On Anaxagoras and νους (mind) cf *CN* I 208, quoting Aristotle *Metaphysics* 1.4 (985a) and *P Lects* Lect 4 (1949) 146, alluding to Plato *Phaedo* 97B-98B.

40. For C's interpretation of Heraclitus on λογος see *SM* (*CC*) 95 and 97, where C is using Friedrich Daniel Schleiermacher "Herakleitos der dunkel . . ." *Museum der Alterthums-Wissenschaft* ed F. A. Wolf and P. Buttman (2 vols Berlin 1807, 1810) i 313-533. Schleiermacher (i 316) distinguishes between the modest number of genuine fragments and the reports and mentions of ancient writers. W.K. C. Guthrie *A History of Greek Philosophy* (1962-) i 419-34 discusses the Logos in Heraclitus.

41. C refers to the fragment in *P Lects* Lect 5 (1949) 175. It is quoted in Tennemann III 9n from Stobaeus *Eclog, Physic.* I c 3 p 38: "the Nous is not the same as the One or the Good, but has a nature of its own". C's version in *P Lects* runs as follows:" I refer to the passage in which we are told that the intelligential powers, by the Pythagoreans and Anaxagoras called the *Nous,* (the *Logos* or the *Word* of Philo and St. John) is indeed indivisibly united with, but yet not the same as the absolute principle of causation, T H E P A T E R N A L One, the super-essential Will. . .".

42. C gives the gist of Aristotle's distinction in *De anima* 3.5; Scholastic philosophers had pointed out its significance—e.g. Aquinas *Summa theologica* Ia. 79, 4.

43. "The intellect", "the intelligible".

44. "In a lower sense".

45. Literally, "eternal truths".

46. "And improperly".

47. I.e. "the mathematics".

48. *Republic* 7.525-6; *Laws* 5.747 and 7.818-19.

49. I.e. "matters of fact".

50. C ascribes this statement elsewhere to "Dr Elliotson, the great standard bearer of Materialism, the Ali of the physiological Mahomet [?Mesmer]. . .". (BM MS Egerton 2801 f 69*V*—watermark 1821). The reference is to a note in John Elliotson (1791-1868) tr of J. F. Blumenbach *The Institutions of Physiology*. . . (2nd ed 1817) 130. C mentioned the book in *Friend* (*CC*) i 154-5n and in a letter to Thomas Curtis in Dec 1818 (*CL* IV 886).

51. Cf the account of Hartley's theory in *BL* ch 6 (1907) i 74ff. See below, pp 265-6n.

52. Cf *BL* ch. 12 (1907) i 174ff.

53. Cf below, p 142.

54. Bacon *Distributio operis: Works* (1740) I 15 (var). Tr: [as an uneven mirror] "by its very nature distorts the rays according to its own figure and section". C quotes the same passage in *Friend* (*CC*) 1 491.

55. The discussion of Anaxagoras in Stanley begins at p 63, following the account of the Seven Wise Men and Anaximander and Anaximenes.

56. Pythagoras. Cf *P Lects* Lect 2 (1949) 97ff and *SM* (*CC*) 50 and n.

57. Cf "*negative* faith": *BL* ch 22 (1907) II 107.

58. Cf *SM* (*CC*) 24 and n 2.

59. "Every notion, of whatever it may be, [is] either general or particular".

60. "The mind is posited: therefore it is, for the positing of mind is mind itself".

61. The table is given in a slightly garbled version in ms—C's marks, indicating footnotes, having been misread. It has been corrected by the editor from another ms in C's hand, which must have been the direct or indirect source of it and of paragraphs 32 and 33: BM MS Egerton 2801 ff 85-6 (for which see Appendix D, below).

62. The state of being other; otherness.

63. Individuality; thisness. Duns Scotus' term; cf *P Lects* (1949) 438-9, quoting a marginal note in Tennemann VIII 765.

64. "This and the other whether thing or form". The same phrase

appears in BM MS Egerton 2801 f 88*V*.

65. See below, pp 62-4.

66. Presumably the four preceding paragraphs. The brackets have not survived transcription.

67. See above, pp 7 ff.

Chapter-3

On the Logical Acts

Chapter 3

1. If we reflect on the operations of our own minds while we were employed in the foregoing process, we shall discover first the act of attention, in which the mind exercises the power of directing itself to one or more objects with a particular force. The same is doubtless exercised by the brute creation, but we have no sufficient ground for assuming that this takes place in them by any energy of the percipient power itself, taken separately form the stimulus applied to it by external impression. We hesitate, therefore, in naming it an act of attention ,the word "act" being here contradistinguished form the results of any mere passive sensation or impress[ion]. Still less are we entitled to *conclude*, however much in the case of certain animals we may be inclined to *conjecture*, we cannot name it an act of the understanding. This exclusively appropriate to the human faculty.

2. But if we attend exclusively, or at least more expressly to one subject there will arise two possible cases. This object may either be really separable from the others which are near it, that is, it may be a concrete, or not really separable. And again we may either attend to it, being at the same time conscious likewise of the objects from which we have separated it; or our whole attention, and with it, therefore, our whole consciousness, [may] have been concentred toward it. In the last case it would be a simple act of attention, in the former it would necessarily be accompanied by a act of comparison. This we have before shown, though in different terms, in the distinction between universal and particular propositions, and on it we have grounded our proposal to name the act exerted in the major of the syllogism, the act of *clusion* where the proposition is universal, and of *seclusion* where it is particular. The latter, it is evident, implies a comparison of the object *secluded* with the object or objects FROM which it is secluded,

and this comparison will be implied, though not always expressed, in the predicate by which the major subject of the particular proposition is defined. It does not follow indeed that this comparison shall be carried on distinctly through all the objects from which the predicate separates the subject of the proposition. When, for instance, we determine a certain class of animals by the epithet "quadruped", we certainly imply a consciousness that there are other animals which are not so, though it may be indifferent whether the comparison be distinctly made of quadrupeds with birds, or with insects, or with the footless reptiles, or with them all in rapid succession.

3. In the second case, viz. where no real separation is possible, where the attention is particularly directed to an accident, property, or inseparable part of a concrete, and this attention is continued for the purpose of reflecting on this acci-dent exclusively, we herein exercise a power which is called the power of abstraction; and both in etymological and logical propriety we ought not to say that we abstract something (*abstrahere aliquid*), but that we abstract from something. When on looking at this scarlet cloth on our table we confine our th-oughts to the colour, we abstract from the cloth. The accusative case understood being the attentient. It would be absurd to say that we abstracted the colour itself, unless indeed we were speaking, not as logicians, but as chemists or dyers, when of course we should not mean the colour but the colouring matter. But I possess the power, having thus once abstracted my attention from the scarlet cloth, [of abstracting it] from all other concretes having the same colour; but in doing this, I exert another power—that of substantiation, on which is grounded the conversion of the adjective into the substantive. We speak of the green leaves, but in abstracting from leaves, grass, etc, etc, we can reflect on the green in nature; and whether in the latter case we say green or greenness is logically indifferent and determinable only by the idiom of the language in which we speak, when it is not, as in many languages it is, gramatically as well as logically indifferent. Observe likewise that the act

of substantiation here spoken of is logical or an act of the understanding and not an act of the fancy which may or may not accompany the former. It is not necessary that I should bring up any image in my mind, unless, indeed, the *word* itself can be called such, and the presence of this as an image is common to accident and to substance. The unity of conception, to which we are now about to proceed, is of itself sufficient to constitute this logical, abstract, and merely logical substantiality. In the strict propriety of language we should, perhaps, instead of abstract conceptions (*conceptus abstracti*), use the participle active (*conceptus abstrahentes*), acts of conceiving, in which we abstract from such and such concretes. The most frequent mistake, however, is that of confounding abstraction with generalisation. In the term "sheep", so far from withdrawing my attention from the animal, I am bringing a succession of these animals into comparison with each other and in consequence of certain essential likenesses, without abstracting from the differences, but on the contrary with a full insight into the compatibility of these differences with the points of essential likeness (or logical identity) I form the general conception "sheep"; now the most abstract conception is that which has nothing [in] common with anything at all different from it. This is the conception expressed in the word "something", for the only conception or term that is different from it is "nothing", and between these of course there is no point in common.

4. Nevertheless, in the process of thinking there is found to be a transition from the abstract into the general, and this we shall perhaps explain most intelligibly by a declaration of the proprieties of the three terms which in ordinary life are most frequently confounded: I mean, "idea", "abstraction", and "generalisation".

5. N.B. It would perhaps be the more proper expression to say that an abstraction is capable of being reduced to a generic conception by its reduction, that is, its being brought back again to the objects from which it had been abstracted, in order to determine whether or no it was universally applicable

or its compatibility with all the differences contained in the concretes. Thus an abstraction followed by an act of comparison of the common conception which by means of this abstraction we had formed, with the differences, constitutes a proper generic conception. Thus an abstraction is in all cases a common conception but not in all cases a generic conception. In other words, the abstract in the most comprehensive sense contains the generic, but in another is contradistinguished from it when we wish to express that it is merely an abstract. An idea, on the contrary, is opposed equally to the abstract and to the generic. We have seen that an abstract conception may be matured by following acts of the mind into a generic.

6. We shall hereafter show in what manner an abstraction at the time that it passes into a generalisation becomes connected or rather coincides with an imperfect image or impression of a whole without distinction of the component parts (which image might not inappropriately be termed an abstraction of the sense in the same [way] as the corresponding conception to this image is an abstraction of the understanding). But an idea must be conceived of as anterior to all image and is that which is presupposed in all form and in every concrete as far as the same is reducible to any determinate law. It has therefore no common point with abstraction and as generalisation is an abstraction, therefore none with generalisation. But what have no point in common are diverse in kind and therefore insusceptible of all comparison, even that of opposition, by a law the importance of which we shall have ample occasion of learning in a more advanced stage of the work—*oppositasemper unigena,* or there is no opposition between heterogeneous subjects.

7. Some of the ablest foreign logicians (and even the greatest logician since the time of Aristotle and the founder of the critical philosophy forms no exception) have incurred or sanctioned this error by their assumption that in the formation of a pure idea we abstract from image, etc, etc, But this is true only in a lax and impermissible sense of the term "abstract",

that act of simply excluding or rather precluding whatever would tend to disturb the mind as impertinent and heterogeneous. It would sound strange, were a man to say that in constructing a watch or describing a diagram he abstracted from the pictures in the room or abstracted from the noise of the children playing under his window; and if, instead of impressions made on the senses, we put images and thoughts equally impertinent to and diverse from the immediate object of our attention, we should be as little justified in this application of the term. "An idea", says Kant, "contains in it all its subordinates". An abstraction has all its subordinates under it, but so that each subordinate contains more than its superordinate, and the first abstraction contains the least of all. Now there is, to say the least, an ambiguity in the word "contain". We will suppose the first abstraction to be "thing". Its subordinates secondly "organisation", thirdly "animal". Though I confess that any order at all which can justify the use of the words "subordinate" and "superordinate" is merely arbitrary. But waiving this, surely the second is no less an abstraction than the first, and the third is as much as either; and how can one abstraction contain more than another when abstraction is contradistinguished from idea in consequence of its not containing any reality at all? In fact the word "contain" or "comprehend" means no more than that such a term is predicable, without contradiction or incongruity, of a quarter or less number of things, and in this sense rather has been, than may be, said to comprehend them.

8. We have seen what the nature of the syllogism is, considered exclusively as the logical canon or the rule according to which the understanding proceeds in conclusive reasoning. What is affirmed [of any thing is true] of every other contained in the same. Divested of technical terms we may give this rule and at the same time explain it by compressing what has been before said. When an act of conscious attention is directed towards an object by means of some mark applying to the same throughout, and we afterwards think of any part or content of

this object as a thing of itself, but with the recollection of its having been included in the former, the mark by which we distinguished the first belongs of necessity to the second likewise, inasmuch as the mark was universal, or applicable to the object throughout, to all its parts and consequently to each. *Quicquid de o[mni] positum est, ponitur de unoquoque.* For object, substitute the conception of an object or its presentation in the mind, and the process becomes logical, that is, subjective in reference to the understanding, aloof from the question of its reality independent of the understanding. On this account what we have before called "object" we now entitle the "subject", and the mark by which it is distinguished and fixed in the consciousness we name the "predicate". It is evident therefore that the value of the syllogism in relation to the purposes of truth and actual knowledge must consist in the legitimacy of the first position, technically called the major of the syllogism, and this again must consist either in the propriety of the mark or predicate of the subject or in the fact of an existence correspondent to a subject so characterised. It is the former, however (the subjective legitimacy, I mean), in which the logical canon is properly concerned. Supposing a syllogism to commence with the assertion of a flasehood, but in other respects without fault, the answer would consist, not in a detection of any error in the form of reasoning. The logic, we should reply, is just and convert it into an hypothetical syllogism by prefixing an "if" or other equivalent condition, it would be as true in logic as it is false in fact. In a former page we have given a syllogism of this king which commences and concludes in an absurdity, and yet as far as the logical process alone is in question is undeniably correct. To use a trivial and somewhat ludicrous illustration, chalk is returned from the [mill] instead of flour, but there is no fault in the mill or the grinding.

9. Let us not, however, think too meanly of the process, whatever the asserted facts may be correspondent to the logical subjects. The combination of the one with the other by the common mark, and the absolute necessity of this combination,

are not only true but real; not only real, but, for the mind, the condition of all other reality. If A = C, and B be contained in A, THEN B is contained in C. This proposition thus stated is a truth of mind: a somewhat that in the mind actually exists, as any object recognised by the senses exists without us. Strictly speaking, indeed, the former may be said to occupy a higher rank, for its evidence is immediate, whereas, that the latter exists *out of us* or *without us* would, if examined-exclusively on speculative grounds, derive its evidence from a truth formed *within* us, and we may appropriately say with us. The proof will have been anticipated by every man who has attempted to return a speculative reply to the well-known position [of] Bishop Berkeley, or who, without this occasion, has endeavoured to satisfy his own mind as to the difference between his sight of an object taken as an impression on the mind through the medium of the senses, and the outward cause and correspondent of this impression. The permanence, the regular recurrence under the same conditions, the absence of all conscious activity in himself, the unconnectedness of the impression with the trains of thought immediately preceding it, the marked character of contingency; these and other grounds of conviction will suggest themselves to his understanding, or whatever else may have occurred to him in reflection and experience as the contradistinctions of our waking perceptions from our dreams or our trains of thought. He seeks reasons on which to ground his assertion of the outward reality and *derives* the evidence of that reality from those reasons. He does so, I mean, as an intellectual being, though he may not perhaps derive his faith in it as a man. For the former, the truth and real existence of the conclusive act in the mind, he brings no reason, for it is self reason and as such having its evidence in itself and immediate.

10(a). This, therefore, is well worthy to be the first position of the dialectic or the sifting or discriminating office of the mind, the criterion or test of the reason and of the understanding. By marks distinguishing the one from the other, thus enabling us to assign to each its proper realm and functions in the acquirement and establishment of truth either directly or indirectly by the detection and removal of error and falsehood, [it] must of course take place of all other criteria, both as being their foundation and as supplying the principle of insight into their nature and value.

10(b). We may commence this inquisition by defining the reason (I mean solely in reference to the logical process) as the source of principles, the understanding as the faculty of rules. The reason is all *end, summa finium.* The understanding all *means, summa mediorum.* Thus, rules are in all cases means to some end. A truth the oversight of which is exemplified and may be profitably illustrated by the false conclusions of certain French critics, who, having borrowed the rules of tragedy which Aristotle had abstracted and generalised from the composition[s] of Aeschylus, Sophocles, and other Greek poets, treated them as ends to which all the parts of every tragedy were to be adapted as means. A conclusion which was of necessity false as often as the end[s] proposed by the Greek dramatists or imposed on them by local and accidental circumstances, e.g. the magnitude and construction of the Athenian theatre, the historical origin of the Greek tragedy, and in consequence of this, the necessity and essential character, adding the minor circumstances which grew out of the preceding and derived their propriety from them, the buskin (*cothurnus*), the tragic mask (*persona*), and the music with the musical recitation of the words throughout, were different from the ends proposed by the modern poets or imposed on them by their local and accidental circumstances. The science of criticism dates its restoration form the time when it was seen that an examination and appreciation of the end was necessarily antecedent to the formation of the rules, supplying at once the principle of the rules themselves and of their application to the given subject. From this time we have heard little (among intelligent persons, I mean) of the wildness and irregularity of our Shakespeare. Nay, when once the end which our myriad minded bard had in view and the local accidents that favoured or obstructed or in any way modified its manifestation are once thoroughly comprehended, the doubt will arise whether the judgment or the genius of the man has the stronger claim to our wonder, or rather it will be felt that the judgment was the birth and living offspring of his genius, even as the symmetry of a body results from the sanity and vigour of the life as the organising power. This subject on the one hand requires so particular and heedful an inquisition and on the other hand is of an importance and fruitfulness so well calculated to remunerate the pains and patience requisite for its investigation that I need not apologise for having introduced it by an instance of its application that at first sight would seem remote and almost alien from the dry pursuits and unattractive interests of a formal science.

11. We have proposed to distinguish the reason from the understanding, and from these distinctions to derive a determinate notion of each as far as the purpose of logic make requisite or expedient. In a science which derives its name and character from the *logos* or understanding, as distinguished from the intuitive faculty, or the sense, and from the *nous* or the reason, there would be some propriety in beginning with the understanding, were it not expedient on many more substantial grounds (and here again permit me to repeat the request, that the student should bear in mind that we are examining neither in any universal application but both alike as far only as the purposes of logic are concerned).

12(a). On the same ground that we have defined reason as the source of principles and the understanding as the faculty of rules, the reason being the *finis finium* or sum of ends, while the understanding is the faculty of means and the sense the faculty of materials, we may proceed further to define the reason as the power of ideas, the understanding the faculty of conceptions, and the sense the source and faculty of intuitions and perceptions. What then, as we are at present treating more immediately of the understanding, what, I say, are conceptions or thoughts? Wherein does the discursive act of the mind consist? In other words, what is that act or effort which declares and manifests itself in any conception, and on which the possibility of conception itself as a species of knowing rests? What is the act that must be presupposed in the conception as the product of that act in order for it to become intelligible to us?

12(b). This act is no other than that by which a multiplicity of given presentations are comprehended in some one representation. By this means the several original presentations acquire a unity, and in this function of unity the act of the understanding or the discursive act consists. But here I must recall to you a former remark, that provided we are aware of the unindividual and transcendent character of the reason as a presence to the human mind, not a particular faculty or component part of the mind, provided, I say, we keep this master truth steadily in view, it is (philosophically) indifferent whether we take the term "understanding" as a perfect synonym of "mind" and then consider the understanding in a twofold application, that is, now exercised discursively and now through the intuitive power, or whether we take the term of "the mind" exclusively as the common term or genus and "the understanding" and "the sense" as its two component faculties or species. Philosophically it is indifferent, but practicably we have found and shall continue to find many and important grounds of expedience for preferring the latter as the avowed and declared terminology adopted throughout the present work, and, let me be permitted to add, in all my other philosophical writings. Were there indeed no other motive than the universally admitted and understood diversity of metaphysic [(μετα φυσικα)], logic and mathematics, and the convenience and exact correspondence of these to the three sources of the reason (νους), the understanding (λογος), and the sense ([?θεωρια]), even this would suffice to incline the scales in favour of the scheme which has been already presented in a synoptic form in a preceding page.

13. In consistency, therefore, with our own nomenclature, we must take the function of unity as twofold; original, namely, or the unity of primary perception, and derived. The latter of which alone is logical and properly belonging to the understanding in our confined and appropriated sense of that word. It is implied in the designations that the derivative unity presupposes the original, the object being common to both. The representation which rises out of the logical function of unity is called a common conception (*conceptus communis*) and depends upon our power of combining a multiplicity of presentations in one and the same act of consciousness. Instead of common conceptions some writers have employed the phrase of "complex ideas" and the innovation has obtained no small currency; but unhappily we think, the first word being indefinite and leaving it doubtful whether it refers to the process and antecedent materials, or to the consciousness, or to the conceptions abstractedly. Applied to the consciousness, the very essence of which is unity, it is absurd, and applied to the conception it is false and a falsity that never fails to arise when we are speaking of one thing with the image of another and a different thing before our imagination: when, for instance, we propose to speak of a thought but in reality are under the influence of some confused image derived from the mixture or combination of bodies, that is, we speak of the constituents or constitution of a thought as if we had been talking of the components of an olio or a pudding. A common conception is as indivisibly one as an individual perception, but if the first term be at best vague and inappropriate, the second, which confounds conception with idea, is altogether a misnomer, as we have already shown. For a common conception is that by which I present to myself the identity of the consciousness in a manifold and different presentation, as in the instance of a house. In the same of consciousness I comprise the presentations of the roof, the chimney, the wall, etc. etc. But this is evidently impossible if these manifold images were not comprisable in one and the same act, though in order to this act there have been many antecedent acts, each including a

narrower and narrower sphere and directed towards a less and yet less complex object. I could not, it is evident, make myself conscious that swans are white unless the sense of whiteness had been previously combined with sundry other impressions in the one impression "swan": nor even so if I had [not] previously combined it with different sets of images or presentations in other total impressions [such] as lilies, cliffs, snow, summer clouds, and the like. For to make myself conscious of anything I must reflect on it. Or rather to make myself conscious of a thing and to reflect on it are but different expressions of the same act. But that on which I reflect (*reflecto* = turn back or turn inwardly upon) must have been taken up into my mind (*apprehensio*) antecedently and in order to the reflection. This apprehension or primary combination of A (we will say) with b, c, d, in the act of *perceiving* the given object corresponding to the impression A, b, c, d, has by some logicians been called the synthetic function of the understanding, and the reflection on the same or the reflex consciousness of this combination *as* a combination, by attending to A distinctly and with the recollection of its existing in combination with E, F, G: H, L, M, etc, etc, as well as with B, C, D—in other words, that A is common to many and different objects or complex impressions. In consequence of which, all these several impressions may be classed together under A as the common mark or character of the class. This reflex or secondary consciousness, I say, the writers above mentioned have named the analytic function of the understanding.

14. Where the meaning is determined and thoroughly understood, there, as far as the containing sentence or period is alone considered, the names may be of slight importance, though even here I could not regard them as altogether indifferent. But where instruction is to result from a connected whole, the parts of which are various yet interdependent, distinctness in the first appropriation of the terms and strict consistency in the use of them are such mighty assistants of the truth, so eminently conducive to the first apprehension of

the meaning and to its connection with other truths whether by likeness or by contrast, each point of distinction serving as hook or eye for that from which it distinguishes as well as the thread for the holding together for all the particulars comprehended in the same distinction, that we need make no apology for preferring any given nomenclature or scheme of terms on the mere ground of its permitting a more perfect consistency in the use of each severally (a recurrence with less sensible variation of purport than in any former nomenclature, but in fact this consistency must commonly, if not always, be itself the result of other and higher advantages, as for instance an exacter correspondence to the differences of the things and objects themselves or at least to our conceptions of the same). Hence no man in the habit of connected thinking, no man for whom distinct conception[s] have become a necessity of his intellectual being, can use a lax and as it were staggering terminology, in which the meaning must in each instance be collected from the context and dilated or compressed according to the demand, without inward dissatisfaction as well knowing that such flexible terms are neither signs nor causes of wisdom on any occasion. And, vice versa, an exact and manageable terminology is at once a secure test of an exact and original thinker, and one of the most important benefits that he can confer on mankind.

15. For these reasons I should not hesitate in substituting the term "mind" for "the understanding" in speaking of the synthetic function and should justify the change by the great conveniencies that result both for the teacher and the learner in using "the mind" as the common term while "the understanding" and "the sense" are reserved for the designation of its two constituent faculties. Let it not, however, be thought that by referring the synthetic function to the sense and the analytic to the understanding, I mean the unity in the former instance to be a mere simultaneity of passive impressions without distinguishable interspaces, as for instance a landscape [in] a small concave mirror or the image of a lake on the

retina of the eye, which is an act of agents external to the mind, if it be an act at all. No! I speak of a function which, as I have before explained, supposes a power of conferring unity in the mind itself, which power in the very introduction of the work we have learnt to recognise as mental forms or primary moulds. In the production of a single line, the first and simplest manifestable form in nature, or in a simple surface as a production of the line in all directions equally, as in the most complex figure that can result from surfaces as bounded by lines, there is a unity presupposed in the mind of the geometrician necessary as predetermining the figure which is to be the product of the act of the indefinite number of points that may be supposed to constitute a circle, or, in more scientific terms, of all the simple acts of position which the geometrician performs in the description of the circumference; the unity of the whole, or the contemplation (θεωρημα) as indivisibly one, must have been present to the mind previously to any or all of the acts exerted, in order to its production. I am well aware that the unprepared imagination will at first find a difficulty in mastering the conception of forms as acts, in distinguishing the act of length from the product which is at the same time the image or representation of that act, and this again from the line on the slate or paper which is but the picture of this image—three stages which some of the later Greek philosophers designated by the terms ενεργεια θεωρητικη, ειδος and ειδωλον. For the removal of this difficulty there is but one way—that of placing yourself in such situations, or as it were positions, of mind as would be likely to call up that act in our intellectual being and then to attend to it as its necessary transient and subtle nature will permit. I have secured to myself to have experienced it often when connecting two bright stars, the one directly above the other as the extremities of the same line. I seemed, if I may so express it, to have a something between a sense and a sensation of length more perfect than any actual filling up of the interval by a succession of points in contact could have given me. I seemed to find myself acting as it were in the construction of that length undisturbed by any accompanying perception of breadth or inequality which must needs accompany all pictures of a line. It was length without any necessity of abstracting from breadth or depth; in other words, it was a self-conscious act snatched away as it were from the product of that act. But the happiest illustration of the act of the intuitive imagination and its close connection with its product in the mental diagram, I believe, the most exact but assuredly the most amusing mode of conveying what I mean, I have seen in the ephemerae and other minute and half-transparent insects who by the exceeding velocity of motion actually present to our eyes a symbol of what Plotinus meant when, speaking of the geometricians and then of Nature as acting geometrically, he says θεωρουσα θεωρηματα ποιει, her contemplative act is creative and is one with the product of the contemplation.

16. Réaumur describes with great eloquence the emergence of a world of ephemerae from a river as seen by torchlight: he represents the moving transparency as composed of ephemerae in jointed and articulated triangles of silver light, and these things the great naturalist appears actually to have mistaken for real and produced by the contact of the flies. "The light of the flambeau exhibited a spectacle which enchanted every one that beheld it.[...] Never had an[y] armillary sphere so many zones, as there are here circles, having the light for their centre. There was an infinity of them crossing each other in all directions, and of every imaginable inclination, all of which were more or less eccentric. Each zone was composed of an unbroken string of Ephemerae, resembling a luminous strip of silver lace, formed into a circle deeply notched, and consisting of equal triangles placed end to end (so that one of the angles of each triangle touched the middle of the base of the triangle preceding), and all moving with astonishing rapidity. The wings of the flies (says Reaumur) [...] formed this appearance".I can, however, add my own testimony to that of Messrs Kirby and Spence in their delightful introduction to entomology,who consider, or I venture to say have ascertained, that this was a visual deception of Reaumur, well as he deserves the praise

of the most accurate observers. "[...] Walking in the day-time with a friend, [...] our attention was caught by myraids of small flies, which were dancing under every tree; viewed in a certain light they appeared (as the ephemerae did to Reaumur) a concatenated series of insects moving in a spiral direction upwards, but each series, upon close examination, [...] was produced by the astonishingly rapid movement of a single fly". So far Spence, but I can add that I have twice seen the ascent of the ephemerae in a strong moonlight, the beams passing through an opening in a branching tree that overhung the water on which the moonlight formed a small island in deepest shade, and here by intensely watching the phenomenon I satisfied myself that the different spiral figures were each produced by the image [of] motion which the single insect left on the eye; each of which overtook the preceding before the impression had ceased, on the same principle as boys produce the circle of light by a piece of kindled charcoal whirled rapidly round.

17. I shall not regret the space or time which this apparent digression has cost me, if it should be found to have assisted in forming the right conception of mathematical lines, points, and surfaces, as acts of the imagination that are one with the products of those acts. For this is of especial importance to our present pursuit, in which we must evermore bear in mind that we are throughout treating of mental processes wholly abstracted from all outward realities, and consequently that we must learn to consider the sense itself, or the faculty of original and constructive imagination, aloof from all sensation and without reference to any supposed passive impression from objects extrinsic to the percipient; but if so, if the passive be wholly separated, what can remain but acts and the immediate results of the same in the subject or agent himself; for this is the very principle from which we commence, that we confine ourselves to the mind, and that the mind is distinguished from other things as a subject that is its own object, an eye, as it were, that is its own mirror, beholding and self-beheld. This

once understood, we are no longer startled by the definitions of Euclid and understand the definition of the point as having no magnitude, the line without breadth, and the surface without depth, as mere popular ways of guarding the boyish geometrician against the supposition that things are the subject matter of the science at the threshold of which he is preparing to place his foot. Perhaps, however, it would have been more expedient even in point of intelligibility to have conveyed the same meaning by the simple declaration that the points, lines, and surfaces of geometry are not bodies nor parts of bodies, but acts of the mind and figures which are the offspring of what the great founder of logic has called intellectual notions having their proper canons or mirror in the imagination of the geometrician, even as the luminous zones and triangles of the ephemerae had their receptive and retaining table in the eye of the observer.

18. The analogy which the processes of outward perception have to these purely intellectual constructions is a subject of deepest interest and highest importance, but the contemplation belongs to the third and concluding portion of my work,in which logic in its most comprehensive sense, as the formal science of the rational understanding, is employed as on organ for the discovery and advancement of real knowledge, whether it consist of realities in the world of the senses or the higher realities of the intelligible world. This primary mental act,which we have called the synthetic unity or the unity of apperception, is presupposed in, and in order to, all consciousness. It is its condition (*conditio sine qua non*) or that which constitutes the possibility of consciousness *a priori,* or, if we borrow our metaphor from space instead of from time, *ab intra.* Both metaphors mean one and the same, viz. an act or product of the mind itself considered as distinct from the impressions from external objects. We may illustrate the sense of these sense of this so frequent and so frequently misused term "*a priori*" by likening it to the stains in the old cathedral glass which predetermine the character of the rays which it transmits and

which it reflects. But above all, and leading us at once to our present disquisition, it is this synthetic unity which first gives meaning and determinate import to the word "is" in all affirmations. The repetition of this synthetic act in the under-standing, or, what amounts to the same, the reflection on this act, completes the consciousness.

19. In the first act we have seen that a principle of unity is contributed by the mind itself. But if there be a uniting power, there must be that which is to be the subject or matter of the union, and by what name shall we designate this latter? At present we know no more of it than that it is opposite to unity: for how else should unity have been superinduced on it? But the opposite to one is the many, and by this name or its synonyms have philosophers in all ages and languages agreed in designating the same; but observe, only in relation to the mind and that which the mind can discover of what is not contained in its own consciousness by a light of its own. But such knowledge, it is plain, can only be negative, and when the external, the immediately sensuous, the supposed impressions from external agents are comprised under the common term of "the many", "the manifold", or "multeity", or "the indistinguishable" (to which we may add the phrases adopted by symbolical writers or mystics,viz. "chaos", "the waters", etc, etc[)]. In all these there is or there ought not at least to be any pretence of determining the nature and character of the external agents considered as powers separate from the mind and having like the mind a principle of subsistence in themselves. For logically, that is, as far as the acts and conclusions of the under-standing or the sense are alone concerned, the mind has acquired no right of affirming even the external existence of such agents otherwise than as an affirmation is implied in the act of distinguishing these impressions, or, in more appropriate language, these stimulations and excitements from itself as not belonging to its own self-consciousness. On the point at which we are at present standing, it is altogether indi-fferent whether it be the matter of a waking perception, as a

perception of a rainbow, or the matter of a waking intuition, as in the imaginative formation of a diagram in geometrical contemplations, or lastly the matter of a phantasm, "the stuff that dreams are made of".The matter is that unknown [?το μη ον] on which the mind is to act and which is of necessity supposed in consequence of that act. We may therefore safely entitle the assumption of its existence a logical postulate. On this ground the existence of A is such as implies the existence of B as its opposite, inasmuch as the form under which we find A existing is no absolute form but that of an opposite, as much (by way of illustration) as the existence of a North implies that of the South: but the opposite found in the act of making one, the characteristic of the opposite to this, must be that of receiving a unity which did not belong to it in its own nature.

20. Without the primary act or unity of appreception we could have nothing to be conscious of. Without the repetition or representation of this act in the understanding [that] completes the consciousness we should be conscious of nothing. It will appear, however, on a moment's self-examination that a mere repetition of this act, a mere representation of the product of the act, could in no respect differ from the former in kind, at least more than the second echo from the former, or a secondary rainbow from the principal arch; something more must take place in order to constitute it a repetition by the understanding, and this something is the act of reflection. Experience has shown us that numerous acts of perception, or, to use our own logical terms, that the function of synthetic unity has been long at work and the products multiplied previously to the dawning of a distinct consciousness or reflection on the same.How indeed could it be otherwise? Then, when the mind has many and different forms as the products of its percipient energies, will it have an interest awakened of distinguishing the one from the other. But in order to this the mind must have acquired a consciousness of that which all have in common: for absolute and total heterogenes there is no need of distinguishing. But that which all have in common

is the coexistence of the many in the one, the many being the characteristic of the subject in its supposed anterior state the one had been communicated thereto and the one or unity as the gift of the mind itself being the object. But for this latter the subject would for us have no existence whatever: or, omitting the words "for us", we need not hesitate to affirm that *the* subject *that* in this case is spoken of would not exist at all.

21. Now this resolution of any given representation into the object and subject and the coexistence of both as one we all a judgment, at least it is the first and most generalised definition of the term, judgment, which is most happily expressed in the Teutonic languages by *Urteil,* and the judgment itself or the judicial faculty *Urteil*[*s*]-*kraft,* that is, the power of resolving a thing into its primary and original constituent parts.

22(a). This then is common to all positions; and having discovered this we are now enabled to proceed in the search of the marks by which one may be distinguished from another and one class from another.

22(b). It has been affirmed and it will shortly be more fully explained and proved that neither the subject nor its predicate to either singly or placed in mere juxtaposition contain the principle, or what is here perfectly equivalent, the mental affirmation, of their reality or objective being. This is accomplished when the mind bears witness to its own unity in the subject represented to it, and this act with this consciousness of the same is conveyed or expressed in the connective "is". "The house is white".Now it is evident that this reflection could not have [taken] place, that this resolution of a manifold into its constituent parts, the house as representing the subject, and the white as representing its predicate or distinctive attribute, if these constituents had not been previously united by the mind, and not, likewise, unless the same predicate had been found united with other subjects and the same subject united with other predicates, as a "white rose", a "red house".Now the act of reflection in all instances [?is subsequent] to this—to this product, I say, of the mind's own synthetic power. It may well be that the subject has no existence but in the mind. For instance, let the position be, "Cerberus is three-headed", or, "the Chimera is triform". The act by which the mind combines the three heads or the three forms with all the manifold which is again united in these into a one-formed shape beheld in one act, that is and must be real, and this reality it is, and not those so-called principles of identity and contradiction, which logicians without exception have hitherto talked [of] as the foundations of logical evidence,which supplies us with the Archimedian standing-room from which we may apply the lever of all our other intelligent functions. The mind affirms firstly its own reality. Secondly, that this reality is an unity. Thirdly, that it has the power of communicating this unity, and lastly, that all reality for the mind is derived from its own reality, and in proportion to the unity which is its form and communication, that is, its own form and thence the form of the subject to which it has been transferred. The whole collectively is comprised in the Latin sentence "mens est forma formans", the mind is, and it is a form, and it is formative.

23. Here then arises an apparent contradiction. We have found object and subject the common constituents of all representations of which reality is affirmed, that is, which are connected by the verb "is", and we have here an object which is said to contain the principle of reality in itself exclusively, nay, in contradistinction from whatever is not mind. This contradiction admits but of one solution. There must be some object which is in one and the same indivisible act or moment a subject likewise and, vice versa, a subject that in one and the same moment is an object likewise; it must be both in one. Now does there exist such an object-subject and subject-object? We reply, "yes! and it is found in the reality of self-consciousness". In contemplate myself. Myself the object is one and the same with the I or subject, and the first rule of logic is in accordance with the first rule of grammatical syntax—that the case which follows the verb substantive, and as such stands for the objective, is the same with the case that

preceds, that is, the subjective case. There may be many SUBJECTS (the living principle, for instance, in plants) which we may call powers, lives, principles, active FORMS, that which manifests itself and without which there is no conceivable *objectivity;* but *that* subject alone is a mind which is its own object; and an object which includes without confounding the subject is the definition of mind, and in the same moment we have the first ground of classific distinction, and we subdivide subjects into those which are in themselves their own object, that is, minds, and those which are not, that is, simply subjects.

24. We have stated that the objectivity or reality which is asserted in every judgment, as the major in all logical syllogism, is expressed in the term "is". We have seen too that this term expresses in the first instance the reality of the act itself by which certain positions were combined or seen as one; for instance, "the house is white". Now the question is, what is the agent expressed in this act? If it be an act of the mind it would seem to follow that when we affirm that a spirit is a simple substance, or any other so-called judgment, we can mean no more than this, "as sure as I am, so surely this is". Now the truth implied in the position "I am" is the ground and condition of all truth: whatever therefore is as true as this must necessarily be true in the highest degree.Such was the reasoning on which the sect of the Dogmatists, Descartes and his followers among the moderns and the Stoics among the ancients, grounded their metaphysical and theological systems; but how erroneously the following distinctions will readily exhibit.

25. It is undeniable that the origin and fundamental knowledge must be somewhat which being thought of must therefore, *be,* and which *being* must necessarily be *thought* of. It is no less evident that if we take this somewhat as the first, and which, being presupposed in all other knowledges is so far anterior to them, there is no other assumed which is then to think of it, it must therefore be thought of by itself; and this primary and preconditional truth may therefore be characterised as that which, thinking, must be, and which,

being, must think. It must exhibit the perfect coincidence or (to use a term at once more vital and more accurate) coinherence of reality and conception. Now this character is found in the *sum* and *cogito,*in either and in both; for *sum* implies *sum cogitans.*for it is not merely self, but a self-assertion of a self, and in like manner *cogito* involves *cogitans*; for what indeed, even etymologically considered, is *cogitans* but the blending of the two terms *cogito* and *ens*, a being that asserts iself. This then is self-consciousness, and the Dogmatist therefore affirms that the primary underived truth commences in self-consciousness. But to prepare for the detection of the sophism which will be found to lurk in this position we have established the distinction between the synthetic and the analytic function of unity. If the question were : "what is the origin of our knowledge of all truths?", if the enquiry were confined to the *principium sciendi,* the *quomodo scimus nos scire*?,the answer must doubtless be self-consciousness, inasmuch as the terms are identical. But we have enquired for something more and higher than this self-consciousness which supposes reflection, and reflection an act antecedent thereto. It were therefore a contradiction in terms to call that a primary truth which is admitted to be secondary or derivative, and we must first secure an absoluteness, an independency, to the position "I am" before we can communicate certainty to other positions on the ground of their being with it or a part of the self-consciousness. But to affirm of any finite being that it is absolute is a contradiction in terms: in order to absoluteness there must be an "is" (*est*) which necessarily involves the "I am", and again an "I am" without which no "is" would be conceivable. This therefore and this alone can be the *principium essendi et sciendi* or the perfect identity of being and knowing and therefore the ground and source of both. Without any present reference to any religious or superhuman authority the title "I Am" attributed to the Supreme Being by the Hebrew legislator must excite our admiration for its philosophic depth, and the verb substantive or first form in the science of grammar brings us the highest possible external evidence of its truth.

For what is a fact of all human language is of course a fact of all human consciousness. The verb (*verbum*), the word is of all possible terms the most expressive of that which it is meant to express, an act, a going forth, a manifestation, a something which is distinguishable from the mind which goes forth in the word, and yet inseparable therefrom; for the mind goes forth in it, and without the mind the word would cease to be a word, it would be a sound, a noise. If we ask ourselves how we know anything—that rose, for example, or the nightingale hidden in yonder tree—the reply will be that the rose (*rosa subjecta*)manifests itself, that it renders itself objective, or the object of our perceptions, by its colour and its odour, and so in the nightingale by its sound. And what are these but the goings from the subject, its words, its verb? The rose blushes, the nightingale sings. (And here again we have an instance of the difference between the *principium sciendi* and the *principium essendi.* If we considered the point relatively to our knowledge, the conception of our going forth or production would be the more general form of the manifestation, the word or the verb: so far at least that we might venture to use this term in cases to which we should hesitate in applying the term "act" in its highest sense, that namely in which the agent originates the act. On the other hand, in relation to the *principium essendi,* all going forth, all manifestation, must of necessity have had their origin in an act, and all that lives and moves derives whatever agency and whatever semblance of agency there be therein in consequence of that act and its continuation.)

26. The sum of the preceding argument may be thus recapitulated.

27. We have been seeking for the principle of our certainty and we have found it necessary to distinguish between the *principium sciendi* and the *principium essendi.* Now such a principle cannot be any *thing* or any *particular object.* For its very purpose is to constitute the objectivity in all objects as far as they are objects of our consciousness (*principium realitatis*

non potest ipsaesse res).Each thing is what it is in consequence of some other thing. The water could not be that particular water were it not for the air, the banks, etc, etc. An infinite and independent thing is no less a contradiction than an infinite circle or a sideless triangle. Besides, a thing is that which is an object of which itself is not the sole percipient, but an object is inconceivable without a subject as its antithesis. *Omne perceptum percipientem supponit*(understand that [?otherwise] the words would have no meaning for us, they would possess no logical import). "Tall" and "short" express a relation the seat of which is in the understanding, εν τω λογω, and neither of these would have any meaning but as being the correspondent opposite of the other.

28. But neither can the principle be found in all subjects in contradistinction from an object : for *omnis perceptio,* that is,*omnis percipiens in actu perceptionis supponit perceptum.*We may borrow an illustration from physics. It is impossible that negative electricity should be assumed as the principle of positive electricity, for it presupposes it, and equally impossible that positive electricity should be assumed as the principle of the negative, for it presupposes the negative, that is, they mutually suppose each the other. But whatever can be though of must be either an object or a subject or some third which is neither separately because it is the root and identity of both. If the principle is to be found, as we have demonstrated that it is not to be found either in any possible object or any possible subject taken separately, [as no other third is conceivable],the principle must be found in that which is neither subject nor object exclusively, but which is the identity of both.

29. The principle thus characterised manifests itself as in the ειμι, *sum*, or "I am", which we shall hereafter express indiscriminately by the words "mind", "self", or "self-consciousness", the preference being at once determined and explained by the context. In this, and in this alone, object and subject, being and knowing, are identical, each involving and supposing the other; it is a subject which becomes a subject in and by the

very act of making itself its own object, or to familiarise ourselves gradually with the technical language of our science, it is a subject which becomes subjective by the act of constructing itself objectively to and for itself; but which never is nor can be an object except for itself, and only so far an object as by the very same act and in the same indivisible moment it becomes a subject.

30. So much for the principle generally; the distinction between it as a principle of knowing (*principium sciendi*) and a principle of being (*principium essendi*) will require still less attention to be understood. If a man be asked, "How do you know that you are?", he can only reply, "Sum quia sum", "I am because I am", that is, "I know myself to be, because I know myself to be". But if the absoluteness, the primary underived and independent character of this certainty having been admitted, he were again asked, not how he KNOWS that he is, but how he, that individual person, *came* to be, then in relation to the ground of his existence, not to the ground of his *knowledge* of that existence, he might, rather must, reply, if he reply at all, "Sum quia Deus est",or, still more philosophically, "Sum quia in Deo sum". I know that I am because I am and am self-known; but that I am and know myself to be, there is but one assignable reason—that Being and Will which we express by the word "God".

31. If then we elevate our conception to the absolute Self, Spirit, or Mind, the underived and eternal "I Am", then and herein we find the principle of being, andof knowledge, of idea, and or reality: the ground of existence, and the ground of the knowledge of that existence, absolutely one and identical; both are alike adequately expressed in the term "sum quia sum","I am because I affirm myself to be".

32. All truth is either mediate, that is, derived from other truth, or immediate. The latter, of which we have been treating under the name of truth absolute or principle of truth, may be designated by the formula A = A, [a] formula which, however, must be here taken to signify not only self-evidence but self-

originated as excluding the conception of any truth previous to it. On the other hand, the former, or truth mediate, that is, of derivation dependent and conditional, certainty which properly and originally belongs to A is attributed to B, and B is known to be true because in some sense or other it is one with A, being included in A it is concluded. A chain without a staple from which the links collectively derive their stability, or a series without any first, has been compared not inaptly to a string of blind men each holding the skirt of the man before him, the file reaching far out of sight, and yet all the individuals moving without the least deviation in one straight line. That it was beyond the reach of sight would scarcely weaken our conviction that there was a sure guide at the head of the file. What if it were answered, "No—there is no head man. The blind men are without number and infinite: blindness supplies the place of sight"? Equally inconceivable is a cycle of equal numerically different truths without a common and central principle, and that the absurdity does not strike us with the same force as in the preceding instance of the line is owing to a surreptitious act of the imagination which automatically and without our consciousness not only fills up the intervening spaces and contemplates the *cycle* (of B, C, D, E, F, etc) as a continuous cycle, A giving to all collectively the unity of their common orbit, but likewise suggests and as it were supplies the one central power which gives to each its place in that circle and renders the movement of all cyclical.

33. Lastly there can be but one such principle, but one asolute truth, self-grounded, unconditional, and known by its own light, yet capable of communicating to other positions a certainty which it had not received. But this may be proved first *a priori*, for were there two or more such principles, and of course *ex hypothesi* equal, they must refer to some other third and higher principle by which their equality is determined, or rather in which it is involved, consequently neither would be self-established, which yet is demanded in the hypothesis. And *a posteriori* it will be demonstrated by the principle itself as soon as it is presented to the mind. The principle itself, I

say, which is here the absolute "I am", will be found to involve a universal antecedency and consequently to preclude both all precedency and all parity of any other in its very conception, and what is here affirmed metaphysically of the absolute "I am" is logically and scientially affirmable of consciousness generally. This will be admitted at once of contingent truths. They of course can have only a borrowed certainty.If we affirm of a board that it is blue, the predicate "blue" is accidental and not implied in the subject "board". We know it to be true by having seen it. But even where the truths are necessary, they are not therefore, as we have already shown, independent. When I affirm of a circle that it is equi-radial, the predicate indeed is implied in the conception of the subject, but the existence of the subject itself presupposes the existence of a mind both as its cause and percipient.

34. Before we proceed, in this our conversation at least, it may not be uninteresting or without its uses in preparing and familiarising the apprehension for after-truth to make a few remarks on the celebrated principles or rather principle of contradiction and identity which in all books of logic hitherto are stated as the ground and universal rule of all logical reasoning—in short, as that truth in which all other truths are contained as far as the form is concerned. But it is questionable whether even these principles properly belong to common or syllogistic logic, and during the disquisition which we have been carrying on lately I have been not unaware that I was anticipating what appertained to the last and concluding stage of our present subject, viz. the transition of the dialectic into the organic, and, with this, the subordination of logic to the noetic or formal science, to that knowledge in which truth and reality are one and the same, that which in the ideas that are present to the mind recognises the laws that govern in nature, if we may not say the laws which are nature. The principle of identity is "A=A" or, if we prefer the refinement of the *Wissenschaftslehre* (Fichte has so called his peculiar system of idealism), "if A=A, then A = A", and the principle of contradiction

that "A is[not] not-A", Both amount, as we have seen, to the position "A is", and even this supposes an assumption of the latter word "is" as either one and the same with A, so that "A is" really means no more than a tautological repetition of "is, is", or in other words a mere and simple assertion of being universally, or that something must be, which again is equivalent to the following fact of our consciousness. In order for me to attach any sense to the word "something", in order to the conception "something", I must have had the conception of "thing", and, in order to this, [a] conception which we will resolve into the "ing", that is, our English termination answering to the *ens* of school Latin.Let us try this in another form, our present object being that of exercise and the agility and flexibility of mind acquirable thereby—it is not food, but as a game at tennis. "A is"—by this position I either assert necessary being and at the same time the necessity of being, by light of reason [νους], and then it belongs to noetics (metaphysics *sensu strictiori*) or I speak of some fact in the light of sense,the inward or the outward, and then the position belongs to history (*sensu generalissimo*).Now *toto genere* different is the question "what is A?" To this question, "A = A", or "A is [not] not-A", would be no answer, for these are the same with the affirmation implied [in] "A is". "What is A?" resolves itself into two sentences, the former assertory, "A is", and the latter interrogative, "but what is it?" The answer must be some predicate of A as a subject and not of A as *ens absolute positum* or that which is its own predicate and which is therefore no more a subject in relation to a predicate or object, for predicate is here but another word for object, its logical synonym. "I am that I am", where (as we have before more than once noticed) the simple term *sum* or *ego* is equivalent to the whole position. Hence in the formula A = A, etc, representing principles of identity and contradiction, the subject (improperly so called) and its *predicate* are always convertible terms. Example : "Quid est spiritus?" Answer, "Ens se ponens". "Quid est ens se ponens?" Answer, "Spiritus". But let A signify wood and B signify black and then A=B is far indeed from B=A. In the one case the predicate, whatever its grammatical form may be, is in sense and logical value a substantive, in the latter necessarily an adjective. Ebony is black, but we cannot say that black is ebony. And it is such positions alone that properly appertain to syllogistic logic. Thus if these famous principles have any property logical it can only be that the proper subjects of logic are λογοι, in distinction from ρηματα, φωναι, ειδωλα; but the λογοι are acts of the λογος, or reflective mind, of which it is a constituent character, that in the act of knowing its own being its knows that it cannot at the same time and in the same sense deny what it affirms or affirm what it denies.

35. For the same reason, therefore, that in a former chapter we have omitted reflection in the list of the particular distinguishable functions of the understanding,viz. attention, comparison, abstraction, because the reflection is the understanding itself, a synonym not a predicate, or at best a tautology, we here dismiss the principle of identity as having no other place in logic than as an assertion sufficiently superfluous, that the forms and functions of the understanding suppose an understanding as their ground.

36. The principle of contradiction is: *impossible est idem simul esse* [*ac non*]*esse*-well, this is a good definition of the impossible but is it therefore a principle? If it be a *princeps,*that which is to go before, there ought to be something that should follow; but what is to follow in the present instance? How can we arrive from this negative to a positive? Through another negative? As whatever is not *ens* and *non ens* at the same time is possible[?] But the rule that two negatives make a positive is grammatical, not logical. Besides, even this is not to be inferred immediately, for it requires an intermediate position, viz. that the contrary of the false is true. Both of them may be entitled axioms but neither of them can be named a principle. The rival position, the *principium identitatis*, is in fact two positions. First, "whatever is, is". Secondly, "what is not, is not". Now the former is merely a repetition during the act of reflection of the term "is". I mean that it expresses no more

than my consciousness that I am reflecting,that is, consciously reflecting the truth of being. The term "is" being a verb substantive, we might without absurdity, though without any change or addition in our knowledge, convert the word "is" to a noun substantive in one case and a verb in the other and say, "is, is", and in fact we do what is tantamount to this when we say, "the necessary being is", or, "God is". Do not yield to the very natural temptation of impatience with these subtleties so thin that, strip them of their clothing, they totter on the edge of nothing. They, or rather the exercise of the mind in reducing them to their true value, will not have been useless if only it has put us on our guard against the frequent error in arguing, an error which has by no means become absolete with the schools in which it sprung and was reared, the error of presenting as particular truths the mere exponents of our universal or essential consciousness—such, for instance, as the one now under consideration, the being of being. Instead of truth, principle, or axiom, it is in reality a mere narration of a fact.I reflect on being. The second position, "Whatever is not, is not", is either a μεταβασις–εις αλλο γευος, that is, the introduction of a heterogeneous term, or it is nonsense; for it either means that "A *non est* Y"—Y being some predicate, as "ebony is not white"—and then indeed it may belong to syllogistic logic, but as a particular, consequently no principle; or else A stands as a universal, and then it amounts to, "omne ens quod non est ens, non ens est",or "A which is no A, is no A", a precious principle with commences with a contradiction. In short, the substance of these boasted principles is a mere assertion of the act of reflection, implying the reason as one universal in all individual reasoners. The "is" we have before shown, is grounded, not in our reflection, or the analytic unity, but in the synthetic, which we do not give to ourselves but find given to us.Though the contents as it were or matter of this datum may be given in the sense, but which, as not being the product of any individual's faculty, we call common sense; yet the *form* and that which gives it immoveable reality for the mind, that is, certainty-*this,* I say, is a truth of reason. The striking analogies between reason and sense are among the most interesting subjects of philosophic meditation. The mathematic,indeed, which has for its subject the forms of the pure sense and products of the active imagination, is not only the first pure science but supplies to all other sciences the most perfect model and exemplar.

37. The highest compliment which we can pay to such truths as "whatever is is" or, "if it is, it is", etc, etc, is to interpret them into these words, "if it be so judged by my reason, it is valid in all reason and for all rational beings who are gifted with reason". Though even here the negative part of the position (that the reason cannot at one and the same time, and of one and the same thing, deny what it affirms) seems to be little more than a way of generalising a form of words familiarised to us by the habit of comparing particulars with each other: e.g. I am accustomed to see jet, and while I am thinking of jet I happen to light on a piece of amber in very many points resembling jet, and with this thought present to my mind, "amber is not black", which in truth must be resolved into, "jet is black, and amber therefore is not jet". But here we are referred to principles of a very different order from those of technical arguing:the metaphysical ideas of identity and alterity, the one and the many—principles, I say, of metaphysical ontology as much presupposed in common logic as sounds are in grammar. And after all that can be said in favour of these abstractions, the habit of abstracting being perhaps their best purpose,it is no slight objection that from their extremely vague nature the terms are unsteady and not marked by that plain and clear opposition which is essentially requisite in all logical antitheses: thus *nego* is not the proper correspondent or antitheton to *affirmo,*but really answers to *removeo.*"I remove this while I place that". The rightful use therefore of these terms, as represented by + and –, is to be found in the doctrine of characters, best studied mathematically and during algebraic studies.

38. As, however, we have proceeded so far and while we

are yet lingering on the origin and comport of the objectivity or affirmation of the same contained in the major of the syllogism, not as the συλλογισμος or ratiocination itself, but as its condition and persupposition. . .the clear way of stating the true force of the negative is as follows. It is a fact of universal consciousness that man possesses the power not only of beholding A and B but noticing that they are two and different. Hence if he reflect on B in immediate succession to A, so that B comes while A is still present to his thoughts, in which memory and the condition of all comparison consists, he soon discovers an abbreviation for the two positions "A= A", "B = B" in the words "A is not B", this "not" having been probably first derived from some painful feeling occasioned by his having looked for one thing which he was desirous to have and finding another which was nothing to this purpose—looking for parsley, for instance, and finding hemlock. The gesture, the motion of the head, the impatient shrinking hemlock from the object, and the correspondent motions in the organs of speech, produced, and still are found to produce in infants, that particular modification of sound which may be traced more or less distinctly in the simple negatives of all languages, the nearest being the Hebrew "ngain" or the "ng:", the roughest and primitive digamma, the sound which, softened and made pronounceable by the vowel prefixed, we retain in the αγγελος. It is not therefore so properly a *perception* as a *sensation* connected with some one perception, in consequence of some other having been and still being in the fancy, connected with the feeling of expectation. It is curious to notice in ourselves that preparation which we make for an increased degree of vividness which we expect from the senses when we are on the point of seeing something which is already present to the mind's eye; a feeling not unlike that which we experience the moment before the presentation of the moon through a glass. But in proportion to the degree and pleasureableness of this expectation and preassurance is the disappointment, and when by the frequent repetition of such occasions the sensation is become evanescent and the tones of passion are no longer heard, that abbreviation, that compression and welding as it were of the two into one, remains in use from its convenience and the "not" becomes the mere sign or character of connection by comparison.

39. There are three assumptions then on which the solidity of logic as the science of conclusion is grounded. The first, the existence of mind absolutely, which we have agreed to distinguish by the term νους. We commenced, it will be remembered, with the division of philosophy into the speculative and the practical, and then announced our present object as belonging to the former.Next, we seek for some principle, from which we might proceed. But this, as a principle, and independent of the consideration whether it is to be a principle of speculative or a principle of practical philosophy, must be *absolute.* For how can that which depends on, or is bounded and qualified by, another and extrinsic power be a *principle*? In the strict sense of the word, I mean. Again: there cannot be two absolutes different from each other. The supposition involves an absurdity. It follows, therefore, that the principle must be the same for both divisions, that is, the principle of speculative philosophy is one and the same with the principle of practical philosophy.

40. Nevertheless, when, as is the case in all speculation, our attention is especially directed to the absolute as the principle of the ideal or intelligential, in distinction from the same absolute, considered as the source of being and action, we may allowably *confine* the terms "nous" and its derivatives to the expression of this special direction, and appropriate the terms, "Supreme Will" or "Supreme Being" to the designation of the same Absolute, as the principle of ethics or practical philosophy. I need not say, however, that these distinctions of terms refer exclusively to differences in our own thoughts and their validity is exclusively subjective and logical.

41(a). Still the same essential character is intended, and the νους is that in which the idea is at the same time the reality; the knowing is the thing known: the *scire* one and the same with the *esse*. This, then, is the first assumption. Secondly, it is assumed that the reason which is present to the mind of man or of which the human mind partakes (*vide* N.T.) is one with the νους; in other words, that the reason in man as far as it is reason implies its own reality, and consequently that the truths of reason are essentially real—real in their own right, and not in consequence of any other thing being real.

41(b). There are two things which we may contemplate as contraries. The one a whole, the parts of which are not necessarily homogeneous, and consequently a whole that derives its right to be so called altogether from the unity of the perception, and so that it supposes no unity in the object but only in the organ of sense through which that object is presented. A heap of corn or still better a heap of grains, chaff, dust, etc, etc, affords an instance. With regard to these we cannot conclude from the whole to the parts, or infer that because it is a part of that whole it is one with it; so that what is affirmed of the major or including shall be predicable of the minor or included.

42. In full contrariety to such merely subjective wholes stand those unities, the parts of which are not so properly called parts: for this term can be strictly used only of objects which in some way or other constitute units by aggregation, as they are repetitions of the units conceived as realising (in technical language putting themselves under given relations).Purely for illustration's sake let us imagine space to posses real being and energy and that to its figurability were added the active power of figure-*vis se figendi relative ad forman et extrinsecam et interiorem;* that is,*ideam figurativam*.The consequence would be that all the possible elementary forms with all their combinations would be contemplated as so many repetitions of space and at the same time representations of its figurability, all which would differ indeed from each other but in no respect from the space which would be their common essence. Now what we have here imagined of space is actually affirmable of TRUTH the moment we have agreed to consider

it as real, that is, as universal reason and not a mere logical whole having its unity in the analytic unity of the understanding, or reflection, as the heap of grains, etc, in the synthetic unity of the sense together with the organ of sense. Between these three is a third possible mode of existence partaking of both, which you will at once recognise under the name "organisation" or "organic body". In these there is a positive and intrinsic unity as well as the unity which is completed in the percipient and has its occasion only externally in the accidental juxtaposition of particulars, each of which, from the endless divisibility implied in body, is as truly a whole, as all collectively, and we need only alter our position or change our arrangement, as it were, and sphere of our attention, to convert the collective all into a part of some more comprehensive whole.

43. We have seen that a judgment or the act of judging consists in reducing a position to its primary constituent parts of subject and predicate, and that his presupposes the division into object and subject. Consequently the functions of logic commence when we consider the subject objectively, that is, as a something that is not the same without own subject or our mind, but an object of our mind. Thus, for instance, when I think of my neighbour's soul I know that it is a subject in and for him; but relatively to me it becomes an object. While for that which, had it appertained to myself, I should have called an object, I am compelled to invent another name in order to distinguish it from the former. In order to this I call the former what it really is in itself, *the subject,* though in relation to me it is an object, and the object of that subject I name its predicate. Hence we may see the ground on which logicians have defined a judgment, viz. to compare a mark with a thing, that is, a predicate with a subject, is what we call judging,the act of comparison being expressed by the intervening verb substantive. There is little perhaps to object to what is here meant, yet somewhat to the way of expressing this meaning. And I am anxious to impress this because more than any other

point it is calculated to elucidate what has been before declared respecting the simplicity and universality of the syllogistic form as uniformly consisting of the three acts of the mind, clusion, inclusion, and conclusion. Strictly speaking a judgment is the determination of a subject by a predicate, not always or necessarily to compare the one with the other. E.g. "a spirit is simple". "Spiritus est aliquid vere simplex".No one will deny that this is a judgment, and yet it would be a strange abuse of language to say that we compared the word "spirit" with its own meaning. But, likewise, "a spirit is not compounded". "Spiritus non est aliquid composit[um]".Now here we do compare or contrast the conception "spirit" with the essential predicate of a different conception in order to acquire at least a negative knowledge of spirit or for the purpose of enlivening our knowledge and bringing it into a distincter consciousness by adding an act of seclusion to that of clusion simply. This, however, is a question of language rather than of things inasmuch as it depends on the different extent in which we may use the term "compare". If it could be proved that other things besides spirit were likewise entitled to the attribute of simplicity in the same sense, we doubtless might be said to compare "the one" with "us", a particular with a universal, or a minor with a major, in order to determine whether or not the former was contained in the latter. I am, however, inclined to think that inst-ead of distinguishing judgment into affirmative and negative, both being considered as comparative, it would be more expedient to entitle the first positive, the other comparative, while determinative is the name common to both.

44. From this point we are now able to see the true use and application of logic; and this twofold. In the first the forms of thinking are realised in the objects of the thought, as that "all men are mortal and therefore Socrates, being a man, must be mortal". Here is an actual inclusion, and in all cases of this kind the process as far as it is a logical process is almost automatic or spontaneous and the only question is respecting the truth of the original perceptions or apprehensions, whether

ideas or facts, and not respecting the conceptions or comprehensions which follow by the very mechanism of our intellect. It is a science of nature's rather than of our conscious self, or, as we commonly say, it is a natural logic.

45(a). But there is another application which, though it may be called verbal, is of far greater need and more frequent utility. Nor will the epithet "verbal" degrade it in our minds who have learnt to distinguish words, λογοι, from articulate sounds, ρηματα, and to consider them as partaking of this communicative intelligence, του λογου, and of its ideas or communicable forms, των λογων, as the echo partakes of the original sound, and that sound of the power which modified while it impelled the motion of the air to its distinct conveyance; or rather as a portrait would partake of the person if we supposed the person contemplating the same and the image varying with the changes in the person produced by the contemplation.

Like to Narcissus, on the grassy shore,
Viewing his outward face in watery glass,
Still as he looks, his looks add ever more
New fire, new light, new love, new comely grace
To's inward form; and it displays apace
Its hidden rays and so new lustre sends
To its true shaow-[. . .]

And this I wot is the soul's excellence.
That from the hint of each self-issuing glance
In shadows se[nsible]she doth from hence
Her inward life and radiant hue advance
To higher pitch, and by good governance
May weaned be from love of fading light
In outward forms having true cognizance
That 'tis not these that are the beauty bright
Which takes men so, but what they cause in human
sprite.

Henry More

The first utility which I shall mention is that of which we have before given an instance, in which if we regarded the mark or predicate in the minor as the predicate of the subject [of the major] it would be a mere synonym of the predicate in the major instead of being included therein. In other words it would be a mere tautology,thus: "God is simple". "God is noncomposite". Where the "non-composite" might be commuted for "simple", and "simple" for "noncomposite", and yet it may be of use both as an auxiliar and as a corrective, to remind a learner that God being simple cannot be sought after by the same organs as bodies or things that are compound. There results therefore a real addition, not indeed to the material truth, but to the mind's property in that truth. We acquire a sort of regulative knowledge from being thus made sensible that the simple is irreconcilable with the composite and inasmuch as the mere prefixing of the negative sign to the latter renders it a synonym of the former.

45(b). Now in the stricter use of the term "understanding" it has been defined [as] the regulative power or the faculty in which all RULES originate. On this being assumed, the judgment may [be] technically distinguished from the understanding, as the determinative faculty or the power of *determining* this or that under the condition of some rule; while the reason gives a necessity or universality to that determination under the condition of the rule, that is, the rule and the accuracy of the rule being taken for granted. Whenever therefore a predicate arises in my mind not self-presented but in consequence of some other predicate in which its truth is involved, or even when on consideration the former is found to mean the same with the latter, if only it requires consideration to be aware of the sameness, we are entitled in both cases in respect to the forms of reasoning to regard the one as included in the other, and such note, mark, or predicate is called by the logicians *nota intermedia.*E.g. "necessary" is an immediate mark or predicate of God; but "unchangeable" is a mark of necessity, and therefore a mediate or intermediate mark of God. We arrive at the truth of God's immutability by reflection that

[that] which exists of necessity can neither have existed from any contingent cause out of itself, nor can it have been affected by any such cause, for then, [it] would no longer be an existence of necessity inasmuch as it must have been conceived to have been or become something that it was not, or something else than what it is. This intermediate mark, like the former or immediate, may be either positive by affirmation or comparative by negation. It may be either "God being a necessary Being, is therefore immutable", or "God being a necessary Being is therefore not subject to contingency" and whether this conclusion by intermediate marks is more than tautological is determinable by no rule beforehand but by the state of knowledge and development of the faculties in the person respectively to the given subject for whom the reasoning is intended, provided only that it is possible to consider one or the other of the terms as the more comprehensive. Thus we should not hesitate a moment in rejecting the following as a logical conclusion. "This cloth is sky-blue and therefore it is cerulean"; though by reversing it, it might be a necessary grammatical instruction that when the cloth was described as cerulean it meant the same as its being sky-blue; but in neither case could the position be entitled a logical inference by *nota intermedia.* Thus, then, we come to the real definition of a logical or rational conclusion. Every judgment by means of an intermediate mark is a conclusion. In other words, to conclude logically is to compare a mark or predicate with a subject by means of an intermediate mark, which in a syllogism is ordinarily named *terminus medius* or "middle constituent conception".

46. Logicians speak of immediate conclusions. The impropriety of the word "conclusion" we need not point out, it being evident that what is concluded must have been previously included, therefore affirmed by means of an intermediate—call them, however, immediate deductions or inferences, and still I much doubt whether they can be properly termed logical by any right of their own, whether they may not all be referred either to truths of reason or metaphysical facts, as in a former

page we have already explained in our sceptical remarks on the principles of identity and contradiction,or else to grammar as mere explanations of synonymous terms, or thirdly, and most often in conjunction with the first or second, to an enthymeme or abbreviated syllogism: in all which the process in the mind is the same as in the regular figure, only that some one term is passed over as obvious of itself, or, as the school phrase is understood, *subintell[ect]um.*

47. A single instance will set the preceding, in full light: "all matter in mutable, therefore what is not mutable is not matter". This is a so-called immediate conclusion, of which the logicians enumerate several sorts—that of logical inversion and that of contraposition being the most important. It is difficult to determine how far such an inference deserves the name of inference, whether in reality it be logically considered anything more than repetition of the very same truth in other words: and whether so or not it is plain that the force of the deduction depends on a rule not mentioned, though understood, viz. that whatever contradicts the essential predicate of a thing contradicts the thing itself. We shall see this in what follows, though we need only alter the words without in the least affecting the meaning and make the "whatever" or logical sign of the universal what it really is, an indetermined particular, to find that this instance corresponds to our preceding assertion, viz. that it is but an abbreviated syllogism "No matter is unchangeable"; then putting "A" for "whatever", "A is unchangeable", therefore "A is no matter". We have, I repeat a regular syllogism.

48. A syllogism formed of three positions is a pure syllogism (*ratiocinium purum*) and necessarily affirnative, that is, in the form of affirmation or negation. Whatever is composed of more than three positions is a mixed or illegitimate syllogism (*ratiocinium hybridum*) and is not coercive by force of the terms or positions mentioned, others being always understood. This most frequently takes place by the interposition of some immediate inference or deduction, as above explained. We will

suppose a friend to reason thus. "Nothing that is corruptible is simple. Therefore nothing simple is corruptible. The soul of man is simple. Therefore the soul of man is not corruptible." Now this contains four positions, but by reflecting on the true grounds of the conclusion we shall discover that this is nothing more than an ordinary syllogism grammatically disguised. "Nothing simple is corruptible" is precisely the same as "the simple is always incorruptible". "Whatever is simple is incorruptible. The soul of man is simple. Therefore the soul of man is not incorruptible." I have been perhaps unnecessarily prolix, but it has been to preclude the worse prolixity which the different forms of the so-called four figures of syllogism would have forced us to. It is a safe rule that a syllogism (*ratiocinium logicum*) consist of three acts. First clusion or seclusion, that is, universal or particular premise. Secondly, inclusion, and thirdly, conclusion. And that whatever is affirmed on other grounds than by a conclusion rising out of an inclusion may be *truths* of *reason,* that is, those of which we render outselves distinctly conscious by an act of evolution (which will be explained in the third part of this work, or the organon),or by equation as in the truth of sense—as in geometry—but are not properly logical. The same criterion may be expressed thus: "Whatever is predicated, the mark (say, B) of a mark (C) of a thing (A) belongs to the thing itself.

C B

Whatever is rational is a spirit.

A C

The human soul is rational

A B

Therefore the human soul is a spirit."

49. This is Kant's rule, but some little obscurity may arise from the first position ("whatever is rational"), which stands as the subject of the major [and] is entitled a mark or predicate; but this we have before explained in the more intelligible rule

that the subject of the major becomes the predicate in the minor and the conclusion. C has for its mark or predicate B. A has for its mark or predicate C. Therefore A has for its mark or predicate B.I should prefer expressing the rule of the so-called first figure thus: when the subject in the major becomes the predicate of the minor, the subject of the minor acquires the predicate of the major, all apparent deviations being nothing more than grammatical equivalents or inversions, that is, saying the same thing in a negative form that had been before said in an affirmative, and vice versa. Now we assert that in this figure only and exclusively are the *ratiocinia pur* or legitimate conclusions possible: and that in the three other figures the syllogisms are mixed or illegitimate, *ratiocinia hybrida.* In the second figure mixed conclusions only are possible.

50. "The rule of the second is this: Whatever contradicts the mark of a thing contradicts the thing itself."But this position is true only because whatever is contradicted by a mark contradicts that mark, that is, if A is precluded by B, B in like manner is precluded by A. But again whatever contradicts the mark of a thing contradicts the thing itself, consequently that which is contradicted by the mark of a thing contradicts that thing itself. Here it is evident that the connection of the minor with the conclusion depends altogether on the convertibility of the major as a negative position, and that unless this conversion be mentally interposed the syllogism has no conclusive force. But his position expressing the inversion is, we have seen, an interpolation or a fourth term. In the technical language of logicians the syllogism has four judgments and is therefore a *ratiocinium hybridum.* For instance:

No spirit is partible,
All matter is partible,
Therefore no matter is a spirit.

Doubtless I have here inferred rightly, but the conclusive power consists in this—that out of my first position, "no spirit is partible",mentally infer the inverse. "Therefore nothing partible is a spirit", and from this the remainder follows. According to the universal rule, the syllogism falls under the first figure, consequently the second figure is no proper part of logic, but a disguise which belongs to grammar or rhetoric or rather to that science between both for which we have proposed the name "rhematic".

Nothing partible is spirit,
All matter is partible,
Therefore nothing that is matter is a spirit.

The original major, by means of which it acquired its place as a second figure, being wholly superfluous to the syllogism, though possibly the occasion by which the reasoner came to the legitimate major," no spirit is partible". Well! that is the same as "nothing that is partible is a spirit". We will substitute the latter :

Nothing that is partible is a spirit,
All matter is partible,
Therefore nothing that is matter is a spirit.

Ah, now we have a legitimate syllogism, but it is a syllogism of the first figure.

51. In the third figure likewise, the conclusive power depends always on a fourth or interpolated judgment. The rule of this third figure is: whatever belongs to or contradicts a thing, that likewise belongs to or contradicts some things that are contained under some other mark of this thing. "All men are sinners," The "sinners" here belongs to "all men". "All men are rational" Here is another mark of "all men". "Therefore some rational beings are sinners. "Now it is plain this conclusion is brought about *per conversionem logicam, per accidens,*that is, a logical conversion partially of the minor position. I reason thus: "all men are rational", but therefore "some rational beings are men". If the term "rational" expresses the whole sphere in which man is included, I do but say the same thing in other words when I assert that some part of that sphere is filled by men. But, this once granted, the whole follows regularly.

All men are sinners,

All men are rational,
And consequently some rational beings are men,
Therefore some rational beings are sinners.

The force of the conclusion depends on the perception of the mind that the term "some rational" is perfectly equivalent to the term "men". It is therefore no syllogism [of the third figure] if you omit this and say, "All men are sinners". "Some rational beings are men, and therefore some rational beings are sinners." It is a legitimate syllogism; but a syllogism of the first figure.

52. The very same holds good of the fourth figure, under which, observe, no affirmative positions are possible. The rule for this fourth figure it is perhaps possible to give, but the mode of conclusion is so unnatural and depends upon so many interposed or understood inferences and equations that any universal rule abstracted from the possible instances would be a riddle or puzzle, the difficulty of which would stand in an inverse proportion to its worth. Instead therefore of a rule I will content myself with pointing out under what conditions the conclusive force is possible. Now this take place when either by logical conversion or contraposition I alter the places of the constituent terms and therefore after each premise can think of its immediate consequence or rather equivalent, so that these steps of the conclusion acquire mentally the same connections which they would have had expressly in a syllogism under the first and in fact the only legitimate rule and figure. Of the first sort, and that by logical conversion, take the following instance.

No fool is learned,
Some learned men are pious,
Therefore some pious persons as not fools.

It would be quite sufficient to prove its want of all claim to the name of syllogism, that nothing is included, but the predicates are aplied by mere accident. Piety, for instance, is no property of the learned as learned, and therefore the term "learned" is altogether idle and the bond of connection therefore, such as it is, is supplied by a word wantonly interpolated. But to adhere to our former test, we will take the thing as it is, inserting those mental interpositions by force of which there is any force in the conclusion.

No fool is learned-consequently
No learned person is a fool.
Some learned persons are pious-consequently
Some pious persons are learned, therefore
Some pious persons are not fools.

Substitute the parenthetic positions, omitting the major and minor of which they are the converse, and we have the regular syllogism with no fault in the *form* whatever, Ignorance as to the fact may be proved by the rash assertion that no learned man is a fool. Of the second sort take the following instance:

Every spirit is simple,
All that is simple is incorruptible,
Therefore something incorruptible is a spirit.

The conclusion as it here stands cannot, it is plain, flow out of the premises; to see this we need only compare therewith the middle or common term. I cannot say "some incorruptibles are spirit"; because it is simple it does not follow necessarily it is a spirit. The syllogism ought to stand :

Every spirit is simple,
But whatever is simple is incorruptible,
Therefore whatever is a spirit is incorruptible.

But the whole includes its parts and therefore "some incorruptible is spirit". But then it is evident that, omitting the mental interposition or fourth term, it differs in nothing from the regular syllogism of the first figure.

Chapter-4
Theory of Logic

Chapter-4

1. The old and famous question with which it was once usual to puzzle the logicians and to force them either to a confession of their ignorance or to the necessity of answering in a circle is that which Pilate of old contemptuously [put] to Him who was indeed in the highest sense the reality of that concerning which he asked: "What is truth?"[1]The verbal definition, viz. the coincidence of the knowledge with its object, is here presupposed and admitted. But the querist wants to be informed and such is the purport of the question, "What is the universal and sure criterion of any and every knowledge?"

2. "Prudens quaestio dimidium scientiae", says Lord Bacon.[2]It is already a great and important proof of understanding and insight to know what can be rationally asked. For if the question itself be absurd and an answer unnecessary, the consequence may be that the querist beguiling the respondent into an attempt precluded from the beginning, that of returning a wise answer to a senseless question, places the respondent and himself in a position which our ancestors describe by observing that the one milked the boar and the other was holding a sieve under to catch the stream.[3]

3. Harris has informed us that "the ancients divided questions into two kinds, the simple, which they call ερωτημα or interrogative. and the complex, which they call πυσμα or *percontatio*".[4]"The first consisted of such questions as permitted an answer, in the same words without addition when affirmative, and with the addition only of the negative particle when negative. 'Are these verses Homer's?' 'These verses are Homer's.' 'Are these verses Virgil's?' 'These verses are not Virgil's.' 'Yes' and 'no' being the abbreviation or way of returning the same answer in the shortest possible manner; but if the question be complex, as, for example, 'Are these verses Homer's or Virgil's?' or, if it be indefinite, as, for instance, 'Whose

verses are these?', it is evident that the former mode of replying would be inapplicable. A certain enquiry is more or less necessary; a choice must be made; the answer to the first instance may be either first, 'They are Homer's', or, secondly, 'They are not Homer's,' or, thirdly, 'They are Virgil's', or, fourthly, 'They are not Virgil's', or, lastly, 'They are neither by one nor the other': and this may be pursued still further or rather without limit in the latter instance, 'Whose verses are these?', either affirmatively as, 'They are Virgil's, Ovid's, etc,' or negatively, 'They are not Virgil's, Ovid's etc, etc.' In all questions of this kind or *percontations,* the answer cannot be given in the same words without addition or with 'not' only added, though here too the language of mankind ordinarily furnishes appropriate abbreviations. Thus, if it were asked 'How many right angles do all the angles of a triangle contain?', we should reply by the single monosyllable—'two'; but unabridged,the answer would be, 'All the angles of a triangle are equal to two right angles'."[5]

4. "Such is Harris's account, and it would be hard to say that it is not sufficiently accurate, and yet we may be allowed to complain that little or no additional light has been thrown on the subject. Perhaps we shall succeed better if we take up the subject at a somewhat earlier point and begin by asking not how many kind of questions there are, but what is a question. Every questioner (if the convenience of this word may excuse this barbarism),[6]every questioner, it is plain, wants to know something by which a deficient or imperfect position or affirmation may be completed and rendered satisfactory. The answer supplies this defect and transforms the imperfect position of the questioner into a complete or perfect one. 'Who is the author of the *Iliad*?' The interrogative 'who' stands here in the place of the unknown subject. The answer names the subject 'Homer', and now the position is complete. 'Homer is the author of the *Iliad.'* 'What is the *Iliad*?' The interrogative 'what stands here in the place of the unknown predicate. The answer names the predicate 'an epic poem of Homer's,' and we

have a complete position. 'The *Iliad* is an epic poem of Homer's.' There is no necessity therefore to [?deal]with any abbreviation,[7]as Harris has done, from the very definition of a question that the answerer needs only give that part of the position which the questioner wished and was unable to supply. The interrogatives have the same function here as the letters X, Y, Z, as marks of an unknown quantity in algebra. The answer gives the value or determinal quantity which must be substituted for the undeterminate mark in order to render the position full and determined."[8]

5. "In like manner the case of the interrogative points out the defective part of the position—where the language possesses such cases. The nominative 'who?', 'what?', 'which?', signifies some main term of the position, subject, or predicate, as may be seen in the instances already given, while the accusative 'who[m]?', 'what?', informs us that an object is wanting, as in the following instances : 'Whom has Homer seen?' 'Whom has Homer taken for the hero of [the] *Iliad*?': answer, 'Achilles'. The ablative signifies the point whence, the dative the point whither, and the genitive the relation in which the subject or predicate stands with some other subject: e.g. 'Whose epic poem is the *Iliad* ?' the original position contained in that question was, 'The *Iliad* is an epic poem of X', that is, of someone but I know not whom. The subject and predicate are here given and determined; but the substantive was wanting with which the predicate is to stand in the required relation. The answer supplies this substantive, viz. 'Homer'."[9]Respecting Harris's fifth possible answer to the question, "Are those verses by Ovid or Virgil", "They are by neither of the two", is no[t] so properly [an answer] as a declaration that the question was absurd or incorrect inasmuch as it confined the doubt within narrower bounds than the truth permitted. [...][10]That kind of question therefore, "which, according to Harris, the ancients called πυσμα (*pereontatio*), and which he describes as complex, belongs in truth to the ερωτημα (*interrogatio*)and is not complex but in and of itself perfectly simple. The number of possible

answers exists" only in the indifference relatively to the logician who is supposing the case or in the indefiniteness of the example.[11] In reality the answer would be perfectly simple, either the name of the author or "I do not know", which of course is no answer at all. The questions which are properly entitled πυσματα, and which again are no more characterised by their compound nature than the former, are such as these: "Are those verses Homer's?" "Have you seen the white bear?",[12] to which the answer is "Yes" or "No". On the conversion of the change of the personal pronouns or the position of the words, "Are these verses Homer's, yes or no?", or "These are or they are not Homer's". "Hast thou seen?" "Yes", "No", or, "I have", or "I have not", in English we might express the πυσμα by "asking", the ερωτημα by "enquiring", or simply by "questions" and "enquiries". The latter have acquired a certain dignity by their constant recurrence in the Socratic reasoning, it being the habit of this greatest of uninspired teachers "to determine at all times the subject and predicate of a position so exactly as to leave no other answer necessary on the part of the disciple but 'Yes' or 'No'. [...] These subtleties, which our Sterne has placed in so laughable a light in his example of the white bears, lead nevertheless to useful enquiries.[13] They remind us at least that all questions must be answerable, that they must consist of imperfect or defective positions which a possible answer may convert into perfect[ible]and conceivable positions.As soon as it is proved that the position which the question intends to have completed is in its own nature incapable of completion,the question itself must be rejected"[14] and instead of an answer the questioner, if he be in earnest and deserve a serious reply, must have this incurable defect in the question pointed out and explained to him.

6(a). We will apply this remark to two or three questions which it is not uncommon to hear proposed and agitated in societies where the conversation turns on speculative subjects, and we will recommence with the question with which we introduce[d] the present chapter: "What is truth?" taken not in the sense of its verbal definition as the correspondence of an affirmation or particular knowledge to its object, or as the test of such correspondence, but as a universal criterion, whether or no in any and every given case this coincidence exists. Now if truth consist in the coincidence of a knowledge with its object, this object must thereby be distinguished from other objects. For a knowledge is false if it does not coincide with the thing to which it is referred, though it may contain somewhat that might be truly affirmed of other things; but we are bound to demand of a universal criterion that it should apply to all knowledges indiscriminately, that is, without distinction of the objects severally appertaining to them; but in order to this we must abstract from all the contents or *material* of the knowledge, which material constitutes in fact what we mean by its relation or reference to the object, and it is evident therefore that as the truth consists in this reference, as this, the material, the substance, or "very stuff" of each knowledge, is what we understand by its truth, the question itself is absurd and rationally impossible. For it is to ask after a distinctive mark of the true contents and matter of each and every knowledge, when at the same time the abstraction from all contents is a necessary condition of the possibility of such a mark.[15]

6(b). To avoid the inconvenience from the awkwardness of the plural word "contents" and the ambiguity of the singular "content" we shall henceforward employ the term "matter" as the antithesis of "form" and as answering to the *Inhalt* (Inhold of the German). Question: "What is truth?" Answer: "If you ask for the meaning of the word, and this relatively to the human mind, I reply, 'the coincidence of the word with the thought and the thought with the thing'". Relatively to God the question has either no meaning or admits of but one reply, viz. "God Himself". God is the truth, the identity of thing and thought, of knowing and of being, and consequently the idea of God is presupposed in the coincidence of the one with the other, which implies the existence of each severally; but this was not the purpose of the question. You ask for some one test by which in all cases you can determine this coincidence between the word, the thought, and the thing, and in this sense the question implies a contradiction. For to be universal we must first abstract from all that is particular in each thought: but this consists in its reference to the particular thing at the time thought of, consequently we remove the very subject for which the criterion was required and properly worded the question should stand thus, "What is the universal criterion of truth when all truth is out of the question?"

7. Truth, therefore, is its own criterion and, in the language of Augustine, at once discovers itself and detects its opposite, even as we discover darkness by light and the light by its own evidence[16]—*vide* fol. third *ab hinc.*[17]

8(a). So far on the supposition that the question respects truth objectively: but there is another sense and a more fruitful one. We may mean subjective truth, in which truth may be defined [as] the coincidence between the thought and the thinker, the forms, I mean, of the intellect. Now as far as concerns the knowledge of the mere *form* abstractedly from the *matter,* it is plain that logic, inasmuch as it presents the universal and necessary rules of the understanding, must in these rules present likewise the criterion of truth, that is, of formal truth, or truth relative to the constitution or constituent forms, laws, and rules of the thinking faculty. For what contradicts these tests is false, because the understanding contradicts its own universal rules of thinking, and therein contradicts itself. And in truth there can be no contradiction. These criteria, however, respecting only the form of truth are in themselves infallible; but not of themselves sufficing; for, though a knowledge may be in perfect congruity with the logical form, and be free from all contradiction, it may nevertheless contradict or be incongruous with the matter or real subject. The logical criterion of truth or the harmony of an affirmation with the laws of the reason and the rules of the understanding is the *conditio sine qua non* but still only the negative condition of all truth, and farther than this pure and proper logic cannot extend, and consequently can supply no touchstone of error or falsehood, when such error lies in the thing, fact, or reality, considered as the substance and matter of the thought.[18]

8(b). But there is a third sense in which the question might be asked, as we have indeed implied in our last definition of truth, in the communication of which always and in its evolutions and presentations to our own minds most often a coincidence between the thought and the word is likewise implied, and here the criteria must vary with the occasion and the purpose. They may, however, be reduced to two. First, common usage, and, in civilised and cultivated societies, the usage and authority of the best writers; but where these are imperfect, and not only different shades of meaning are found expressed by the same word, but even diverse meanings, then we have no other criterion than to determine the word to some one of these meanings and if there should be another word used synonymously and, as most often happens, equally equivocal and unsteadfast in its application, to appropriate this, and if there be not, we must either borrow a term from some other language or invent one in the mint and from the materials of our own, or lastly be content to convey our meaning in a periphrasis, and supply the want of the proper term by the definition. For rude and ponderous masses, our corn, hay, coals, and timber, the weighbridge will suffice, and for the commodities of the market generally the steelyard[19]and the ordinary scales differing more in their dimensions than their accuracy, but medicine must have its appropriate weights and the goldsmith and the jeweller their gold and their diamond scales, and the experimental philosopher seeks from the artist an accuracy yet more nice, even though at the cost of a more complex machinery and the final result not obtainable without the aid of calculation.[20]We may apply this to the investigations of truth speculative, moral, or historical. The common usage is but the weighbridge,and even the authority [and] sanctions of celebrated writers [are] only the steelyards and the weights and measures of the market enjoined by public authority; the investigator must use the gold scales of precise definition; never, indeed, want only deviating even from the common usage, still less rashly rejecting the sense attached to the term by his more celebrated predecessors in the same pursuit; but yet preferring the interests of truth to all ("amicus Plato, amicus Socrates sed magis amica veritas"),[21]and well knowing that accuracy which in this case demands the fixation of the magnetic needle to one point, a thing possible, indeed only when we are masters of our own poles and can, as it were, construct our own world, or, at least, to suffer no variation without giving at the same time the requisite warning.

9. The second instance : "What are the things in and of themselves independent of our sensations, representations, and conceptions?"[22]In this form an idealist would state the question. "What [are] the things in themselves, independent of their qualities and properties, that is, what is the substance wherein the qualities and properties inhere? What is that to which they belong?" For so the materialist would state it. In either case, this somewhat, metaphysicians have named the thing-in-itself, *res in se, res ipsa,* or *res absoluta.*[23]Now before we think of the answer we will, according to the rule above given, transform the question into the imperfect position which it contains: the things independent of all sensations, representations, and conceptions (or independent of their qualities and properties)are = X. And for this unknown quantity X the respondent is to substitute some "A".[24]We will suppose this done. Now it is evident that this "A" can by no possible means represent anything by which it can be distinguished from the former X, for if it be a known quantity, there must exist some means of knowing it; but the means by which we can know an object are contained in our sensations, perceptions, representations, and conceptions wholly and exhaustively. Not only are there no other means, but no other is it in our power to imagine, even as possibility, and again, on the second statement, the means by which the thing here assumed as

external and self-subsistent can make itself known to us are all contained in its qualities and properties, consequently the A is equal to X and therefore = to not-A. The question therefore supposes a contradiction, in other words, no answer at all, as the only answer of which it is capable.

10. A shorter, but less obvious, way of annulling the question would be found in the definition, and possibly in the etymology, of the word "thing"; for possibly the word itself is the same with the "ing", a termination frequent in the names of towns and districts in the countries in which the mother language of the inhabitants was a branch of the Gothic, whether Scandinavian or Teutonic, and a diminutive of which our own language retains in the word "ingle" for hearth, that is, a smaller inclosure within another space likewise inclosed. The "ing", therefore, is the universal exponent of whatever is inclosed, bounded; but what is inclosed, considered abstractedly, must be known by that which incloses it; and these are the qualities and properties or the correspondent acts or effects in the percipient.[25] It would be no less absurd therefore to enquire what a thing, that is, an inclosure, is, supposing the inclosure out of the question, as to ask what a circle is, exclusive of its circumference, or a square, exclusive of its sides and angles. I scarcely need warn the reader that the inclosure is here taken metaphorically, or that the external image, or particular in which all words originate, must lose its particularity when its sense is extended. Whatever may be thought of the etymology as an historical point, the sense is out of all doubt: a "thing" in all languages is that which is contained in the answer to the *quale* and the *quantum*.[26] And it is to the perception of the contradiction implied in the extension of the enquiry beyond the *quale* and the *quantum* that has occasioned the third interrogative term, *quid,*[27] under the name "quiddity",[28] to mean anything at once subtle and senseless.

11. In this instance, however, as likewise in the former, there is another sense in which the question might be asked, and to which the preceding reasoning would not apply. It is,

however, full and conclusive in reference to the terms in which the question has been stated, of those things, namely, which are considered as objects of our sensations, perceptions, and conceptions, whether they are supposed to arise like the images in certain pieces of clockwork from the mechanism in the mind itself; or as holding the place of the reflection in a glass to the object, or of the object to the reflection; or lastly of the image in a picture to an invisible painter, under which illustrations we may accurately represent the systems of egoism or ultra-idealism; of Locke and Hobbes, and lastly of Berkeley.[29]

12(a). The third instance: "'Has the universe any motion of place? or can the universe move out of its position, and change its place in empty space?' I ought to speak of this query with some hesitation, for it was proposed by the great Newton himself. And yet it is evident that in order for the question to be answerable, the position 'The universe hath changed its place' must be distinct, and by some intelligent being or other capable of being distinguished from its contrary,' The universe hath not changed its place'. Now this is impossible by the very terms of the proposition; for in the infinite vacuum there cannot possibly exist and mark by which the portions of space and consequently the differences of the places can be distinguished.[30]"More plainly, we need only , as in the former instance, require a definition of the term, "Place", and when we find that it means no more than the change in the relations of space of one or more bodies to one or more other bodies, it is evident that by excluding the latter half of the definition, namely"other bodies", you destory the meaning of the whole: for if the universe change its place, it must needs be in relation to some other bodies likewise under relations of space; but then it would be no longer the universe; and "Leibniz was justified in rejecting the question *a priori* as unanswerable".[31] If , however, it should be objected that the universe might change its space, though, supposing such a change, no human or even no human or even no angelic understanding could discover the difference, it might perhaps be permitted, as with a smile, to recommend the propriety of suspending the question till it could be proposed to an intellect capable of returning the answer. But it would be wiser and more fruitful to demand of the respondent, which in this case may be one with the querist, by what right he assumes that a superhuman is not at the same time a supersensual intellect? But if supersensual, by what right he is entitled to suppose that a supersensual intellect contemplates the objects under the relations of space or with the predicates of inward and outward distance or proximity? I have said that this would be the more fruitful method, for it would lead us to an investigation of primary and indispensable necessity as the portal and even preliminary of all philosophy—of all speculative investigations, I mean, the object of what is conveyed in the heaven-descended precept, γνωθι σεαυτον.[32]

12(b). We might increase the number of these instances almost indefinitely; these, however, would be sufficient for our present purpose, were I not tempted by the frequency of its occurence to add one other, different, however, from the preceding inasmuch as the questions are all answerable if only we take the preparatory caution of ascertaining all the senses in which the words may be used and to answer each separately: that if one answer only were demanded, the question would belong to the former class, and be fairly put aside by the old tale of the tailor who was required to make a suit of clothes for the moon which should fit her through her phases.[33]I think I have given the example elsewhere, but it deserves to be impressed on the memory, and for this reason I will repeat it more at large as I find it in the prelections[34]of the excellent Mendelssohn.

13(a). "Let a four-sided pyramid A be supposed to float in the air so as to receive the light equally on all sides and consequently not suggesting the notion of its solid figure and contents to the eye of the spectator. We will suppose eight or nine spectators in different positions, and the question afterwards arises what shape the phenomenon had. The one had stood just underneath at C and declares that it was a proper square; a second who stood just on the one side, *vide* B, assures them that it was a triangle that they had seen, whether equilateral or otherwise according as he had contemplated it more perpendicular[ly] or from the point downward. A third, D, saw two sides, and affirms the figure to have consisted of two right-angled triangles applied to each other. 'Nay', exclaims a fourth, E, 'two triangles there were, but two unequal triangles'. The fifth, F, has seen a triangle with a trapezium hung to it. A sixth, G, a quadrangle with a cross. A seventh, [H], a parallelogram divided into three triangles. The eight, I, declared himself to have seen three unequal triangles.The student in perspective is aware that many more positions might be imagines."[35]

13(b). No let us suppose the question to be, assuming no known difference in the competence and integrity of the eight contending evidences, which of these was the true figure. It is evident that in each the answer might be either "this" or "not this", and, to all collectively, "all and none". How, then, should we proceed? Contradictions cannot be true, and there is no possible way of avoiding a contradiction in this instance but on the supposition that there are two senses involved in the word "figure" in the question "Which is the true figure?", and our first endeavour must be to discover the possibility of this generally and then [to turn] to the application of the difference so discovered in the particular case. The general possibility has been already given in the different senses [?φαινομενα, νους], object and subject, objective and subjective; and in applying this difference to the particular case we shall have to examine in which of the senses of the terms we should be entitled to reply that B, C, D, etc, are objectively false but subjectively true. First we shall find that the term "subjective" is not used in any defective sense, in which, indeed, the word "true" itself would become equivocal: e.g., suppose the question instead of [to the] figure had related to the colour of an object, and that one of the dissentients had seen it as yellow or in that colour which is produced by the insensibility of the eye to blue. Here we might indeed say that the person had answered truly, but scarcely that the answer was true, or truth and veracity would be confounded, or the question at least would be sifted, viz. from "What colours is that object L?" to the query "Did the object L appears to the person M?"

14. There are then two modes of subjective perception, the one, which is in congruity with the object and finds its explanation in that object taken conjointly with its possible relations: and the other, in which the perception, that is, the phenomenon resulting from the perception, has no proper cause in the object, but must be explained, not merely by the opposition of subject and subjective to object and objective, but by the peculiarity of the individual subject. In the former instance the absence of all such peculiarities is taken for granted. The answers are therefore supposed to be subjectively true, and therefore the question leading to the final answer must be, "What figure is that which, being taken objectively, though different from any of the figures seen, will yet account for them all as the necessary consequences of the real figure under each particular relation?" And this, though in reality it might never have been, or be capable of being, an object of immediate vision for any human being, as, for instance, the true magnitudes of the sun, Jupiter, and the fixed stars, is yet not only an object of human experience, distinguishing it from mere images, and the fleeting stream of impressions connected with the sensation of their outwardness.

15. Having once mastered this general distinction, and having filled up the outline sufficiently so as to put us in possession of the possible difference in the application of the terms, a new sense will arise in all or the greater number of the preceding instances, and this too of such importance as to leave no doubt of the correspondent use and necessity of tracing these differences, those, I mean, of the objective in the object, and of the subjective under the generic term of the subject, to their sources, and as far as is possible to causes and occasions. We have seen one proof of this in the question respecting the

change of place of the material universe, and we may find another in our second instance; and for the more close investigation into this point we have an additional motive, inasmuch as the answer, or rather the negation of all possible answer, which, applied to things as phenomena, whether considered as outward images or impressions therefrom, as true and conclusive, might give occasion to a dangerous error, if it were returned to the question, "What are things in themselves, as contradistinguished from appearances?" Nay! the most noticeable stratagem of the present age, the true *sophisma pigrum*, or sophistry of indolence,[36]and mode of justifying ourselves in the indisposition to any energy of reflection, much more to the yet higher effort of beholding the truths that have not even their origin in the senses, and in the contemplation of which the senses affort us either no assistance or an ambiguous and unsafe one, may be referred to one or other of the two maxims, the use of which we have ourselves exemplified in the instance preceding. The frist is the way of settling the question by denying the difference, or in other words by reducing the difference to a mere difference of words. How often and in what self-complacent terms have I heard men, who had never troubled themselves with the first elements of self-knowledge, who had never looked at a Plato or an Aristotle, or any of their celebrated compeers in later times, except on a shelf, assure their auditors that all the points noted by the metaphysicians were mere disputes about words, utter logomachy, and these the men who would have stood silent to the simple question: "What do you mean by a word, or has it any other meaning than that of an articulated sound?" Or lines in various connection or juxtaposition representing the same?" For should there be another and higher meaning, namely the meaning itself, should the word differ from the mind only as the breeze differs from the air-should it, I say, mean the truth, contemplated as conveyed and communicated, and the truth itself be a living power, or, to bring all to the one point, should two diverse things be included in the common term "definition", which in one therefore must be the essence of the thing and in the other the mere accident, namely an articulated sound or its visual representative, should the ρηματα (flowing sounds) which are not λογοι (intelligible words) be distinguished from the latter, whether appearing with the accident of the former or otherwise, and, lastly, should all words have their ground and highest source in the "Word"that was from the beginning,[37]it might appear that a dispute, if by dispute serious and earnest discussion only be meant, that a dispute concerning words is the most important subject on which the mind of man could exert its reasoning powers, a contemplation worthy [of a Bruno],[38]and which might remind the objector and the educated worldling, wherever he be, of the truth that we do not live by bread alone, but by every word which cometh from the mouth of God.[39]

16. But I have been led unintentionally into too high a strain, and perhaps ill suited to a subject in the treatment of which the mind should not only remain dispassionate, but even free from emotion, however ennobling the latter might be on its own account and in its own connections. Neither is it from worldlings only, or as an excuse for indolence, or a trick by which ignorance is transformed into a merit, that we hear the same maxim from many excellent and intelligent persons who have taken up their notions of the Schoolmen and even of their master Aristotle on hearsay, or from books that have copied from copyists and repeated for the hundredth time the repeaters of Lord Bacon's assertions, and even men of philosophic minds, but who have taken up their first grounds too superficially, or at all events not at the true depth, have for the last century and more accustomed themselves to a mode of thinking and expression exactly coincident with the following sentence of Mendelssohn, himself an amiable and every way respectable representative of the class last mentioned. "You are aware", says he, "how inclined I am to consider the controversies of the philosophic schools as mere disputes about words, or at least to trace them up to some logomachy as their original first source."[40]How predominant this maxim was in the mind of this philosopher may be seen in almost every page

of his work; in all the polemic passages, I mean. I do not hesitate, however, in coincidence with the founder of the critical philosophy, of which Mendelssohn witnessed the dawn only to express a very different and almost the opposite conviction.[41]I believe that the existence and number of false synonyms, that is, of different words in the same language used to convey the same meaning, as well as the opposite but always accompanying evil of one and the same word used at different times to convey very different senses, have been and are the growth of later times; and that the countervailing excellence we in no small measure owe to the labours of these supposed logo machists, the logicians, theologians, and divines from the thirteenth to the sixteenth century; but that the possibility of the remedy and the means of administering it were given by their labours and are to be found in the study of their works. I know of no controversy of any long continuance or which had excited any strong interest in the mind of the learned world that can be fairly reduced to a mere dispute on terms. On the contrary, whatever imperfections had previously existed in the language, whether in the Latin or vernacular tongue, these controversies were the surest and most efficient means and occasions of their removal, by forcing the controversialists to compare the term with the thought that had been conveyed or the object intended, and trying the consequences by this test, that is, truing them up to the thought or object from which they legitimately followed, to perceive the differences of the thoughts, and the correspondent necessity of a difference in the terms. But the difference of the thought once secured and in any language once fixed becomes a mark and a guide for all other languages.

17. The old mapmakers were allowed the privilege to fill up the interior of Africa with giants or pygmies, mountain or abyss, griffins, elephants, and wildernesses of land rendered doubly uninhabitable by monstrous serpents. A liberty not altogether unlike this, the critics and metaphysicians of the last century and more have taken with the writers of the Mid-

dle Ages; or it would be incomprehensible how the charge could have originated against the Schoolmen and the earlier reformers, of neglect and laxity in the definition and discrimination of their terms. It is impossible to turn over fifty pages of any one of the Scholastic commentators on these sentences and not to perceive that the fault that might truly be laid to their charge lies in the opposite extreme—excessive anxiety in the detection and display of distinctions almost always just and subtle, but too often unfruitful.It might seem as if the whole mass were crystallising into needles. I am not ignorant, nor unwilling to concede, that their premises too often stand in contrast with the process, as must needs be the case when the first ground is not taken at a right and sufficient depth: though even in this respect it would not be difficult to give the most convincing proof, by a series of instances containing the most important subjects of human disquisition, that they are superior to the age that succeeded them, almost to our own days, in all questions properly philosophical, or when the subject does not consist in the objects or notices of the bodily sense. When, however, facts or matter of fact are concerned, the student would find it neither uninstructive nor unamusing to compare (I will not send him so far back as to the masters of the school, no, nor even to the systematised divines of the fifteenth or the former half of the sixteenth century), let him compare a volume of miscellaneous tracts published during the interval from the death of Elizabeth to the Restoration with a similar volume form the last century. I am much mistaken if there should not be found at least as marked a superiority in the logical connection of the sentences, in the correct use of the conjunctions and other exponents of the connecting acts in the mind, in short as marked a superiority in the propriety of the statement and the legitimacy of the consequences on the part of the elder writers as there is of good sense and accurate observation in those of our contemporaries.

18(a). From this digression, though in common justice I ought rather to term it a prolongation of the subject, we will return by giving one striking example of the fallacy concealed in the maxim which occasioned these remarks, viz. that the controversies of most note [on] which the schools of philosophy and divinity have been divided are reducible to mere disputes in words. The same Mendelssohn from whose *Morning Hours* we have quoted this maxim[42]has applied it to the great and inveterate question or controversy on freedom and necessity, which whole dispute he would reduce to a mere equivocation in the word "must", or, as we might as well or better express it in our own language, to a neglect in distinguishing the difference between compulsion and obligation, a physical and a moral necessity.[43]But this is attempting to stop an inundation of the Danube or Ganges with a hay-band or a bundle of straw. It is most true that such an equivocation did exist, and perhaps in the minds of too many may exist still in the term "necessity" and, till the reign of Charles II, even in the word "compulsion". And Hobbes repeatedly speaks of the will as compelled by certain causes where an accurate speaker would now say impelled by such and such motives or tendencies.[44] But this ambiguity has long ceased to exist among men conversant with the history of this celebrated controversy and at all entitled to renew it, and its removal having been effected by and in consequence of the controversy furnishes a proof in point that the most noted questions in philosophy not only are not mere logomachies easily reconciled by showing that, though both parties use the same word, yet each understood it in a different sense, and thus that, like the two knights respecting the gold and silver target on the signpost, both were right;[45]but that the discussion of such questions is one of the most probable means of detecting and disarming all equivocal terms. And whether the controversy ends by the solution of the problem, or is still carrying on the pursuit, or is fairly tired out, yet it is almost sure during its continuance to remedy some one or more imperfections, and, as no important question having been once started can ever be more than suspended except by the discovery of a satisfactory answer, to shorten the labour and direct the attention of those who may recommence it, and to render our conceptions clear and more distinct even when it has failed in giving deeper insight or an enlargement of view.

18(b). The several modes by which this is effected form one of the most important parts in the logic of discussion and can be here introduced only by anticipation. One mode is that of stating the question in a higher formula, that is, in such terms as to comprehend both of the two or more senses contained in the equivocal term complained of, and this was the mode adopted in the present instance—whether the occurrences in the world under which term the voluntary actions of men are comprised are or are not determined in the series of the antecedent causes. Now this is evidently no longer a mere strife of words, but a question of profoundest interest, which in all ages it has excited wherever the duty and tendency of self-knowledge is felt and allowed.

19. So much for the first maxim, which, we may be permitted to add, is calculated to produce different effects in different characters. To the idle and vain it furnishes a self-complacency with a pretext and a disguise for mental ignorance and a self-complacency in the ignorance resulting: but to individuals of active minds, more acute than subtle and not more agile than desultory, minds more delighted with the pursuit than intent on the truth pursued and fonder of beating up for the game than of being in at the death, it too often seduces into sophistry.

20. The works, but particularly the dictionary, of the celebrated Bayle furnish abundant instances how easily a man of an acute, quick, and discursive intellect in his eagerness to detect logomachy falls himself into the more dangerous fault of logodaedalism, that is, verbal sleight-of-hand and word-trickery.[46] He brings as it were two meanings together on a damp or sinking ground and when they run exclaims, "See, they are both one and the same."

21(a). Before we conclude our reflections on this first maxim, there is one other caution to be noticed, of yet greater practical importance and frequency of application: before we can safely decide whether a controversy is fairly reducible to a dispute about words, we ought to understand clearly and distinctly what is meant by "words", even when a word is proved equivocal and when the delusion is effected by placing the word in one sense in the premise while the conclusion [follows] from or on the supposition of the other. "Ridentem dicere verum/ Quid vetat?"[47] The mere wish of relieving the subject might be a sufficient apology if from the crowd that present themselves to the mind I select a trivial and ridiculous instance in preference, but in truth I have other and more serious purposes in view, and such preference forms part of my plan, for reasons which I shall hereafter explain. To the instance, however, A country squire, one of the reverend vegetables so exquisitely portrayed in the 86th No. of the *Tatler,* having for the first time left his home, for inland, for Ramsgate, had been further tempted to join a sailing party in a trip to Calais. From the state of the weather the opposite coast was invisible till within a league of Calais. Our worthy voyager still keeping his face toward old England, when all at once the mists dissolved and the French cliffs bursting on the view, the master of the boat turned him suddenly round, exclaiming: "There Sir! that's France!" "You don't say so", quoth the Squire, "That's France! and pray, which is Spain?"[48]Now here it is pretty evident that the words "France" and "Spain" were both equivocal, each had two meanings, one the country so called, the other the portions of paper in the map of Europe or the world representing those countries, and that the good gentleman had started with the former, but was overtaken by the latter, that is, by the feeling that had been habitually associated with the image in the map and probably by some dim and imperfect relict of the image itself; but a moment's reflection will make it equally evident that the origin and proper cause of this blunder is to be sought for in the failure, irregular action, and faulty habit of the recollective, comparing, combining, and concluding faculties, and above all in the too habitual passiveness of the mind to the automatic trains of the memory and the fancy, the sequency of which is mechanically determined by accidental proximity of time and place in the original impressions (*vide Friend,* volume third, page 138),[49]and that the words are merely the modes in which the errors in thought are conveyed and expressed, and so far from being in the first instance causes of the confusion the pre-existence of such confusion is the *conditio sine qua non* of their own existence as equivocations.

21(b). Nor can we rest here, for it is in the exposure and detection of these ambiguities that we have the best means of making men sensible of the faulty and relaxed state of their intellectual powers and functions, not only in individual instances but to the enlightening of the public mind with and by the improvement of the general language. Were I asked what the most effective means would be, I should answer, as I have elsewhere already done, "a dictionary constructed on the one only philosophical principle, which, regarding words as living growths, offlets, and organs of the human soul, seeks to trace each historically through all the periods of its natural growth and accidental modifications".[50]A work worthy of a royal and imperial confederacy, and which would indeed hallow the science! A work which, executed for any one language, would yet be a benefaction to the world, and to the nation itself a source of immediate honour and ultimate *weal* beyond the power of victories to bestow or the mines of Mexico to purchase. The realisation of this scheme lies in the far distance, but in the meantime it cannot but beseem every individual competent to its furtherance to contribute a small portion of the materials for the future temple, from a polished column to a hewn stone, or a plank for the scaffolding; and as they come in, to erect with them sheds for the workmen and tempo[ra]ry structures for present use.

22(a). The second maxim will not long detain us, but the observationwhich it suggests is most important. When, says the self-presume advocate of common sense, you have been told what a thing does or suffers, how it acts and how it is acted on, there is no sense in asking further what the thing is: it can have no answer because it is, properly speaking, no question. As by means of the former maxim the majority of the most celebrated philosophical disputes are settled by compromise, by means of the second maxim the remainder are to be got rid of by a nonsuit.In the first instance, now, in the form in which we cautiously stated the question, this answer, or rather denial of the possibility of any answer, is strictly just. What the student has not to impress on his mind is that the question was purely logical, and not philosophical; for logic, we have long learnt, consists in the abstraction from all objects. It is wholly and purely subjective, and though in the preceding statement we had left it to the choice of the proposer whether he should say impressions and sensations, or properties and qualities, nothing is more easy than to demonstrate that the latter are reducible to the former. As far as the understanding and the senses, or, comprising both in one, as far as experience alone in concerned, the least reflection will convince us that these qualities and properties supposed to inhere in, or proceed from, outward things are a mere inference from our sensations and impressions in connection with the forms of the mind, which it is supposed are called into action by them; but that this hypothesis is nothing philosophical, that is, that it has no respect to any reality independent of the mind or comprehending both the mind and outward nature, may be readily proved by substituting the mere term "cause" for these supposed qualities and properties, and the position would stand thus. The understanding is under the necessity of applying the notion of cause to all the images and thoughts on which it reflects, and when these cannot be referred to any volition of the mind itself, [to] the notion of an external cause. But this notion is itself abstracted from the forms of the understanding and consequently purely subjective. How else could it be accounted for, that this supposed object is in all instances one and the same with the supposed impression, and even in the images of memory a perfect duplicate? Can anything be more evident [than] that this hypothetical object is a mere projection of the image in the mind, not indeed ordinarily detected as long as the individual is in a similar state with that of other individuals around him, but recognised at once in fever, delirium, and even in dreams?

22(b). This remark contains the true answer to the Berkeleyan system.It professes to be a subjective philosophy, the *perceptum* substituting in the *percipi,*[51]and all the phenomena attributed to some outward reality under the name of nature or the material world being mere modifications of the percipients's own being.Now we reply that this may be logic; but it cannot be philosophy inasmuch as herein alone consists the difference between logic and philosophy, that the latter seeks for a truth which is not merely subjective. But again, though the Berkeleyan scheme, most inappropriately called Idealism, is logic in the extensive sense of the world, it is far, however, from being either a system or a science of logic, were it only that it takes its ground in the sensations, that is , in modes of consciousness that are utterly heterogeneous both from the understanding and from the pure forms of the sense. *Dantur non inteliguntor*.[52] Add to this that the deduction of visual forms from the mere cessation or diminished intensity of the Istimulus of colour is one skimmed form the mere surface of the mechanical philosphy and which the admirable author would have rejected with contempt at a later period of his life, while at the same time it is an *argumentium in circulo*,[53] for as the sensations subsist in the sentient and as colour, according to Berkeley, is a sensation, it is evident that cause and effect are one and he same thing. To be sure, nothing can be more simple in appearance thaqn the series of proof in support of this scheme. All sensations subsist in the sentient exclusively. All preceptions are modes of sensation, and all appearances are mere perceptions. (Their essence consists in being perceived). But by external nature which man knows, or is capable of knowing, we mean nature which man knows, or is capable of knowing, we mean only the aggregate of appearance, therefore, the so-called external nature subsists in the sentient and is merely and altogether subjective. Pity that the constructor of this scheme had not furnished us with his proof of the first position,[54] on which all that follow, together with the context depend.

23. It is certainly no part of our immediate consciouness, and as little is it any part of the general belief of mankind, much less is it an universal belief, which it should be to be of any force at all in the present question. Now if instead of the assumption that the perception are forms of sensation we should take perception as the generic term and assume that sensation is a form or mode of perception, viz. a simple perception, or perception confined to one object, which in this case is the percepient's own being, while those involving the act of comparison and which be called complex are perceptions commonly so called, the whole superstructure of Berkeleyanism would fall. Now we are perfectly entitled to do this, for the defect, if it be such, of removing the diversity which the common sense of manking finds between sensation and perception, feeling and seeing,is common to both assumptions; the result of the former are in direct contradiction to the universal and involuntary faith of man, while those of the latter would be found in perfect coincidence with it.

24. Add to this that the latter hypothesis has this advantage over the Berkeleyan in the very outset, that in agreement with common sense and all known language it makes "feel" and "see" verbs active with a distinct objective case; while the philosophers who assert that all perceptions are to be resolved into sensations, and that sensations are but modifications of the sentient ought not if they spoke consequentially to say, " I see a chair", but " I see or I see myself in the form of a chair", "to see", "hear", "touch", etc, being with them verbs reflex and intransitive.

25. Returning, however, to the second maxim, the validity of which we have admitted in all questions purely logical, but that it would be of false and most dangerous application if assumed as univesally true, it would be only necessary for us to reflect on the way in the which we form our idea of God as the highest intelligence. We contemplate in Him, pure,

perfect, and proper reality, a something which is not merely real in opposition to pure negation of reality, but in opposition to the apparent, or phenomenal. Thus the motion of the sun, it rising and setting are real appearances *(realitas phaenomenon)*, but Copernicus, Kepler, and Newton[55] have taught all but the most ignorant that they are not the true reality. I beg leave to draw the student's attention more particularly to this remark, viz. that the opposition of real to not real, or mere nothing, is verbal and belongs to the grammar and the dictionary, not to logic; or to philosophy, if it were anything, it should be called the contrary of reality, not the opposite; but reality can have no contrary, and in accurate language we should say that "unreal" is the contrary word to the word "real". All opposites, like the extreme points of all lines, must have a mid—term common to both. Now in the present case reality itself is that mid-time; for what can we think of antecedent to reality out of which reality might proceed or be evolved? But this granted, we can at once perceive the nature of the two opposites, viz. substantial reality and apparent reality. A full illustration of which we have given in a preceding page in the example of the suspended pyramid.[56]Equally evident is it that all which we receive through the senses must belong to the latter kind, and indeed we comprise them all under the common name of *phaenomena,* that is, "appearances". It is probable that [the explanation of] the adoption of the Greek term when a term exactly corresponding was found in our own language and this too a word in common use, viz. "appearances", is that this word itself comprises, or rather is equally applied to, two species: appearances that belong to mankind generally and constitute the common world of the senses and which under the name *phaenomena* we distinguish from appearances that result from accidents and peculiarities of the individual subject, and which therefore we do not honour with the name of real in either sense, but consider as closely bordering on pure nothingness, in the subtle language of the old Scholists as *non entia tantum non vere non entia,*[57]that is, nonentities that are only not quite not absolute nonentities or nothings next door to utter nothing.

26. A ghost and a shadow supply an apposite illustration. the shadow is a real phenomenon, though not a substantial reality. A ghost is a mere appearance, a fancy or disease of the individual beholder. But in the idea of the Supreme Reality we dismiss all that is phenomenal. He is invisible essentially and, in one word, absolutely supersensual; but though we attribute to Him neither hear, nor cold, nor colour, nor shape, nor hardness, nor softness, is our idea merely negative? Does it consist in the abstract term "reality" without knowing what we mean by it, save only that we do not mean any one of all the realities of which we have any conception? Do we not far rather attribute to him intelligence, will, bliss, power, etc? We attribute these indeed to God in their absoluteness without limit in extension and unfathomable; but diminish these in the degree as much as you will, still they remain the same in essence, realities that are not phenomena, that are not appearances in any sense, even in the highest and that which comprehends all human beings, e.g. the aspect of the solar system as seen by an eye supposed to be placed in the sun, which are not therefore merely subjective, for they must be presumed in order to conceive the existence of the subject; and as their substance or quality is not changed by differences in their degree, they amy be attributed to other beings as well as to the Supreme; and in these therefore we possess properties of things, or rather the things in themselves, which are not only capable of being thought of, but which present the worthiest, nay, the only worthy, objects of the thoughts of a wise man, inasmuch as all others, if not directly or indirectly in reference to these as the ultimate aim, are vanity of vanities,[58]the dreams of an individual or the dreams of a multitude.

27. Still, however, our former speculation is not hollow, nor without its practical uses. Still it remains true that these realities, the first and the last of philosphy, are not objects of logic and therefore cannot be submitted to a discussion or reasoning purely logical.This for many reasons, one of which

will suffice for the present and is, indeed, the only one suited to the present stage of our investigation. They cannot be submitted to logical reasoning because they are of necessity presumed and presupposed in the very first step, as the student will not recollect to have been proved by us in our analysis of the syllogism respecting the force of the copula "is" in every logical position, which communicates the reality to the subject and predicate. Before we could proceed to the sources of falsehood in subjects properly logical, it was necessary, for a moral expedience ought to be considered as a necessity, to establish those truths which, being transcendent to logic, are not deducible form it, and which because they could not be fairly deduced, and because every attempt so to do has been proved fallacious and sophistical, have been themselves regarded, nay! treated, as falsehoods. The first source therefore of falsehood in logic is the abuse and misapplication of logic itself. But if not of the understanding, of what other power are these truths the besetting objects? This is the question with which this second division of our work will end, the answer to it forming the contents and subject of the third and last.[59]

Footnotes

1. John 18.38

2. *De augmentis scientiarum* bk v. ch 3: *Works* (1740) I 148-9 (var). C's tr in *Friend (*CC) I 489 : "the forethoughtful query . . . which is the prior half of the knowledge sought".

3. The proverb has English predecesors (e.g. *Spectator* No 138 [8 Aug 1711]). but C is probably giving an English turn to Kant's version, which involves a he-goat; paragraph 1 and 2 are adapted from Kant *C d r V* 82-3 (97).

4. C is quoting Moses Mendelssohn (*Morgenstunden* notes p xx), who in turn is referring to a footnote in James Haris *Hermes* bk I ch viii: *Works* 1 299-300n.

5. A free translation of *Morgenstuden* notes pp xvii-xx.

6. for "jeder Fragende."

7. "Es ist also nicht nöthig, mit dem Harris eince Verkuzung anzunehmen : "it is unnecessary, therefore, to accept an abbreviation as Harris does". *Morgenstunden* notes p xxi.

8. Ibid pp xx-xxi (var).

9. Ibid pp xxi-xxii (var).

10. "Respecting Harris's fifth . . .truth permitted" is a free paraphrase of ibid p xxiii.

11. A free rendering of ibid pp xxiv-xxv.

12. The question is from ibid p xxiv.

13. *Tristram Shandy* vol v ch 43.

14. *Morgenstuden* notes pp xxv-xxvi.

15. The paragraph is a free translation of Kant *C d r V* 83(97-8).

16. Thinking perhaps, of Augustine on John 18.38: "When therefore Christ bears witness to the Truth, undoubtedly He bears witness to Himself, seeing it is His word, *I am the Truth*: and indeed He hath said in another place, *I bear witness of Myself*". Homily cxv 4 in *Homilies on the Gospel According to St. John. . .* (Oxford 1848-9) II 1021.

17. See above, pp 110-11—three folios earlier in ms.

18. The paragraph is a fre translation of Kant *C d r V* 83-4 (98).

19. An instrument for weighing luggage etc.

20. The metaphor is an elaboration of one used in *P Lects* Lect 12 (1949) 355, which in turn seems to be derived from Kant *Träume eines Geistersehers, erläutert durch Traume der Metophysik* (Königsberg 1766) pt 1 ch 4: *VS* II 304-5.

21. "Plato is a friend, Socrates is a friend, but truth is a gre-ater friend". Traditional adaptation of Aristotle *Nicomachean Ethics* bk 1 6 par 1.

22. *Morgenstunden* notes p xxvi. This is Mendelssohn's first instance of the class of unanswerable questions.

23. "Thing in itself, thing itself, absolute thing".

24. The passage "the imperfect . . . substitute some "A" is from *Morgenstunden* notes pp xxvi-xxvii (var).

25. A discussion of the particle "ing" appears in a letter on elementary logic C wrote to his son DC in late Nov 1818: *CL* IV 885. Cf also his report of an encounter with Horne Tooke: *TT* 16 Aug 1833.

26. The "what kind of" and the "how much".

27. The "what".

28. The term is used, e.g., by Berkeley *A Treatise* . . . and *Three Diologues Between Hylas and Philonous* : *B Works* II 75, 256 Cf *TT* 20 Apr 1811.

29. I.e. the egoism exemplified by Locke and Hobbes, the theory that what "I" perceive conveys adequately the reality perceived; and the ultraidealism of Berkeley, in which what is perceived by God is, by definition, reality.

30. *Morgenstüden* notes p xxviii (var).

31. Ibid p xxviii., See Leibniz and Samuel Clarke *A Collection of Papers . . .Relating to the Principles of Natural Philosophy and Religion* (1717) Leibniz's Fourth Paper 6ff pp 94ff. See below, p 159-60.

32. "Know thyself" C is quoting Juvenal *Satires* 11.27—a favourite passage. See below, e.g., pp 143 and 205.

33. Traditional. Cf Burton *Anatomy of Melancholy* 1 sect 3 mem1 subsect 4: "you may as well make the Moon a new coat, as a true character of a melancholy man . . .". C may have noticed its occurrences in Horne Tooke Επεα πτεροευτα I 46.

34. For *Vorlesungen*.

35. *Morgenstunden* notes pp xvi-xvii. C also uses the example in a letter to Edward Coleridge on 27 Jul 1826 (*CL* VI 597) and in 1829 included the letter as an appendix in *On the Constitution of the Church and State* (*C&S-CC*-178-9). See Illustration 3, facing this page.

36. Of which Leibniz gives a clear and amusing illustration in his *Theodicee* pt I § 55.

37. John 1.1.

38. I.e. of a philosopher concerned with reconciling opposites. For C's knowledge of Bruno, see Alice D. Snyder "Coleridge on Giordano Bruno" *MLN* XLII (1927) 427-36. See also Dorothea W. Singer *Giordano Bruno His Life and Thought* . . . (New York 1950) 196-

200.

39. Matt 4.4 (var).

40. Untraced. The sentiment, if not this wording, does appear in Mendelssohn: "Es wäre nicht die erste beruhmte Sterifage, um welche die Menschen sich veruneinigi, ja einander gehasst und verfolgt haben, und die am Ende auf eine blosse Wortfehde hinauslief" ("It would not have been the first famous subject of controversy over which people have fallen out, indeed have hated and persecuted one another, and which in the end resulted in an empty quarrel about words"). *Morgenstunden* 118-19.

41. See e.g., Kant *C d r V* 368-9 (309-10).

42. C's only direct reference in the *Logic to the Morgenstunden.*

43. *Jerusalem oder überreligiose Macht und Judenthum* (Frankfurt & Leipzig 1791) 5-12. C's copy in the BM is bound with the *Morgenstunden.*

44. C is drawing on *Jerusalem* 12 here. A favourite example : cf *BL* ch 4 (1907) I 64n and *P Lects* Lect 5 (1949) 174.

45. Cf C's note on a flyleaf of Jacob Rhenfred *Opera philogica . . .*(Utrecht 1722) (BM copy): "The controversy . . . was like that of the gold and silver shield—the phrase meant either—and which of the two must be determined by the context." The fable of "The Party-colour'd Shield" appears in Sir Harry Beaumont [Joseph Spence] *Moralities: or, Essays, Letters, Fables: and Translations* (1753) 99-102; its moral is, "never enter into any Dispute . . . till you have fairly considere'd each Side of the Question". The story was a commonplace, however; see WW *Prelude* XI 79-82 and Scott *The Antiquary* (Edinburgh 1816) I 133.

46. Pierre Bayle *Dictionaire historique et critique* (Rotterdam 1697). C mentions elsewhere Bayle's "acuteness and dexterity in the management of words and tricks of argument" (BM MS Egerton 2901 f 3). and calls him "the Founder and Father of Modern Scepticism and religious Indifference" (f 2*V*). Cf *AR* (1825) 119, BM MS Egerton 2801 ff 50 and 74*V*, and the early references in *CN* I 277 and n, and 280.

47. Horace *Sares* 1.124-5. Tr H. R. Fairclough (LCL 1966) 7: "what is to prevent one from telling truth as he laughs ...".

48. C heard the story told of Sir Gregory Page Turner (*CL* IV 942: 12 May 1819). He writes: "I would have given half a crown for such a Story when I was at Jesus. It is really an excellent one—I picked it up at Sir George Beaumont's last Monday." Sir Gregory (1748-1805) also appears in *The Watchman,* speaking in a debate on dog tax. *Watchman* (*CC*) 257.

49. *Friend* (*CC*) I 456. C refers to the 1818 ed.

50. See p 58, above. Cf *BL* ch 12 (1907) I 165n and, above, p 15 n 3.

51. The "thing perceived" subsisting in the "fact that it is perceived".

52. "They are given, not understood". Cf below, p 162.

53. "Circular argument".

54. I.e. that "all sensations subsist in the sentient exclusively". See Berkeley *A Treatise Concerning the Principles of Human Knowledge: B Works* II 42f. C's warmth comes from finding Berkeley trying to confute materialism with an inadequate argument.

55. For C's opinion of the relationship of Kepler to Newton, see *AR* (1825) 393-4 and *TT* 8 Oct 1830.

56. See above, p 117.

57. E.g. Duns Scotus.

58. Eccles 1.2.

59. I.e. the projected organon again. See above, pp 57, 100.

Chapter-5

On the Discussion of the PREMISES in All Logical Reasoning

Chapter-5

1(a). What in ordinary language we call the "premises" of an argument is expressed technically by the major and minor of the syllogism. Independent of the subject and the predicate, and, indeed, in a certain sense antecedent to them, the student's attention was drawn to the copula which, connecting both, asserts the reality of the whole; and this copula we found expressed by the verb substantive, "is". In what this reality consists was likewise declared, viz. that it contained a truth which being antecedent to the act of reflection, and of course therefore to all other acts and functions of the understanding, asserted a being transcendent to the individual subject in all cases and therefore to all subjects thinking under the same laws. Of this primary reality we discovered two sources-one above the reflective and discursive powers, the other below them. The one was the reason, and the other the impressions from the senses. Concerning the reason, we have in the preceding chapter spoken sufficiently for the purpose which we had in view, which was, to satisfy the claims of morality, and secondly to prevent, though at the price of anticipation, any misunderstanding (which by the way is as often occasioned by the absence of an important truth as by the presence of an error or falsehood). We have therefore now to treat of the latter source, viz. the senses.

1(b). And yet a knot of uncommon difficulty meets us here at the very outset, of such difficulty indeed that, if the reader will excuse an apparent contradiction, resulting from the necessary inadequacy of every metaphor (*simile non est idem*, or as we say, no likeness goes on all fours),[1] it must be first cut in order that it may afterwards be untied.[2] We have used the term, "impressions on or through the senses"; but what is impressed, as far as we have hitherto seen is not the forms; for these the purely subjective nature of our science has compelled us to place in the mind itself, that is to say, either in the forms of the pure sense or in the forms and functions of the understanding, both which by a coarse metaphor indeed, but not more coarse or imperfect than the diversity between mental and material objects rendered inevitable, we attempted to explain by considering them as primary moulds or forms, conceived as the cause and origin of all shape, and consequently not subject to the necessity of having any shape of their own to be explained; for it would be absurd to speak of shape respecting a subject which we have assumed as the antecedent of all shape, and not less contradictory than the question of ignorant atheists: "What was done during the time before time had a beginning?"[3]

2. If not the shapes of objects, what remains? Shall we answer, a sensation which, though of necessity inherent in the sentient subjct itself, the subject cannot refer to any act or volition of its own and which being accompanied with the sense of contingency and its succession being altogether irreducible to the spontaneous processes of the mind carried on under the law of association, seems to authorise, but at all events compels, us to consider in reference to something self-subsistent and present to us as other from ourselves and no less real. Such is the faith in the existence of an external world, a faith confessedly pre-existent to, and, indeed, presupposed in, the arguments by which it is confirmed[4].

3. We refer these sensations to objects without us; can we then divide or practically distinguish the one from the other? I have a peculiar sensation, as, for instance, a thrill or any other feeling, and then infer that a table or house is present and acting on me. In all the objects with which the intellect is principally concerned, the very contrary is the known fact. In the impressions of sight as long as they remain healthful there is no appreciable sensation at all, and to distinguish the sensation in its latent mode of existence all languages have adopted a different word. And we say a sense of sight and [?cavil] at a visual sensation as only not a contradiction. As

little, on the other hand, can we in any particular instance detect or separate the share contributed by the mind itself, though, as in the kaleidoscope, we may have had it satisfactorily demonstrated how large a portion of all that we behold is given by the organ or machine itself.[5] What then remains but that in the first instance we should take the objects as universal nature and our own conjointly present then to us? Enough that we have learnt that the unity in which all form and whatever can be called a whole must consist is not dependent on any power that we can call ourself. That whether in the mind or out of the mind or both at once, it is a nature and the only reality of objects considered in the primary antithesis of object and subject. It may not indeed be the primary reality, for in this the distinction of object and subject does not exist; but though in this sense a secondary and so far a derivative reality, we might even already anticipate that it would be found one and the same with the reality of the reason, and that the difference will be found in the different relations to the individual subject.

4. Our first rule, therefore, may be termed the rule of common sense, *nihil in intellectu quod non prius in sensu.*[6] In other words, that the objects must have been perceived aright before they can be rightly conceived, and, as a corollary, that they must have been rightly conceived before we can form legitimate abstraction or generalisation, and the like manner that we must have rightly abstracted and accurately generalised before we are in the condition of attaching appropriate abstract or general terms to the conceptions.

5(a). Does nature, however, for by this term we have agreed to understand the cause and substance of all reality apprehensible by the senses and cognisable by the understanding—does nature, I say, present these objects to us without exciting any act on our part, does she present them under all circumstances perfect and, as it were, ready-made? Such may [be] the notion of the most unthinking; for even with these it is too opposite to their own experience to be a distinct belief: but our readers need direct their attention, were it only to have the power of recognising it, or, as the phrase is, to bring it under their cognisance when perceived; but the very senses by which we are to perceive will each again require the aid of a previous scientific insight-anatomical, physiological, and physical. Take, for example, the act of beholding: the instrumental agent of vision, viz. light, with its laws and properties, give[s] birth to the science of optics; yet these laws cannot be safely applied without an acquaintance with the laws and properties of the atmosphere together with the nature of vapours and their varying densities; and this again will be imperfect and insecure if the nature of transparence, translucence, and the transparent and translucent bodies generally be not understood, and the rule by which the phenomena are generalised grounded in some higher principle. Thus the several sciences of hydrostatics, aerology, crystallology, and chemistry, preceded and accompanied by a knowledge of the pure mathematics, may be all required in order to a ligitimate judgment on a single phenomenon, i.e. before the image can be safely declared to possess objective reality—before it can be recieved with safety as a fact of experience. So erroneous would the assertion be that an object of the sense is the same with the impression made on the senses, or even that what we appear to see in the same with the image formed on the retina, if it were possible to conceive an act of seeing wholly separate from the modifications of the judgment and the analogies of previous experience. Nor have we yet enumerated all the requisites. A delusion might result, and in many cases necessarily would result, if the knowledge supplied by anatomy and physiology were wanting, and even with these the source of error is not yet wholly closed. All inttention to the laws and rules, pure and empirical, of the imagination, volition, and the feelings might occasion the beholder to mistake a product or disturbing force of his own being for the object which then only supports that name when it is contemplated free from all such pre-existence of itself, as given to it when [?it has] attained the character of memory—thus in nature the germ presupposes the blossom even as the blossom presupposes the germ, numerically different indeed, and different in the relations of time and space, but essential and, in all its intelligible characters, the same. For an absolute first is a position with regard to which the understanding may submit in silence but which can by no artifice be thought of by the understanding or reduced under its forms. What follows? Even this—in order to discuss aright the premises of any reasoning in distinction from the reasoning itself, a knowledge of the matter is the first and indispensable requisite. This may appear a truism, but though equally certain it is not equally obvious that the same necessity applies to the very means and acts with and by which we acquire the materials of knowledge: not only must we have some scheme or general outline of the object by which we could determine its nature, which we could determine its nature, informed that there is a previous discipline of the senses, that even in the general functions of touch and taste and smell and sight and hearing we pass from our birth into a school beginning at the lowest forms and at our death have not yet attained the highest. And as there is a seeing and hearing which belongs to all mankind, even so in the different kinds and species of knowledge there is a separate apprenticeship necessary for each. All indeed reducible to the common form of attention appropriately directed and rendered proportionally intense, but varying in degree of excellence with the greater or less knowledge already possessed by the oberver of the object to which, the medium through which, of the faculty by which, and lastly of the state in which, the observer is while he is thus attending, for such is the mystery both of man and nature that every perception presupposes itself, and no knowledge could be acquired without subjective influences.

5(b). We freely admit, or rather I have purposely introduce the preceding remarks for the purpose of announcing and impressing the truth, that in cases like those supposed in these remarks, where the reasoning is grounded on some distinct external object, the business of common logic is simple, indeed, and that the application may be safely trusted to the common sense of mankind. For first the main end in investigations of this kind is most often the establishment of the object itself, which, once established, contains or rather is coincident with its inferences, and secondly, when this is not altogether the case, the sole logical exercise of the mind would be confined to the examination whether the second term was or was not included in the first, as the more comprehensive, or, which will more frequently occur, whether the application of the general rule is or is not legitimate. A power acting inversely as the square of the distance is the power of gravitation, but the law acts by a power, etc, therefore the law acts by a power of gravitation. We may now therefore readily understand the observation of Lord Bacon respecting the insignificance of common logic and its utter inadequacy in the investigations of nature, and, he might safely have added, in those of the pure reason, but let it not be forgotten that the great philosopher at the same time asserts its utility, nay, its indispensableness in all the moral and forensic concerns of life.[7] But if we abstract all speculation and all discourse that fall under the class of moral, historical, and forensic, how small a portion shall we reserve for the majority of mankind. We need only reflect on the infrequency of any discussion in which the object is singly and directly presented to the sense or the senses.

6(a). For the purposes of ordinary observation the few and safe rules generalised from uninterrupted experience, aided with a few of the principal results obtained by scientific investigation, and which are practically intelligible without any insight into the process by which they were originally obtained, will be sufficient to give us a justifiable confidence in that which alone we men have a social interest to ascertain, viz. the coincidence of our individual perceptions with the average perceptions of our fellow creatures. Here indeed, plain and simple as these criteria are, spontaneously and almost instinctively as we apply them every hour of our lives, and simple as the rule pre-established in the logical canon [is]—that in order to a conclusion we must assure ourselves that A has been rightly secluded and that B is actually included in A—yet the habit of repeating this process consciously and on all subjects of importance, above all, and in all cases where the apparent conclusions of the understanding are at variance with our moral convitions or the persuasions of common sense, is of vital importance and efficacy, for the results can be no other than that of a healthful dissatisfaction or premonitory discontent with whatever is vague or flitting. A mind so disciplined acquires not only a facility of recurring frequently to the sources and fountainheads of truth and there renewing the elasticity of reimpressing and sharpening the stamps of his intellectual being; but this process becomes a want, an habitual desideratum of his nature, the cause the more pleasurable because he progressively finds himself more and more amply remunerated both by the power which he acquires over others in anticipating the conclusions of minds formed in the same school with his own, and the delusions of others which he overlooks, as one placed on an elevation in the centre of a labyrinth of paths not only sees his own future direction but can safely prophesy the entanglements and wanderings of the groundlings at every turn and in the whole detail of error.

6(b). Of the application of the rule implied in the canon as reduced in this work to the three forms of clusion, inclusion, and conclusion, we will give a single example as an instance of the mode [of] applying the rule and a proof of the services which it is capable of affording. In the writings of Plato we find the following apparent syllogism:

'Ερως μεν αει φιλοκαλος

των δε καλλισιωυ Σοφια

'Ερως ουν αει φιλοσοφος

i.e. "to desire beauty is the essential character of love. But wisdom is a thing of all other[s] most beautiful, therefore to desire wisdom is the essential character of love".[8] Now here it is plain that the minor is included in part only of the major, viz. in the term "beauty"; and secondly, that the immediate consequence of the minor would be therefore, "to desire wisdom is to desire beauty": but with this it would be a syllogism of four terms, which, where the result is not directly false, always proves that some one of the four terms is out of place, and we must add another syllogism in order to give the coercive power to the conclusion, for instance: "Whatever is harmonious in itself and in its relations. Therefore wisdom is beauty." "To desire beauty is the character of love. But to desire wisdom to desire beauty. Therefore to desire wisdom is the character of love." Here the syllogistic reasoning formally considered is complete, and we have only to ask whether wisdom is actually included in beauty. Now a little reflection will convince us that wisdom is not a phenomenon, does not derive its being from relations, while beauty which is beautiful in itself is a nonentity or a mere lax and metaphorical use of words. For beauty subsists in relations and common sense. Sense instructs us that wisdom may be beautiful, i.e. may manifest herself in relations the constituent forms of which harmonise with each other and combine to a common unity in the total impression, yet we cannot say that beauty is wisdom or that the beautiful is necessarily wise. The conclusion therefore would be, not that love would desire wisdom for itself, but that it would affect the beautiful in wisdom; and this would be a mere movement in a circle. The minor was not included, and the apparent progression consists in nothing but a repetition of the major or original position in the different forms of words.

Footnotes

1. Cf above, p 11 n 4, and below, p 143.
2. The Gordian knot. Cf p 235, 132,
3. Cf *CN* III 3763 and n, where a version of this question is traced to St Augustine *City of God* 12,15 as being beyond "even the greatest fool. . ."
4. Cf *BL* ch 12 (1970) I 177-8 and Schelling *System des*

trasncendentalen Idealismus 343-4.

5. Cf *AR* (1825) 258n; *TT* 14 Apr 1833.

6. Traditional summation of Aristotlian thought: "there is nothing in the understanding which was not previously in the sense". (C's tr; see below, p 226.) Cf pp 183-4, below, *BL* ch 9 (1907) I 93, and *AR* (1825) 73.

7. See *Distributio operis* and *De Works* (1740) I 13-14 and 137-8. *augmentis scientiarum* bk v ch 1:

8. *Symposium* 204B (var).

Chapter-6

Essence, Form, and Rules of Universal Logic

Chapter 6

1(a). We have now reached the point at which it will [be] expedient to half, though but for a moment, in order to review the road we have passed over, that we may thus be able to form a distinctconception of the journey that yet remains. For in order to see distinctly what a thing is we must ascertain what it is not. Hitherto, then, we have exhibited the essence, form, and rules of common or universal logic. Now the common logic is either pure or applied; in the first, which alone we have given in its completion, we abstract from all empirical conditions under which the exercise of the understanding takes place; we abstract from the influence of the senses, from the interference of the imagination, from the laws of memory, from the weight of customs, of inclination, of passion, and, inclusively, from the sources of human prejudices—in short, we abstract, from all cause from which any given and particular cognitions arise, or out of which any counterfeits of knowledge proceed—because all these respect the understanding, circumstantially, under certain contingent occasions of its application, or of objects to which objects, to which and by which the application was determined. But in order to the knowledge of these, experience is required. But the pure common logic appeals wholly to principles *a priori*, i.e. principles derived from the construction of the machine itself, not from its uses; from the construction of the understanding altogether abstracted from the materials on which it acts or the causes by which it is called into action. It is therefore, and so we have called it, a canon of the understanding . And inasmuch as the understanding is the organ of the reason, if not directly by affirmation yet indirectly by negation, it is a cannon of the reason likewise, but only in respect of the formal, let the subject matter be what it may, drawn from outward experiences or from inward consciousness and reflection.

1(b). By way of illustration we will take a sextant or other optical instrument. Now we may consider this in three different ways, viz.. with regard to the objects and particular images which it presents, or, abstracting from these, with regard to the way in which it presents these images, however different in themselves, and which is common to them all, or lastly with regard to the construction and constituent parts of the sextant itself. But before we apply this instance it must be premised that in the mind the way in which the instrument acts of necessity, to a certain extent is determinable without the knowledge of the construction or constitution of the instrument, its exercise being inseparably accompanied with a sense of its necessity *inherent* in itself, and this necessity it is that forms the essence of a knowledge *a priori.* We do not say it has always done so and so, and therefore we have no doubt that it will continue so to do; neither the analogy for the past nor the anticipation of the future enters at all into the contemplation. Proofs of which we have in every position of geometry and arithmetic as well as in pure logic. The mathematician rests perfectly secure that his axioms and propositions are necessary and universal truths, without troubling himself with any analysis of the faculties by which he constructs his figures and demonstrates their relations. With this previous explanation we may now apply the instance above given. A knowledge directed to the particular objects or images, as presented by the sextant—after the corrections and rectifications suggested by the variation from other optic instruments and necessary in order to arrive at a common result—such knowledge would represent the sciences of experience, though it might well happen that the knowledge of what experience itself is, wherein it consists, and under what conditions it is possible may form no part of this knowledge. Images which all men having their right faculties under the same given circumstances are capable of receiving passive[ly] or by reproduction and naming, i.e. referring to a class and in which each individual is conscious that the appearances with order of their sequence are not the creatures of his own volition, nor yet explicable by the law by which the spontaneous acts and products of his own faculties are determined, form the content and materials of experience, which, as is indeed involved in this view of its constitution, is as necessarily accompanied by a sense of a contingency, as the truths *apriori*, from which the facts of experience are contradistinguished, are characterised by a sense of necessity. The second sort of Knowledge [is] that which respect of common way in which the sextant represents all images so that the image does not properly belong to the instrument unless it be so presented (e.g. in the case of an accidental speck or reflection on the object glass). This, we say, if applied to the forms of the pure sense, constitutes the sciences of measure and number, or geometry and arithmetic, and, applied to the understanding, gives the science of common or purely formal logic. There remains then one other knowledge, that viz. of the constitution and constituents of the instrument itself, without which we cannot certainly distinguish either what share the instrument itself has in the image presented by it, and, therefore, as little what is that we are justified in referring to a correspondent object subsisting independent of the instrument through and by which we arrive at the knowledge of its existence. In the case of the sextant, we may indeed arrive at a probability which, sufficing for all practical purposes, may be called an empirical certainty, by comparing the result with those of other optical instruments, the human eye itself considered as one, in the same manner as we rectify the notices of one sense by those of some other or of all the other senses.

1(c). But the instrument of the human mind is one and all, and when we have once learnt from experience, and with that degree of insight which experience is capable of affording, so far to generalise the operations of the mind as to distinguish the individual peculiarities or the accidental subjective, we are at the end of our resources. We know empirically that such and such (a way of perceiving, for instance, as when all objects appear yellow, or when no colour requiring blue for its composition is seen) do not belong to the perceiver as a man but as this or that individual in whom it constitutes such a defect or disease; or, when the difference existed in degree only and not in *kind,* possibly as an individual perfection; but whether the seeing of objects generally is an attribute of the object or a communication from the subject will remain uncertain as before.

1(d). Now the desideratum is to distinguish the *subjective* from the *objective in toto,* not partially as hitherto in common logic by mere abstraction from the knowledge given by experience, by which we do indeed know [that] that to which we are exclusively directing our attention is purely *subjective,* but by no means that the matter or materials *from* which we have *withdrawn* our attention are properly and wholly objective—i.e. that they have a subsistence independent of the mind which contemplates them. They may for aught that the common logic can affirm or deny consist of a wonderful and seemingly indecomponible union of the mind and an external agency, as the tune of the breeze and the Eolian harp.[1] It being of the utmost importance that the nature of this threefold distinction should be thoroughly understood, and even made familiar, let us attempt yet another illustration. We have heard of the automaton chess-player.[2] Let us imagine an automaton potter. While we are watching the procedure of the machine, we may either fix our attention on the different clays which by some machinery out of sight had been presented to the potter's hand, or rather to the vessels, inasmuch as according to our supposition the clay does not appear to us previously to its reception of the form, or we may fix our attention exclusively on the series of motions which the hands and arms of the automaton execute in all the different vessels which it is capable of forming. We abstract this action of the machine both from its effects or products and from the machinery which is its cause and agent. Having thus abstracted its acts or motions we then generalise them, i.e. we fix our attention on those of constant occurrence or bring all the varieties under some common conception (as, for instance, circles and ellipses may be brought under the common term of "a revolving line"), or lastly we may examine the automaton itself, and resolve the machine into integral constituents with their relation and subordination, and again each constituent into its component parts, co-ordinate or subordinate. We have before had occasion to remind our reader that no simile quadrates:[3] but in questions that include the powers and processes of the mind in the subject matter it is more obviously true that every likeness must halt or be inapplicable in some point or other. Thus in the preceding illustration the materials on which the hands of the automation work are supplied wholly from without; but in the mind the machine itself and all its acts and processes are equally fitted to be the objects of its action as the vessel with the substance from without that must be presupposed as the basis and recipient of the form. But if only we bear this in mind, and intellectually supply this defect, the illustrations will assist us both in apprehending and remembering the several natures of the three divisions of knowledge which we are here interested in rendering perfectly intelligible. The vessels will represent all the knowledges which we derive from experience. The constant movements of the machine on the clay will represent the formal science generally; that is, according to the faculty which we chose to represent by the hands of the automaton. If we refer to the sense, these motions will represent the pure forms of the sense and the sciences of number and measure. But if, as in the present instance, and in truth with greater similitude and propriety from the narrow compass and simplicity, both of the motions and of the science represented by them, the understanding is the faculty in question, then these movements will represent the science of common logic, the analysis of the automaton itself. The investigation into the composition and constitution of the mind itself yet remains the weightiest and worthiest of all contemplations if the poet have said rightly.

e coelo descendit γυωθι σεαντον[4]

and that the knowledge of our intellectual nature is the substance and life of all our knowledge and the ground of intelligibility of all other objects of knowledge.

1(e). Were it only conceivable as an object of hope, instead of being, as indeed it is, a demonstrable truth, that the human mind is the compass in which the laws of all outward things are revealed as the dips and declinations,[5] this would of itself suffice to make the investigation to which we are now introducing the reader more than a subject of interest; it must make it an object of duty to all who, filling or destined to fill the higher and middle stations or society, possess opportunities of leisure which have been fearfully abused if they have not been made opportunities of reflection.[6] For these classes generally, though with especial reference to those who are forming themselves for public and professional life, the pulpit, the bar, the senate, the professor's chair, or for that which belongs to all and includes the qualities of all, the public press, this work was written, and to these I will now address myself as though they were personally present.

2. My friends! you enjoy an immunity from bodily labour and you are placed or seeking to place yourselves on an elevation to which the majority of your fellow-countrymen are to look up with respect and perhaps with reverence. The titles, the comforts, the revenues, which you possess or aim at, may designate your rank but cannot constitute your moral and personal fitness for it. Be it enough for others to know, that you are its *legal,* but by what mark shall you stand accredited to your own consciences as its worthy, possessors? Not by common sense or by common honesty; for these are equally demanded of all classes, and therefore mere negative qualifications in *your* rank of life, or characteristic only by the aggravated ignominy consequent on their absence. Not by genius or splendid talent; for these as being gifts of nature are objects of moral interest for those alone to whom they have been allotted. Nor yet by eminence in learning; for this supposes such a devotion of time and thought as would in many cases be incompatible with the claims of active life. Erudition is doubtless an *ornament* that especially beseems a high station:

but it is *professional* rank only that renders its attainment a duty. The rank in question must be so far *common* that we may be entitled to look for it in *you* from the mere circumstance of your situation, and so far distinctive, that it must be such as cannot be expected generally from the inferior classes. Now, either there is no such criterion in existence or the desideratum is to be found in an habitual consciousness of the ultimate principles to which your opinions are traceable.[7] Now, a steadfast reflection on the terms of the postulate might enable you to anticipate the conviction which the following section will, I trust, not fail to produce and perfect, that this is impracticable as long as we remain ignorant what, and of what kind, the senses are, and this again supposes a knowledge first of that which, though common in kind to all men, we yet, each of us, are entitled to call "mine", or "myself", as contradistinguished from that which is "not mine", "not of myself"—that, viz which we have so often spoken of as a knowledge of the subjective in contradistinction from the objective. And secondly a knowledge of that which is not myself, or of me as contradistinguished from that which the mind possesses in itself or communicates from its own stores, i.e. a knowledge of the objective as contradistinguished from the subjective. And lastly a knowledge of that which is distinguished from both, as transcending both and [being] of both the root and identity.

3(a). Now it is evident that the knowledge mentioned in the second place, which we may call the universal subjective, or that which is common to the race without distinction of individuals, must be acquired before we can form any judgment of the first, the properly objective. At least from the point on which we have hitherto stood and [are] still standing, viz. the point of reflection. This must be necessary inasmuch as our knowledge of [the] objective is merely negative. We affirm it to be objective—in other words, that the objects of such knowledge subsist independently of the mind-only because it is not accompanied by the mark of the subjective, viz. its validity *a priori,* and because it is not included and therefore not to be evolved out of that which we know to be the subject itself. But on the other hand, though less obvious, it is no less true that as the second or the knowledge of the constitution of the subject is a necessary precondition of any distinct knowledge respecting the object, yet this must presuppose the existence of that [first] and highest insight—an insight into the existence of a somewhat that is the common ground of the subject and object, were it only that it is in the order of its formation anterior to reflection, in which power the antithesis of subject and object has its birth and origin.

3(b). There is, as we have already learnt, a somewhat which, whether we refer it to an agency without ourselves or acknowledge it as an immediate presence to and as it were within the mind, we in both cases express by the affirmative "is". And hence we distinguish from the reflective faculty two species of reality—the reality in nature and the reality of reason. The one[is] characterised by its apparent contingency, as proceeding from a power separate from our own will and spontaneity, and the other by its absolute necessity, not the conditional necessity which inheres in the forms and functions of the understanding and the rules generalised from these, and which necessity with its consequence, the property of being affirmed *a priori,* we have aptly compared with the movement of a machine that results solely [and] inevitably from the construction of the machine, supposing it to act at all, though this is itself not universally necessary but must be limited to the mind from the faculties of which such and such cognitions result. Our present business is [?confined] to the latter, and this again we must subdivide into two kinds, each forming a distinct science—these are, first, the universal forms of the pure sense and the knowledge [that] has been entitled "transcendental aesthetic", a term borrowed from a fragment attributed to Polemo, the successor of Speusippus, who succeeded Plato, the great founder of the Academic School. In order to distinguish the faculty of sense itself abstractly from the sensations and from the modifications of the senses or organs of sense, Polemo designated the former by the words

Αισθησις επιστημονικη,[8] or sciential perception or apprehension. The term "transcendental" means the same as "sciential", but with an additional significance. All knowledge is excited or occasioned by experience, but all knowledge is not derived from experience, such, for instance, is the knowledge of the conditions that render experience itelf possible, and which must therefore be supposed to exist previous to experience, in the same manner as the eyes must pre-exist to the act of seeing, though without that act of seeing we never should have learnt that we possessed eyes. Now to distinguish the truths that are necessarily presupposed in all experience as its condition and co-cause, from the facts or knowledge not only occasioned *by*, but actually derived from, experience, whether it be the experience of the world without or the experience acquired by reflection on ourselves, and yet at the same time to distinguish the former knowledge from pretended cognitions and assertions that transcend our intellectual faculties or, what is equivalent, for which the human mind can be shown to possess no appropriate faculty and which assertions are therefore called "transcendent", the term "transcendental" has been chosen. And I have found it expedient to give this explanation, because the "transcendent" and "transcendental" are stated a perfectly synonymous.[9] In this, however, the lexicographer[10] was not justified by the usage of our own divines and metaphysicians in times past or by the present use in the continental schools. Transcendental knowledge is that by which we endeavour to climb above our experience into its sources by an analysis of our intellectual faculties, still, however, standing as it were on the shoulders of our experience in order to reach at truths which are above experience, while transcendent philosophy would consist in the attempt to master a knowledge that is beyond our faculties, an attempt to grasp at objects beyond the reach of hand or eye or all the artificial ends and, as it were, prolongations of eye and hand, of objects therefore the existence of which, if they did exist, the human mind has no means of ascertaining, and therefore has not even the power of imagining or conceiving; that which the pretended sages pass off for such objects being merely images from the senses variously disjoined and recomposed, or mere words expressing classes of these images and by addition of other words associated with obscure feelings, a process pardonable in poetry, though even there quickly degenerating into poetic commonplace, as, for instance, fountains of pleasure, rivers of joy, intelligential splendours, and the like, but as little to be tolerated in the schools of philosophy as on the plain high road of common sense.

4. The transcendental aesthetic is the first, and as there must be a perception, or, if we dared apply the word in this sense, a ception, before there can be a conception, the transcendental aesthetic must take place of[11] that investigation into the constitution and constituent forms of the understanding, which in analogy with the former is termed transcendental logic or the λογος [a]επιστημονικος[12] of Polemo. However, though we deemed it expedient not to leave unnoticed or unexplained the terms which the most profound of modern logicians and the proper inventor and founder of transcendental analysis[13] has adopted, we prefer the more intelligible and less uncommon title of the *critical* or judicial logic, i.e. a criterion of the general and particular judgments passed by the understandings as the faculty of reflection, derived from a knowledge of the constitution of the understanding itself and of the universal forms of the sense to which the legitimate exercise of its functions is confined.

5. A criterion, indeed, and that, too, comprehended under the terms" aesthetic" we have already given as an appendix to the common or syllogistic logic, i.e. the logic as a canon of reasoning;[4] but not a criterion, scientific and of course *a priori*, nor derived from the sciential or transcendental aesthesis, but abstracted and generalised from general experience and involving the exercise, active and passive, of the senses. Insufficient therefore for the safe application of common logic itself as being limited to those cases in which the affirmation as the major and minor of the syllogism respect[s] the objects of the senses as concretes. These criteria therefore could not

be omitted among the precognitions require as the tests of the material truth of conclusions formally legitimate, but holding a very subordinate place to the criteria which we are now about to investigate, whether we consider the extent and universal application of the latter, the weight and deep interest of the subject to which it is specially applied, or finally the circumstance that the former comes to us spontaneously at best with an accuracy sufficient for the ordinary purposes of life and as the necessary result of the comparisons and half-unconscious experiments which we are compelled by nature to make in order to exercise our senses for the purposes of self-preservation. Though in making this confession we are not to forget that the main point in the marks that distinguish the man of superior mind consists in his doing that consciously, in the light of distinct knowledge and the sense of pure-agency, which the many do unconsciously or rather can scarcely be said to do at all inasmuch as it is their common nature, rather, that does it in and for them.

Footnotes

1. Cf *The Eolian Harp: PW* (EHC) I 100-2.
2. For a description, see Sir David Brewster *Letters on Natural Magic...* (1832) 269-83. An example was exhibited in London in 1819. Cf Descartes' discussion of automata in *Discourse on Method* (1637): *D Works* I 115-16.
3. See above, p 11 n 4.
4. Juvenal *Satires* 11.27. See above, p 116 n 3.
5. C quotes from *SM (CC)* 78-9. The quotation from Juvenal, in English, is given there a few lines later.
6. Cf the audience addressed in C's second "Lay Sermon". See *LS (CC)* 119.
7. Paragraph 2 up to this point is a free quotation from *LS (CC)* 121.
8. C appears to have confused Polemo with speusippus here. Cf Tennemann III 8n, quoting Sextus Empiricus *Adversus*

mathematicos VII § 145, which may be translated: "[Speusippus] said that the criterion of truths of reason (νοητων) is the sciental reason (επιστημονικος λογος) but of things sensible it is the sciential apperception (επιστημονικη αισθησις)."

9. The distinction, as well as some of what follows in the paragraph, is based on Kant *C d r V* 330 (299).

10. Samuel Johnson. Cf *BL* ch 12 (1907) I 164n.

11. I.e. must precede.

12. C uses the term in appositon to "Discursive Intellect" in a note on the endapapers of Tennemann VII I (pt2). See also p 146n 1, above.

13. Kant.

14. See above, pp 70ff.

Chapter-7

Judicial Logic, Including the Pure Aesthetic

Chapter 7

1. Among the consequences of the overbalance of the commercial spirit[1] [—]not from any excess of trade and commerce in themselves, but from the decline or deficiency of the requisite checks and counterforces, and among these more especially (for our present purpose at least) from the gradual neglect of all the austerer studies; the long eclipse of philosophy, the transfer of that name to physical and psychological empiricism, and the non-existence of a learned and philosophic class, constituting a *publicum in publico,*[2] and to all which we may add a cause which the age is accustomed to hail as a matter of triumph and self-congratulation, the aversion to theological controversy with the majority of well-educated Englishmen, and the revolution in the feelings and opinions of the public respecting the rank and value of polemic divinity[3]—among the consequences from the conjoint operation of the causes, we have had frequent occasion to lament the vague and equivocal import of the terms and phrases which we are obliged to use in philosophic disquisition, and which yet we cannot use without awakening the meanings engrafted on them by the market, or at least the confused state of apprehension, which the wearing out of the original impress and superscription by promiscuous handling is too well calculated to reproduce. Some advantage, however, will be derived from this inconvenience if it should work a conviction of the necessity of examining into the original meanings of the words we have occasion to use, to compare these with what we ourselves actually meant, and thus to understand with a clearness and distinctness which cannot fail to produce a correspondent effect on our practice the full force of the words "*propriety* of language".

2(a). If I mistake not, there are few words to which this remark is more applicable than "intuition" (and "intuitive"). The word is by no means of unfrequent occurrence in general conversation or in popular writings, but I have found it no easy matter to determine what the users exactly meant by it, except indeed that it seemed to be nearly, if not altogether equivalent to instinctive, natural or innate; and yet, on the other hand, the proper sense of the term is one of prime necessity in all philosophical enquiries, and most of all in those that have the constitution of the mind for their express subject; and I know of no other convenient English word but "intuition" by which this sense is to be conveyed. Hooker, indeed, has expressed the meaning by an "immediate beholding",[4] but this, I need not say, is not so truly a proper term as the explanation of one and, like all periphrases, unknown in technical use. As an explanation we therefore adopt, it, and "intuition", from the Latin *intuitus* or *intuitio,* from *intueor,* to look at or on a subject, to have it present to the sight, and then by a wider use, present to the senses generally, whether the outward or the inward senses, signifies a simple beholding, both the act of beholding and the simple product thence resulting, indistinguishably. Indistinguishably, I say, for we cannot separate the one from the other without reference to some hypothesis or theory. Our consciousness contains no such distinction, we are aware of no such twinship or duality, and it is a simple fact that we wish to convey, and for which therefore we must have a simple and perfect unequivocal term. It is on this ground that the words "intuition" and "intuitive knowledge" (and it is to be regretted that we have not a correspondent verb [such] as the Latin *intueor* and the German *anschauen*) are not superseded by the words "perception", "perceptive"; and "perceive" not only nor principally appertains, it might seem, exclusively to the organs of sense *per quae* (through which) *sensa capimus,*[5] but because the simple verb *capio, capimus,* anglicised by the syllables "ceive", "ception", evidently refers to an act of the understanding or the reflective faculty. We have all had experiences which we could no otherwise describe than by saying [that] such a thing was present to me and I must have seen it, for it has since recurred to me, that I was so lost in thought or my attention was so fixed on some other object that I did not perceive it. And indeed, though now it is not obsolete, degraded into a vulgarism, such is still the meaning of our native English of *capio.* It is not uncommon either among our rustics or our more knowing Londoners to hear a fellow ask another, "Do you take me?" I.e. not, have you heard my words or seen my winks or gestures, but do you understand them—do you conceive me?

2(b) Now we want an expression for the act of the sense and its accompanying product, independently of any other act or product of any other faculty; but in all beholdings or presentations by means of the bodily senses there is, we have seen, a sensation combined which escapes our consciousness, from use and the rapidity of the impression, but the existence of which is demonstrated by our perception of circular bodies and in general of densities as distinct from surfaces, the counterfeiting of which, rendered possible by the law of association, constitutes the mechanical part of the art of painting (*vide* Berkeley's *Essay on Vision,*[6] or any popular work on optics). Such presentations therefore we must entitle "mixed intuitions", or "empirical intuitions", to distinguish these joint products of the sense and its inherent forms, and laws of action, from some other allied power acting from without and by its coincidence with, coagency of, the sense, supplying the understanding with the ground and materials of experience. But as in the term "nature", or, in the equivalent terms, "from without" used in contradistinction to "from within", we include our own bodies and bodily sensations as far as they are not the creatures of our own will or the products of our own faculties either voluntary or spontaneous—these mixed intuitions are excluded from our present subject. To these indeed as well as to all other facts of experience the science of logic may be applied. Of course they must be known in each particular case before we can judge whether a conclusion *formally* legitimate is likewise materially correct. Nevertheless, if we avoid the absurdity of giving an encyclopaedia under the title of logic applied, we must confine ourselves to the rules and maxims generalised from the common experience of mankind, and which refer to no knowledge that every man in possession of his human faculties is not supposed to possess. It would indeed be more accurate to say, the most important of these rules, of those the variations of applying which are of not frequent recurrence. Of those, the portion that refers to the objects of the outward senses we have already brought together under the title of aesthetic experiences, as an appendix to canonic or formal logic.[7] The remaining, and of greater claim to be inserted because less obvious, will be given as an appendix to the present section, under the head of psychological experiences.[8] We may now recur to our enquiry respecting intuitions.

2(c). In whatever way and by whatever means any affirmation of the mind is referred to an object, that to which the last immediate reference is made is an intuition;[9] and in order fully to understand the nature of intuition *transcendentally* (i.e. where neither the thing nor the knowledge is the subject of investigation, but the faculty by which the thing is known, for this perhaps is the most intelligible explanation of the term "transcendental"), it will be expedient [to] throw ourselves back, as it were, into the ordinary apprehension and language of mankind, as if no question had been stated respecting the outwardness of things or of their being the perfect duplicates of the images by which they are presented to us. From this point of view it is plain that an intuition can take place respecting any natural object only as far as the object (or its component parts at least) is present to us.[10] But this again, viz. the object as the datum of the intuition, is only possible inasfar as it affects the mind in some determinate manner (we use the word "mind" in this place as nearly equivalent to the soul, as the sum of all our faculties, whether active, passive, or spontaneous).

2(d). The capability of acquiring representations, which our elder logical and metaphysical writers entitled "receptivity", is what we call the sensibility or sensuous nature, or the property of having the sense or sentient faculty called into action. But this sensibility of course includes the sensations. When therefore we mean to abstract from the sensations, we want a distinct term to express this intent, and we then call this faculty THE SENSE. If we conceive this sense altogether and perfectly free from sensation (from the sensations, for instance, of pleasure, pain, heat, vividness, colour, and all the degrees and opposites of these) we obtain a notion of the *pure* sense. Either, however, by the pure sense or by the sensibility as including both the sense and sensation, the objects are given us, and consequently in this faculty alone are we to seek the origin of the correspondent intuitions.[11]

2(e). The understanding, on the other hand, is the faculty that enables [us] to *think* of these objects. As the sense is the *birth-place of intuitions,* the understanding is the organ of our *thoughts* and *conceptions.* We find, however, that we are incapable of presenting any object to the understanding by means of the sense except under the forms of space and time.

2(f). We find, too, that these forms of space and time do not belong exclusively to our intuitions or perceptions of things as really present to us; we are equally incapable of *imagining* or *conceiving* any object otherwise than in time and space. Nay! so universally true is this that even objects to which our reason forbids us to attach either time or space we are still compelled to imagine and conceive as existing in both, and hence in the most awful object, tc which the attributes of time and space are both and equally inapplicable, reason and religion forbid us to imagine at all, but at the same time prohibit all attempts to *conceive* or *comprehend.*

2(g). It must needs therefore be a question of deep interest (even were it not indispensable as the condition of all other insight, whether of positive insight into the nature of the things which are the proper objects of the sensuous intuitions, or, negatively, of those which transcend the sense) what time and space themselves are. Not what we *mean* by the terms: for this would be as absurd as to ask what we mean by the terms "yellow", "red", or "blue", if, as would be the case in the present instance, by asking for the meaning of a word we understand the being asked for some other words more plain or that more intelligibly would convey the same sense. No, our question looks in a different direction. Are time and space realities subsisting for themselves independent of the mind? Are they subsistences? or, if not so, if they are only determinations or relations of other things, yet are they such as belong to things in their own nature abstractedly from their particular relation to *our* minds?[12] Dare are confidently affirm them as being the predicates and necessary attributes of the things in themselves as contradistinguished [from the] phenomena by which their existence is made manifest? (See pp [130-1] Introductory Chapter to the second section.) Or lastly, do they attach wholly to the form of the intuition, to the subjective nature of the mind, so that but for this constitution of our own faculties neither time nor space could have been predicated in any instance?

2(h). In order to arrive at some satisfactory answer to these question we must begin with an exposition of the conceptions space and time. By an exposition we mean the removing the parts of anything from each other and again uniting them in order to form a more distinct notion of the parts and of the manner in which they are combined to one whole to understand , in short, the composition of the thing and its components.[13] Thus we make our children take a map to pieces and then reconstruct it. Such is the literal sense of the Latin word *exponere* and such is the force of our own English "set out" or "set forth" and the German *auseinandersetzen*.

[SPACE]

3. First, then, space is not an empirical (experiential) conception. It is not a conception that has been drawn from outward experiences. For in order to my referring any given sensations produced in me to somewhat external to me, i.e.to somewhat in different place of space from that in which I myself am, and

in like manner, in order to represent the component parts of any total impression as outward to and beside each other, therefore not merely as being different each from the other, but as being each in a different place or point of a given space—to be able to do this, I say, we must already have the representation of space itself to begin. The conception is evidently presupposed in the very question " Where is it?" It is presupposed in the universal sense of a thing out of us. If we ask ourselves what we mean by at thing, as opposed to a thought, we shall find that we mean a somewhat extended—a somewhat that occupies a portion of space; and in like manner in the division which experience has taught us to make between objects, into those that merely occupy a space, as a rainbow, and those which fill a space, as a solid body, both in the one and the other the space itself is preconceived. The representation space, therefore, cannot have been borrowed from those relations of outward appearances made known to us by experience; but this outward experience is itself possible only the supposition of space.[14]

4(a). 2nd. Space is necessary representation and, like all representations combined with a sense of necessity, a representation *a priori* as the pre-existing basis of all external intuitions. Try the experiment; attempt to imagine that there is no space—try to fancy it away[15]—you will find it impossible, though without difficulty you may fancy away all objects and imagine a space in which there is nothing, though it be altogether out of your power to conceive a form without a space for it to appear in. Space therefore is the precondition of all appearance. It is that without which apparent thing could not appear. Therefore it is no property of the things appearing, for, were it, so, they could no more be separated in the imagination (fancied away) from space than the space from them. Besides, the appearances are one and all accompanied by a sense of their contingency relatively to us, but space we know to be necessary conception forming no part of our conception of the things existing therein but a representation necessarily and universally antecedent to all and every appearances.[16]

4(b). Now as by the world without us or outward nature we mean only the sum and aggregate of appearances, and that as far as the senses and understanding are concerned we know of nothing which is not either mind or nature, subjective or objective, what is proved not to belong to the one must belong to the other. If space be neither an outward thing nor any property of outward things, it must in some sense or other be a quality or faculty or the necessary result of some faculty or quality in the mind itself.

5. 3rd. Space is no common or general conception of the relations of things in general. Or rather, as all conceptions are discursive, and more or less general, it is, properly speaking, no conception at all, but a pure intuition—in odther words, space is not a conception which we have generalised from any number of objects, like the conception of swiftness, whiteness, weight, and the like. For in the first place we can represent only one single space ; as, if ever we speak of manyspaces, we mean only portions of one and the same space, or, more truly still, we speak only of things existing at certain distances form each other and attribute to the one undivided and indivisible space the diversion and plurality that belong to the things that appear in it. These universal parts cannot be presented for themselves antecedently to the conception of the whole as its components which can be imagined as brought together and constituting and composing spaces—we can merely think of them as parts by a play of the imagination, transferring the properties of A tc its constant accompaniment B. If we talk of a space being separated from another by a wall, we know at the same the wall itself occupies the space between and consequently thus there is a space to be occupied.[17]

6(a). 4thly. We represent space as an infinite given quantity. Now were space a conception, an infinite conception would be one which consists of an infinite number of possible representations as the common character or mark of these.

But no conception can be formed by the mind as containing in itself an infinite number of possible representations. Yet this is the case with space in which an infinity of parts are thought of as simultaneous and co-existing.[18]

6(b). Space therefore is no conception; as little is it an eternal truth of the reason. For we are by no means permitted to assert or are capable of demonstrating that all things exist in space, nor even that anything always will so exist. That there may be a state in which time and space shall be no more, may or may not be a *groundless* assertion; but it is not nonsense, which every assertion must be that contradicts a universals truth of reason. But if neither a conception of the understanding nor a universal truth of the reason, it must be an intuittion, and if not derived from particular things, forms, or images, it must be pure intuition *a priori.*[19]

CONCLUSIONS FROM THE ABOVE

7 Space:

A. By space we mean no property of things in themselves, nor of any single thing, nor do we by space represent any relations they bear to each other arising out of the nature of the things themselves and which would remain after we had abstracted all the subjective conditions under which they are beheld. For neither absolute nor relative properties or determinations of things can be represented previously to the existence of the things themselves to which they belong, and cannot, therefore, like space, be contemplated *a priori.*[20]

8(a) B. Space cannot be contemplated as any single particular intuition. For it has been proved to pre-exist as the necessary condition or antecedent of all particular intuitions. The only remaining possibility is that space is nothing else but the common forms of all appearances of the outward senses—the subjective condition of that sense of sentiency,and that under which alone intuition is possible. Now since the receptivity of the subject, or the mind's capability of being affected by objects, must of necessity exist antecedent to all particular affections and therefore to all intuitions of these objects, we may easily understand how the form of all appearances, that which is the accompaniment of all alike, one and the same in all their particular differences, is to be assumed as previous to all actual perception or things, i.e. to all reference of particular intuitions to determinate objects.[21]

8(b). The difficulty that attends this conception arises from the impossibility of illustrating it by any particular image, but this difficulty will be [avoided] if only we reflect that we are not to seek after any image and then consider that every imaginable figure in which my image can be presented to us is a modification of its extension, but that [that] of which every particular form is a modification must be common to all forms and itself therefore the common or universal form. Or perhaps we may attain the same end still more simply by repr-esenting to ourselves any body of large extent and reflect [ing] on its extension before we have arrived at the boundary which constitutes its figure. Here in the first place we are conscious that the figure arises by a negation of the extension and not by anything added thereto, and, secondly, that the extension, considered independently of this, constituted a part of the image presented to us. But this extension is itself not a thing, in the sense of anything substantial; for this would be a contradiction in terms, the extension being equivalent to surface, and, if we may so say, essentially and exclusively superficial—but, if not substance, nothing remains but that it is a form, not indeed as a shape, but that in which all shapes consist as far as they are shapes and not any particular shape. In common language we might say that space is the way in which we perceive all outward things.

9. It follows, therefore, that as little as we can attribute the form of a cast to the materials which had flowed into the mould, as little can we attribute space to the things that appear under the relations of space; and would we contemplate it as a reality in itself, as a thing outwardly subsisting, there would

arise the absurdity of a thing having all the predicates of nothing, which in fact is the word used by the common people when they mean to speak of space as out of themselves. What is between me and yonder wall? "An empty space", might be the reply of the scholar.The common man would answer, "Nothing". Much less has been disputed respecting the ideality of space and of the celebrated controversy between Clarke and Leibniz[22] on this question, in which both parties were in the wrong. Leibniz was so far in the right that he denied the subsistence of space independent of the mind;[23] but he grievously erred in representing it as nothing more than a confused perception arising out of the indistinctness of all particular figures whether from the distance or the minuteness of the object.[24] Clarke and the English philosophers rightly and unanswerably replied to this that space was preconceived in order to these very confused perceptions, that this very confusion supposed a space, in which it existed no less than the most determinate figures.[25] They contended with truth that space was not abstracted from any object nor generalised from any class of objects: but they erred in the too hasty conclusion that therefore it must itself exist objectively.[26] The truth is that it is the subjective condition of all objectivity, and whatever reality is attributed to outward experience must *a fortiori* belong to that without which no outward experience is possible. If therefore we use the term "real" in opposition to "mental", or "*ob*jective" in opposition to "*sub*jective" in its widest sense, then we must reverse the position.

ILLUSTRATION

10. Those who cannot emancipate themselves from the notion that space, and the same we shall find hold good of time likewise, are inferences or adherences of things in themselves, may perhaps find some assistance in mastering a full conviction of the contrary by exercising their ingenuity on the following paradox. Suppose that two things, as, for instance, two conch shells, in all circumstances, of quantity, and quality, and figure,

fully alike, and only numerically different—it follows that the one might be substituted for the other without any possibility of discovering the change, and in fact so it is with two sovereigns from the same mint, as far as they appear only numerically different. If I had put down one sovereign on the table and my companion had left the room for an instant, he would not discover that I had changed it, nor should I myself afterwards be able to determine which of the two I had first put down, unless I had adopted some extrinsic means of securing the knowledge. It holds good indeed with all the plane figures in geometry. But various spherical figures afford proof, notwithstanding this perfect identity in all intrinsic characters, in every point that can be understood by the simple contemplation of the figure itself, [that there is] yet such a difference in outward relation that the one cannot be put for the other. Take, for example, two spherical triangles of both hemispheres that have an arc of the equator as their common basis. The triangles may be fully alike in respect both of the size and the angles, so that to describe each separately by itself, and this in the fullest detail, yet nothing will be found which will not be repeated in the very same words in a similar description of the other. The description in each case shall be adequate, nothing omitted which could be made intelligible as belonging to the object singly and without reference to any other object existing independently of the same. And yet we know that the one cannot be put in the place of the other, that which belongs to the one hemisphere cannot be transferred to the opposite. There is then some inherent difference of both triangles, which yet the understanding cannot represent as inherent—in plain words, which we cannot make intelligible, and which manifests itself to us solely by the outward relation of each in space.[27] That it is a real, an *inherent,* difference will appear more readily perhaps if instead of the triangle we refer to a similar difference in the hop and scarlet bean, a difference which can be expressed by some outward comparison and which our gardeners do commonly express by describing the perfectly corresponding yet opposite w[inding] as with or against the sun,[28] yet the difference exists in the plants themselves (and there is of necessity an efficient ground and cause of this difference in the qualities and structure of the seed), but we cannot discover this otherwise than by submitting it to an act of comparison, each with the other, and this too in order to place both in a relation of space. Thus we see that so it is and we know that there must be a ground, independent of ourselves and of our own faculties, of our being thus distinctly affected in each instant, but still we cannot *understand* the difference (*datur, non intelligitur*).[29] It is not therefore the understanding that is affected, for our conceptions remain unchanged and wholly alien from this knowledge. It is the faculty of sense alone that is affected, and the difference is made known to us as an immediate intuition, we *per*ceive it instantly, though we cannot *con*ceive. Now, if space were an objective property and belonging to the things themselves, we should be able to describe this difference no less than those by which the two objects are both alike distinguished from others, as, for instance, the spherical triangles from plane, or the hop and bean from some other climber. A still more obvious example we have before us in the looking-glass. What can be conceived more perfectly like to my hand or my ear than its reflection in the glass, and yet the hand seen in the glass I cannot put in the place of the original. If it by my right hand, the hand in the glass is the left, the image of the right ear becomes the left. Here, it is true, there are no intrinsic differences that it is in the power of any understanding even to think, and yet the differences are intrinsic as far as our senses can teach us, for we well know that we cannot put [a] right-hand glove on our left hand, and know that we could not do it even if by some miracle we could substantiate that [?image] perfectly identical of the reflection in the glass. What then is the solution of this riddle? No other is possible than that the difference in question, i.e. as seen by us, and not the cause of this difference, is neither to be found in A singly nor in B singly, but in C, as the result of the different relation in which A and B stand to it, as a third, affected at the same moment by both.

11(a). What is this third corresponding to C? It is, evidently, the subjective sense, and the difference consists in an affection of the subjective sense calling forth that mode of action which results from its own constitution and characteristic property. This mode or form is modified. An unknown agency from without is in part doubtless the modifying cause; but it is the faculty itself or its inherent mode of action that is the subject modified. That it is an affection of space is wholly owing to the sense. That it is that peculiar affection is derived contingently from the nature of the external object. In this simple contemplation, therefore, we obtain an insight, first into the difference of the subjective from the objective and in the purely subjective nature of space as an affection of the subject; and secondly into the differences in the subject itself, viz. the difference of the sense and its forms, from the understanding and its forms, inasmuch as in the instances above given, the sense is affected and its forms called into act while the function of the understanding remain[s] altogether neutral and indifferent.

11(b). I cannot conclude this chapter without introducing one other at once the most beautiful and the most simple elucidation of this point: that which is presented to us in the well-known kaleido-scope, an instrument well calculated to suggest thoughts, the interest of which will long survive the innocent amusement to its powers of supplying which the instrument owed its popularity. We put into the instrument from fifteen to twenty fragments, bits of coloured glass, a steel filing or two, ends of thread, cuttings of wire, small pieces of silk—in short, from twenty to thirty substances—and at every motion that we make there arises some new and distinct form of beauty in endless succession, the number inexhaustible and all beautiful, though not all equally delightful. We find the same differences and the tastes of different persons differently affected, as if a series of beautiful *flowers* or *chefs d'[o]euv[res]* of jewellery were presented to the same person and to different persons. None could be denied to be beautiful, but we should hear the exclamations, "How beautiful!" "How very beautiful!"

"This is pretty, but it does not strike me so much". "This is the most beautiful of all that I have seen", etc., etc. For my readers' recollections will present the delights of a kaleido-scope at its first introduction better than I can dramatise them.[30] Let the twenty or thirty bits and fragments be removed from the kaleido-scope to a dice box and try as long as your patience will permit to throw them or any portion of them on the table so as to form a beautiful figure. You will in all probability waste an hour or a week without succeeding in any single instance. The difference therefore in the former arrangements cannot arise out of the substances themselves, but is attributable exclusively to the instrument or medium through which they were seen and in which their arrangement was effected. What shall we call this difference, this property, I mean, common in kind to all the thousand successive figures presented to us? Evidently symmetry, and this subsists wholly in the instrument itself; in the constitution and constituent laws (or modes of action) of the kaleidoscope itself this symmetry originates and by these it is communicated not to the fragments themselves but to the figure in the beholder's mind resulting from this arrangement, and that they are all so arranged as to fall under one common form, viz. that of symmetry, is the work of the instrument itself. But further, the effect common to all, to what does it refer? Not to the sensibility considered as the capability of sensation. This indeed is affected, diversely affected, and it is its affections by which in great measure our preferences are determined and the greater comparative delight which we receive from one figure rather than from another—or from our selection of some substances rather than others; of bits of coloured glass, for instance, for common glass, or of the variety in colours rather than one or two kinds, and in some measure from the larger number of the substances included, though here the action of the instrument itself is concerned in the effect. If not to the sensibility, therefore to the sense. Instead of the kaleidoscope [as] the instrument of the sentient faculty let us take the faculty itself as its own instrument, or an instrument of the mind-instrument at once and a constituent part. In like manner, for symmetry or peculiar modifications of the relations of space, we will take space itself, and we may then apply the results without change. All intuitions of objects outwardly present have their origin both in the senisbility and in the sense. As far as the sensibility is affected we are justified in resolving this effect into an agency and proper character of the *object*, modified, however, by the nature of the sensibility which it modifies. All else must be referred to the sense, with this exception, however—if indeed it is an exception and not included in the former class, viz. The affections of the sensibility—I mean the contingency of the determinate forms or the fact that the universal form, that of space in the present instance of the faculty, and that of symmetry in the presentations of the kaleidoscope, is such at this moment, as far as it is not referable to an act of our own will, whether the external object be external in the ordinary use of the term or the spontaneous act of our own organisation as in our dreams. In all such cases, however, the determinable form subsists in and of the sense itself: whether the particular determination of the form originates in the will or the sensibility and again whether in the will, calling the sense into determinate act according to the laws of reason, or for the purposes of the understanding, or the will acting on the sensibility in wantonness or for amusement: and in like manner, the sensibility, whether affected by objects from without or by the organisation with which it is connected and on which it depends. The distinction [is] that the first only—the determination of the will according to the laws of the reason and arising form the constitution of the sense itself and the inherent properties of its constituent forms—is accompanied with a sense of necessity and capable of being known and determined *a priori.* The nature of these determinations we shall investigate after our enquiry into the remaining form of sense, viz. time, to which we now proceed.

TIME

12. If space be then the *forma formarum*[31] or common form of the outward sense, it might be anticipated that time would be found to stand in the same relation to the inner sense. The process of proof must consist therefore in a repetition of the former and like the former will fall under two heads. First, the analytic exposition by which the constituent parts of the conception or intuition are *set forth,* so that a distinct attention having been given to each we may thereby obtain a more distinct and clear consciousness of the whole. Our purpose is not to attach a new meaning to the term but to reflect on that which we already possess *implicitly* so as to render it *explicit.* Not acquisition but explication of a knowledge already acquired is the aim of all analytic disquisition; not addition but distinctness. And secondly, the *transcendental* exposition or its relation to some faculty. For this as we have before observed, is what is meant by transcendental[32] We being therefore with the analysis of the term.

13. Time is, first, not an empirical conception that has been or can be abstracted from any possible experience. For simultaneity or succession could not have been perceived if the representation of time did not pre-exist as its ground and condition *a priori.* How should we distinguish simultaneity, or the being together in the same moment, from succession, if the idea of the same moment and not the same moment, of present or not present, and in the not present as past or as yet to come, i.e. the idea of time itself, were not already in our possession ? All knowledge from without must have originated in particular and must be capable of reduction into the same. But no particular can be imagined or conceived which did not or does not presuppose the universal in this case. The utmost that can be attributed to the former is that they may have furnished the occasion of reflecting on the latter: and the first particular that does this gives us the consciousness of the whole, a consciousness not of something then given, but of a something already possessed.[33]

14. Second. Time then is a necessary representation in which all our intuitions are grounded, or shall we say that it is the root of which all particular intuitions are the unfolding under the influences of their exciting occasions. As in the instance of space, so in this: attempt to think away time itself while at the same time you present any number of phenomena co-existing and in succession. It is found impossible, though without difficulty [you may think] away any one or any number of the phenomena themselves. What is the reason ? You cannot think away the thinking itself, for this is presupposed. Time, therefore, is given *a priori,* the *semper datum et suppositium*[34] by means of which all actual phenomena are possible.[35]

15. Third. In this necessity *a priori* or, if you please to vary the metaphor, in this necessity *ab intra,*[36] the possibility of demonstrative apodictic or self-evident principles of the relations of time, or what are called axioms of time generally, is grounded. Time has but one dimension. Different times are not co-present but follow each other. To suppose the contrary would be to assert that *different* time are the *same* time, an absurdity of which (otherwise than by a wanton abuse of words) it is not in our power to be guilty. And yet without any absurdity, or rather by a necessary insight, we assert that different spaces are not one after the other, but are together or co-present. These axioms cannot have been deduced from experience, for had that been the case they would possess neither strict universality nor demonstrative certainty. We should be able to say the common sense of mankind has hitherto coincided in this experience, and we see no reason for supposing that it will be otherwise for the time to come, but not, so it must be and cannot be otherwise for all beings that contemplate objects in the relations of time and space. We could only say, all the bodies that have hitherto come under the notice of my senses or my imagination have presented space to me as consisting of three dimensions, while all the motions of bodies and all succession of bodies have presented time to me as having but one dimension, and I have no reason to suppose

that the experience of any other man has been or ever will be different. But we mean something more and other than this when, with a sense of [the] necessity and universal truth of the position, we affirm that space has three dimensions and time but one—that so it must be—for the contrary is an absurdity, i.e. an arrangement of articulated sounds or their representative characters, a collective sense for which can neither be conceived nor imagined. Hence it is that these axioms of time and space serve as rules under which all experiences are possible. They are not borrowed from these experiences. For in all experiences they constitute the experience itself. What we experience may be the product of conceiving causes; but that we experience at all is owing to time and space and presupposes them as its cause and necessary condition.[37]

16. Fourth. Time is no general conception representing any class of particulars. It is no conception that has been nor can be formed discursively by alluding to a number of particulars and then fixing the attention and reflection exclusively on some character common to all. Different times are only portions of one and the same time, the division of which does not exist in the time itself, but is attributed to it metaphorically from the objects existing in this relation to ourselves. They are not so properly parts of time as measures, each of which indeed is divisible *ad infinitum*. But a representation that can be given only by means of a single object is an *intuition* as contradistinguished from a conception. But this is true of time—it applies totally to each object to which it applies at all. Time therefore is an intuition, not a conception. Even the simple pos-ition that different times cannot be simultaneous cannot be deduced from any general conception. In order to give the words their full meaning we appeal at once to the intuition—simply and without exercising any one of the functions of the understanding, which are, and must be, exercised in the formation of a conception; we refer to no instance, we compare no number of instances, and consequently we neither abstract

from that which is peculiar in each nor generalise anything that is common to all. The position is self-evident and admits of no further proof that it is so-if [for] no other reason than because so it is.[38]

17. (a) Fifth. The infinity of time signifies nothing more than that all determinate qualities of time are possible only by limitations of one single time supposed in all, which limitations, however, have no imaginable subsistence in time itself as the common measure and ground of all, but in the contemplation by occasion of the objects. Time is infinite in the sense that considered in itself, without reference to the object or its beholder, it contains in itself no bounds—*infinitum est, quia nullos habet fines in se*—and herein consists the difference in the infinity of time from the infinity of space. That of the latter is positive and essential. For where space is, it is essentially infinite. The infinity of time, on the other hand, is negative and consequent on the abstraction from all the boundaries or partial measurements that originate and exist in the objects only.[39]

17(b). To give an insight, however, into the nature and ground of this difference would require an investigation beyond the bounds of a purely analytic enquiry and [one] which wo uld not belong even to a transcendental exposition, which rests in the ascertainment of the faculty the existence of which we know only by means of reflection, i.e. by an exercise of one of the functions of the faculty. But to *understand* the faculty of the sense is impossible, for every act of the understanding presumes the sense as its datum. But to *understand* the faculty of the understanding is the same as to understand that which stands undermost—an attempt not more fortunate than that of the eastern speculators who having put the earth on a bull and the bull on a bear found it still necessary to put the tortoise under both.[40] Whether there exist any other source of insight, and [one] that can more properly be styled both a *source* and a source of insight, is an enquiry not included within the province of logic, in the stricter sense of the word, whether canonic or transcendental. If within the spheres of human knowledge at all, it appertains to the science of *pure* psychology, as a branch of metaphysics.

17(c). Now it yet remains to be seen whether such a science as that of metaphysics (in the sense of a first philosophy) is *possible*,[41] or whether it be not *transcendent* of the human faculties instead of *transcendental,* i.e. referable to the constitution of these faculties; in which latter case it would be the same as transcendental logic and the name would be superfluous. But this possibility cannot be ascertained except by the means of transcendental logic, and the determination, whether affirmative or negative, presupposes the knowledge so obtained. There is indeed, as we have already noticed, a higher sense of the term "logos", in which it signifies the reason as including the understanding. On this assumption there would arise relations of the understanding to the reason and of the reason to the understanding, and the knowledge of these relations would constitute a higher, or rather the highest, branch of logic, viz. the logic of ideas and first principles.[42] But as distinct terms are often the condition, and always the assistant, of distinct conceptions, we have proposed to designate this branch by the name of "noetic" and have taken it as the subject of our last section, to the introduction to which the discussion of the question ("Is a first philosophy possible?) is deferred.

TRANSCENDENTAL EXPOSITION

18. What sciences derive their possibility as pure sciences from the notions *a priori* of time and space and law is an enquiry that strictly belongs to the transcendental exposition of these notions; but as I shall be under the necessity of treating the subject in the next chapter, to this I shall refer the student in order to prevent the waste of his attention by repetition[s] when they can be avoided with no greater inconvenience than a slight relaxation in the rigour of form. I proceed at once to the transcendental conclusions from the

conceptions displayed in the analytic exposition.[43]

19 A. Time is not anything that subsists for itself or belongs to things as their own property or objective characteristic. In either of which cases the conception of time would remain after we had abstracted from all the subjective conditions of its intuition. For in the first case, that without any real object would nevertheless be itself real; and as for the second as a property or inherent order belonging to the things themselves, it could not possibly be conceived as antecedent to these things as their ground and indispensable precondition. But that so it is and must be contemplated we have already shown and shall further prove in the disquisition next following, from the nature of the sciences that peculiar evidence of which is grounded in this priority.[44]

20(a) B. Time is the form of the inner sense, i.e. of the intuition that we have of ourselves and of our own inward state. It is this and nothing else. For time is no inherent property or quality of outward appearances. It belongs neither to shape nor position, while on the other hand it determines the relation of our representations in the widest sense of the word, including both thoughts and feelings in our own inward being. So true is it that time has nothing to do with shape, position, and the like, because this inward intuition and universal form of all inward intuitions is itself shapeless.

20(b). We seek to supply this defect by analogy, and as this is found in all known languages, we may say that mankind have been led as by a common instinct of their intellectual nature so to supply the defect and to represent the succession of time by a line proceeding infinitely in which the manifold constitutes a series of one dimension only, and out of the properties of this line all the properties of time are concluded, with one exception, that [those of] the former, viz. the line, are simultaneous, while those of the latter, the moments or things signified, are necessarily successive. It follows too as a corollary that the representation of time must itself be an intuition inasmuch as all its relations are expressible in an outward intuition.[45]

21. At all events it is of the nature of an intuition, and to object to its being called an intuition would be little else than to quarrel with language itself and all the principles on which language is possible. (Instead of saying, what no one would deny, that we cannot actually have an intuition of time unaccompanied by some intuition of space.) The mechanism or construction of the representations of time by space, and vice versa of space by time, belongs to another place; the fact only is mentioned here.

22 C. Time is the formal condition *a priori* of all phenomena universally. Space as the pure form of all outward intuition is, when considered as a condition *a priori,* confined to outward phenomena exclusively. On the other hand, as all representations, whether they have outward things for their objects or not, yet in themselves as determinations, or to use as [?affirmations] of our sentient being, do of themselves necessarily belong to our inward state and as this inward state again falls under the formal condition of inward intuition, consequently of time must be the condition *a priori* of all phenomena, of all appearance, universally. It is the immediate condition of the inward proceedings of our consciousness and thence mediately of the outward phenomena likewise. An illustration of the nature of time (as given in B) is suggested by the words "phenomenon", "appearance", as applied to the experiences of our inward state; as they fall wholly under the form of time, so, like time itself, they are in themselves shapeless, and, as in the instance of time, we are compelled to borrow the expressions from our outward intuitions, i.e. from the forms of space.[46]

23(a). If we abstract from the way in which we intuitively contemplate our inward state and by means of this intuition are capable of representing to ourselves all outward forms, when we abstract from this and consequently speak of the objects as they are or may be supposed to be in themselves and independent of our mode of contemplating them, then time is nothing. And if we use the term "objectively" to express the object in the absence of, or perfect abstraction from, all that is communicated to the representation of this object by the mind or the subject as the instrument and medium of the representation—in the strictly *metaphysical* sense of the word—time is nothing objective, but wholly subjective.

23(b). If, on the other hand, we take the word in the more usual and practical sense as applied to the phenomena themselves, and mean by it that such and such appearances are common to all men under the same circumstances and do not arise from any peculiarities in an individual subject or any particular sort and number of individuals, and that they may therefore be safely reasoned on and confidently anticipated—in this sense time has an objective reality, viz. the very same reality, whether is be of the appearances themselves [?or] of all [?of] which it is mediately or immediately the inseparable condition and constitutive form.[47]

23(c). But we are not entitled to extend this assertion of its reality beyond these appearances, or beyond the human mind collectively takern. We are not entitled to assert that enen all finite beings, whether higher or lower than man, must necessarily perceive objects, or that the objects must necessarily appear to them under the relations of time; much less dare we thus limit the infinite mind. It is certain that we can neither conceive nor imagine any appearance not under the relations of time, and this is a sufficient proof that it is universally subjective as far as man is concerned, but it proves nothing more. It may, however, suggest a truth of the highest importance, that there are objects the existence of which we may hold with the clearest and most distinct insight of reason, though we are capable of forming neither a conception nor an imagination of the same. And this reflection we may make use of as a preservative from two opposite errors, both equally perilous. The one, that of attributing an absolute reality and self-subsistence to that which is subjective only and which therefore is real only as far as the mind is real, of the constitution of which it is the necessary result, and this is what we mean when we say that time is subjective reality; or, real in relation to the human mind as the subject—and in this sense we may contradistinguish this subjective reality from the yellow colour of bodies to jaundiced indiviual or from the apparition of the late Mrs Veal to her surviving laundress in St Bride's Lane, Fleet St, recorded by the Rev Dr Drelincourt, or the translator of his work,[48] which may or may not have been subjectively actual, i.e. have actually appeared to one individual subject, whether feverous or dreaming, but has no pretensions to reality, i.e. permanence and universality, subjective or objective, i.e. relative or absolute.[49]

23(d). From inadvertence to the truth that subjective reality does not cease to be reality arises the only plausible objection to the view of time obtained in this chapter. The changes of objects are real; we have the same experience and consequently the same evidence of these as of the objects themselves; but these changes we have ourselves admitted are not possible except in time, therefore time itself must be real. We answer the position by admitting it. Both the one and the other, the succession and the time, are real, and the experience and the objects of the experience, viz. the phenomena whether of the outward or of the inward sense, are real; but they are all alike subjectively so, and a moment's reflection on the meaning of experience itself will convince us that an experience not subjective would be a contradiction, or an experience which was no one's experience. But I refer the student to the beautiful tale in the *Spectator* of the line of changes, and successive events that happened to the Vizier in the interval between the immersion and emersion of his head in the cold bath.[50] These changes, it will not be denied, were subjectively actual, and the student has only to reflect what was wanting to make these subjectively real and which of these additions would in the least alter the subjective nature of the changes themselves. Will the subjective be done away by multiplying the subjects, or will the rainbow be less a reflection by being reflected from a thousand waves at the same moment or from ten thousand myriads of dewdrops?[51]

Footnotes

1. Which C had analysed in *LS(CC)* 169 ff.
2. " A public within the public" Cf C's later calls for a "clerisy": C&S (CC) 53-4, 54n.
3. To which C had referred in *LS* (*CC*) 199.
4. The quotation is attributed to Hooker elsewhere C—gg." On the Principles of Genial Criticism" *BL* (1907) II 230 and *AR* (1825) 216. Was C thinking of thc following passage: " The truth is, that the mind of man desireth evermore to know the truth, according to the most infallible certaintly which the nature of things can yield. The greatest assurance generally with all men, is that which we have by a plain aspect and intuitive beholding"? *Of the Laws of Eccelesiastical Polittie* bk II 7: works(1682) 119. If so, his rendering has acquired a Kantian turn; of "Anschauung, unmitterlabre offenbarung", ("Intuition, immediate disclosure") In Kant VS III 80 and "Ein unmittelbares Bewusstseyn heisst Anschauung ("An immediate awareness is called intuition...") in Fichte *Das System der Sittenlehre* pt I ch 3 (Jena & Leipzing 1798) 50.
5. "We take [i.e. receive] things sensed".
6. *An Essay Towards a New Theory of Vision* (1790).
7. See above, pp 70ff?
8. The missing appendix, presumably, referred to again on p. 196, below.
9. C is heavily dependent on Kant's "Transcendental Aesthetic" for much of what follows in this chapter and the next. Details are recorded in the notes.
10. Paragraph 2(c) up to this point is based on C d r V33(65).
11. Paragraph 2(d) is closely related to C d r V 34-5(66).
12. The sentence is translated from C d r V 37 (68).
13. Paragraph 2(h) up to this point is translated from C d r V 38 (68).
14. Paragraph 3 is based on C d r V 38 (68).

15. Here and throughout the paragraph, 3, parapharing Kant, uncharacteristically uses "imagination" and "fancy" as synonyms.

16. Paragraph 4(a) is from C d r V 38-9(68).

17. Paragraph 5 if from C dr V 39 (69).

18. Paragraph 6(a) is from C d r V 39-40 (69-70).

19. Paragraph 6(b) is an expansion of the final sentences of the first paragraph of C d r V40(70).

20. Paragraph 7 is from C d r V 42 (71).

21. Paragraph 8(a) is from C d r V 42 (71).

22. Leibniz and Clarke *A Collectin of Papers* (1717).

23. Ibid pp 57, 181-3.

24. Ibid pp 195ff.

25. E.g. ibid.

26. E.g. ibid.

27. Paragraph 10 up to this point is from *Prolegomena* § 13 (1783) 56-8.

28. C refers to this difference between the hop and the scarlet runner bean (*Phaseolus multiflours*, " One of the few plants that twine in a direction contrary tot be apparent motion of the sun"—EB 11th ed article "Bean") for the same purpose in a letter to Thomas Clarkson of 13 Oct 1806 (CL II 1193). In each case he is drawning on an example in kant *Metaphysische Anfangsgriinde der Naturwissenscharft* (Riga 1787) 7-8, from which p 161 line 22 to p 162 line 5 in freely translated. Kant attributes the phrases "with the sun" and "against the sun" to "Seelute" (mariners) rather han to gardeners. Cf also kant Sammlung einiger bisher underkant geblienener klenier Schriftenla (1800) 75 and *VS* iv 75. (C's copies of all three books are in the BM.)

29. "It is given, not understood" From this point on, paragraph 10 is based on *Prolegomena* 13 (1783) 58-9.

30. C first mentions the instrument in 1818 (*CN* III 4411), hard on the heels of its appearance. See *Description and Method of Using the Patent Kaleidoscope,Invented by Dr. Brewster* (1818)—an attempt to market the device—and David Brewster A *Treatise on the Kaleidoscope* (Edinburh 1819). In 1818, SH called it

"entirely the plaything of the Adults" (SH Letter 144; see also 140 sand 142), and Shelley mentions the rage for it in Itly (*The Letter of Percy Bysshe Shelley* ed Frederick 1. Jones-Oxford 1964—II 69).

31. "Forms of form".
32. See above, pp 146-7.
33. Paragraph 13 is from *C dr V* 46.
34. "The thing always given and posited".
35. Paragraph 14 is from *C d r* V 46 (74-5).
36. "From within".
37. Paragraph 15 is from *C d r* 47 (75).
38. Paragraph 16 is from *C d r* V 47 (75).
39. Paragraph 17 (a) is from *C d r* V 47-8(75).
40. *Cf CN* III 3973. A similar remark occurs in Locke *Essay on Human understanding* bk II ch 23 § 2, and, following him, in Leibniz *Nauveaux essais* bk II ch 23 § 2.
41. Kant's first question in the *Prolegomena* Einleitung (1783) 4-7.
42. A fuller discussion appear in HEHL MS HM 8195, " The Divine Ideas".
43. Paragraph 18 is from *C d r* V 48-9 (76).
44. Paragraph 19 is from *C d r* V 49 (76).
45. Paragraphs 20(a) and 20(b) are from *C d r* V 49-50 (77).
46. Paragraph 22 is from C d r V 50-1 (77).
47. Paragraphs 23(a) to 23(b) are from C d r V 51-2 (77-8).
48. Defoe's authorship of *The True Relation of the Appition of One Mrs Veal* was known. See. e.g., George Chalmers The *Life Daniel Defoe* (1709) 74.
49. Paragraph 23(c) is from *C d r* V 52-3(78). The examples of jaundice and of Mrs. Veal are C's.
50. Presumblay a reference to the story of Alanschar's daydream: *Spectator* No 535 (Thursday, 13 Nov 1712).
51. Paragraph 23(d) is based on *C d r* 53-4(79).

Chapter-8

The Common Principle of Analytic Judgments

Chapter 8

1. The principle common to all analytic judgments is that of which we have before spoken as the *principium identitatis et contradictions,*[1] i.e. whatever is, is. Whatever can be said to be, cannot be said *not* to be, and vice versa; or it answer[s] our purpose to say that all analytic judgments are grounded on the principle of contradiction:[2] that which forbids us to assert contraries of the same object at the same time, or, in the language of the vulgar, to say black is white. Now as this principle is a principle of reason, [it is] not deducible from any special faculty of the mind, whether of sense or of understanding, but [is] necessarily presupposed in all the exercises of both and of either, and consequently in all the knowledge which we acquire by experience, i.e. the coincidence of contingent impressions with these faculties, and therefore in the highest sense *a priori*. All analytic judgments are cognitions *a priori*, whether the conceptions that constitute them, and as it were form the materials of the judgment, be empirical or transcendental.[3] That, I mean, which gives a necessity to the assertion is *a priori* and contained in the mind itself, and that which the mind derives exclusively from itself. X may in fact be black, or be white, or neither, and without experience I could not have known which of the two it was; but far beyond all contingency, and altogether independent of experience, I determine with the fullest insight into the necessity and universality of all truth that X being throughout black cannot be at the same time white. We will express the proposition and the reason for it in the technical terms of logic. As the predicate of an affirmative analytic judgment already thought in the thinking of the subject and thought of affirmatively, it cannot without a contradiction be made negative, i.e. denied or exchanged for its contrary, when it is represented by itself and distinctly. In like manner, the contrary in an analytic negative judgment is necessarily negatived of the subject in conformity with the

same principle of contradiction—thus, "Every body is extended" is an affirmative analytic judgment. "No body is unextended." This is a negative analytic judgment.[4] Therefore all analytic positions are judgments *a priori,* however empirical the terms may be—for instance, "gold is a yellow metal"—in order to know gold I must indeed have had experience; but in order to the position, "gold is a yellow metal", I need no other additional experience. My knowledge of the predicate "a yellow metal" pre-existed and was contained in my knowledge of the subject "gold".

Footnotes

1. "Principle of identity and contradiction".
2. The paragraph up to this point is from *Prolegomena* § 2b (1783) 25-6.
3. The sentence is from *Prolegomena* § 2b (1783) 26.
4. The paragraph from this point on is from *Prolegomena* § 2b (1783) 26.

Chapter-9

Of Synthetic Judgments and Their Principle

Chapter 9

1. *Synthetic* judgments require another principle beside the *principium contradictionis.*[1] They, no less than the *analytic* judgments, must be in conformity with this principle; but this principle is only the condition under which they are judgments at all, and *not* the ground on which they rest as synthetic judgments.[2] To the synthetic class belong all judgments of experience, that is, all positions in which the predicate could not have been attached to the subject but by means of an experience as distinct as that of the subject itself. As an instance of synthetic judgments take the following. "This person is a father." I might have a sufficient conception of the person, but without another experience, viz. that of another person as a child, I could not have brought the two terms into connection in the position, "the person is a father". This, however, is admitted on all sides. The very word "experience" implies it, and the common phrases "increased experience", "growth of experience", and the like, openly declare it. The existence of synthetic judgments *a posteriori* is beyond all doubt; but are these the only synthetic judgments, or do there likewise exist [synthetic] judgments *a priori*? And on what ground does their evidence and cogency rest, viz. as *synthetic* judgments? We have seen that all *analytic* judgments are judgments *a priori,* and that they rest on a principle *a priori*, and that this principle is the principle of contradiction. But synthetic judgments are contradistinguished from *analytic* by not resting on the principle of contradiction. And synthetic judgments *a priori,* if any exist, cannot rest on experience as their ground; for by not resting thereon, they *become* synthetic judgments *a priori* in contradistinction from judgments equally synthetic, but *synthetic* judgments *a posteriori*. Their principle therefore must be *a priori,* and in addition to the principle of contradiction; and what may this be then? [These] are questions of the highest importance, the solution of which we shall attempt to give in the following chapter.

Footnotes

1. "Principle of identity and contradiction".
2. The paragraph up to this point is from *Prolegomena* § 2c (1783) 26-7.

Chapter-10

On Synthesis *a priori*

Chapter-10

1. Bishop Berkeley has remarked, and, if I mistake not, an observation to the same import occurs in yet earlier writers, that in speaking of objects in nature as antecedents and consequents we might more safely and appropriately name the former signals rather than causes.

2. Though this remark of the philosophic bishop contains the substance of David Hume's chapter on cause and effect, little or no attention was excited by it. It was reserved for the Scottish philosopher by the publication of his essays in the year [1748][1] and for the celebrity given to these essays by the praises of [the] French, repeated and echoed (according to Gray)[2] by the *literati* or Britain, to bring the subject of casuality into public discussion.

3. This second spark, therefore, cannot be said to have fallen on incombustible materials. It produced great heat and volumes of smoke; but in reference at least to the *literati* of France and Britain it kindled as little light as the former.[3] The reason is obvious: Hume's opponents came forward not as investigators but as adversaries who saw nothing in the subject that required investigation. Whether they understood Hume's intentions as to the moral and religious application of the result, it is most certain that they altogether misapprehended the nature and import of the problem itself. Accordingly, all which the most eloquent among them could effect was the demolition of a man of straw or Guy Fawkes of their own manufacture, after they had amused themselves in contrivances more or less successful, to make it look as hideous as possible.[4] Before we therefore proceed to the solution of the problem, it will be necessary to state the problem itself at large and to explain wherein the difficulty lies: and I cannot perhaps do this better than by following what the Koenigsberg philosopher supposes to have been the course of Hume's own reflections.[5]

4. It stands as an axiom in philosophy, which the metaphysicians asserts and which naturalists have hitherto admitted to be of universal application, that "whatever is not the first cause has (or must have had) a cause"; or, as it is sometimes expressed, whatever takes place, *becomes* (γινεται) or *comes to pass,* has a cause. Now we may use the words "cause and effect" in two ways : first, in the abstract as *entia logica*; secondly, as things to which this name is given when they are described as standing one to the other in the *relation* of cause and effect. To make the subject as intelligible as possible we will take them both successively, beginning with the former. And in order to elucidate the full sense and scope of this axiom we will represent the relation of cause and effect, which we shall hereafter name the "*causal* relation", or more briefly still "causality", under the more general formula of A=B, that is: A, of which B is no constituent part, is nevertheless so connected with B, that if B be given A is of necessity presumed. In other words, the notion of a cause is that of an A which does not *include* B, but yet *infers* it; and the notion of effect abstractly is that of a B which not being included in A is possible only on the assumption of A.

5. This is the true force of the judgment contained in the axiom "whatever is has a cause, with exception of the first cause", or, to avoid the scruple which might be excited by a universal principle (that commences with an exception to its own universality). "all that takes place has a cause". And this judgment is evidently not analytic. The position indeed has neither meaning nor pertinence if B be not different from A. When, for instance, I affirm that all body is extended, no one who understands the meaning of this words would describe the connection subsisting between "body", the subject and "extension", its predicate, as a connection of *cause* and *effect.* In order to a causal connection. I must pass *out* of A and affirm some other not contained in the conception A, viz. B, and vice versa; in order to establish B as an effect I seek for a somewhat not contained in the conception B, but other and

distinguishable therefrom (as a watchmaker from the timepiece) which is to be its *cause.* Now Mr. Hume called on the metaphysicians of his age to make known by what right they asserted the existence and necessity of such a connection, in other words, he required of them to tell him how they came by their notion of effect and cause, by what right they affirm it in reference to natural objects as a *necessary* connection; and further, by what right they transferred it from physics, and the phenomena of the senses, to metaphysical deductions and objects assumed as *super*sensual, and affirm at last a *universal* principle.

6. In the second and improper acceptation of the words in which by "cause and effect" we mean only the "causant" and the "effected", that *res causans, res* [*causata*], as when we say of any two bodies *that* is the cause and *this* is the effect, the exposition may be given in few words. By A=B, in this sense, the metaphysician asserts the existence of a link = X, necessarily connecting B with A. This X is the *notion* of cause, which is here marked problematically as an *unknown quantity*, inasmuch as the notion of cause is incapable of any further real explanation. So true is this that even the words and terms of the *verbal* definition (viz. the necessary connection between A and a B not included in A) drive their positive meaning and intelligibility from the notion of cause, and not the notion of cause from this definition.

7. Mr Hume denied neither the existence, nor the expedience, nay! not even the subjective necessity, of applying the notion of causality to the phenomenon of antecedence and sequence in nature. What he called on the metaphysician to do was to assign the origin of this notion, to give proof that it was not a mere prejudice, and to ground this *feeling* of a necessity on the rational conviction that accompanies insight. Nor ought we to forget that the metaphysicians on whom Mr Hume called were, for the far greater part at least, avowed disciples of Mr Locke—men who no less than himself had exploded the doctrine of innate ideas and had adopted without limitation the principle

of "nihil in intellectu quod non prius in sensu".[6] Hume, in short, took the very same position that had been previously taken by Berkeley in the introduction to his *Principles of Knowledge* and dialogue between Hylas and Philonous,[7] the crude yet *racy* first fruits of his philosophic speculations, and with a more vehement and prolonged pressure deepened while he refreshed the footmarks which his predecessor had left.[8] On the grounds contended for (and which at that time he doubtless considered as having been fully established) by Locke himself did our English metaphysicians attack Locke's abstract triangles or the abstract idea, triangle *in genere* (the main weight of the confutation resting on Mr Locke's own definition and usage of the term "idea"), and afterwards flashed forth the luminous remark cited at the commencement of this chapter. And on the very same *grounds* and with arguments derived from the same premises did the Scottish Philosopher support his sceptical queries concerning the idea of cause and effect; and however dissimilar, or even contrariant, the ultimate objects, the practical aims, of the two men may have been, I should be sorry not to believe that the interests of science and speculative truth were common to both.

8. It would be still more strange, though less uncharitable, to suppose that Mr Hume was ignorant of the actual import of cause, or that if he had needed the information he was so unread in books familiar to all men of ordinary learning as not to have known from Cicero that neither antecedence nor concomitance constituted the essence of the notion. "[Non] praeire sed efficienter praeire neque comitari sed efficienter comitari."[9] It would be too hard, I repeat, to presume Mr Hume ignorant that the phenomena antecedence and concomitance might, and often did, exist without any notion of a causal connection, ignorant, in short, of one of the commonest rules of common logic by which every schoolboy of fifteen is guarded against the sophism, "*cum* hoc: ergo *propter* hoc" or "post hoc; ergo *proper* hoc".[10] No, Mr Hume was well aware that the notion of efficiency was involved in every assertion of a causal

connection, nor did he deny that we were under a subjective necessity of applying this notion in all synthetic judgments respecting external objects. He knew too and admitted that judgments grounded on experience are always synthetic. It were absurd to ground our analytic judgment on experience, however certain it might be that to experience we owed our knowledge of the subject, concerning which the judgment was formed, for as that which we judge or predicate respecting the subject is actually contained and implied in the mere conception of it, on what ground should we go further? Would we seek the *radii* of a circle on the outward side of the circumference? That a man is a rational animal is a judgment requiring no other condition than that of knowing what we mean by the word "man"; but that a man is a father requires that with the subject "man" I should combine the conception of another subject; it is synthetic and so that the latter being given, viz. offspring, the former is necessarily supposed. Therefore through the whole extent of human experience, Mr Hume admitted the existence and validity of synthetic judgments, and admitted too that by the same experience we were entitled, because impelled, to apply the causal connection or notion of cause. Neither did the difficulty which attended this conception escape, nor was it indeed likely to escape, so acute a thinker, viz. that of explaining the necessity involved in our conception of cause and effect. Now is it possible that the phenomena themselves, viz. antecedence and sequency, or concomitance, not merely exciting but being contradistinguished by a sense of their contingency, this contingency being indeed the very mark and criterion of their objective reality, yet the connection resulting from this, should contain a sense of necessity, and this too in the very essence of the conception ? No, he saw the difficulty and proposed a solution. And this solution it is which I confess, highly as I appreciate Hume's acuteness as a disputant and his talents as a writer, makes me sceptical as to the depth and comprehension of view which Kant, judging by the effect produced or occasioned on his own prepared and susceptible intellect, has attributed to David Hume on the score of this particular essay.[11] Hume's solution consists in assigning the origin and ground of the notion, and the necessity conceived therein, to custom, association, thus confounding, in the first place, the conception of necessity as a positive and essential constituent of the conception "cause" with a confused negative inability to do otherwise; in the second place, assigning as the cause of causality a something which itself presupposes a something, which the writers deemed classical on this subject, Hartley, Priestley, and Condillac, and before them Hobbes,[12] had by reducing all the phenomena of association to the law of contemporaneity reduced them under the common law of cause and effect, but which phenomena, according to Mr Hume himself, who has borrowed without acknowledgment a much more correct statement of the laws of association from Aquinas's commentaries on the *Parva naturalia* of Aristotle, do at least presuppose the principle they [are] thus brought in to explain;[13] and, in the third place, [adopting a theory] irreconcilable with the facts and contradictory to the very experience which is asserted to engender this conception. This last point has been ably set forth by Brown, the son of the celebrated medical theorist.[14] He has shown what indeed needs but be mentioned to be remembered as the result of facts, that the function allotted to experience is that of checking and limiting the application of the notion, that children instinctively predicate a causal connection in almost every case of coincidence, that every influence which by withdrawing the mind from reflections on its actual experience produces the same effect on adults that the want of experience does on children, induces the same promiscuous attribution as superstition, hope, fear, etc from the purse or coffin from the fire,[15] the stranger on the filmy grate,[16] the letter and winding-sheet on the candle,[17] the numbers on the hackney coach which my grandmother had twice dreamt of for the prizes in the lottery,[18] the gris-gris of the African[19] and the amulets and charms of the European empiric. In short, it seems like the air we breathe to be ready everywhere to flow in where not forbidden and absolutely excluded by experience, or rather, shall we say, like the faculty of breathing which it requires an express volition to suspend?

9. But a still stranger, though less obvious and less striking, confutation of Hume's solution is derived from the nature and construction of experience itself; and custom is but an abbreviation for a customary or repeated experience. It would carry us too far for our present purpose to enter fully into this subject, the necessity to, being in the part [satisfied] by the preceding investigations respecting the intuitions of space and time as necessary preconditions of experience. In like manner we have only seriously to suppose a time in which the notion of cause and effect, or, if you please, that necessary predisposition to the same which may be called into effect and into consciousness by occasion of impressions from without, but can be no more given by it than the specific form of an oak can be given to the acorn by the outward elements of air, light, and moisture. We have only, I say, to suppose the moment when this notion was yet to be formed, or, to use the language of Mr Locke, to be by means of the senses put or conveyed into the mind. And on what ground, in cases where the effect or impression is coinstantaneous with the phenomenon assumed as its cause, should the mind make this arrangement? Or better still, perhaps, remove altogether the conception of causality and what do we mean by the mind itself? And what is the experience of the mind taken abstractedly from the mind but as empty a word as thoughts without thinking or motion without a moving body?

10. These remarks are not wholly digressive; for whether the manifest insufficiency and superficial character of the solution proposed by the propounder of the problem does or does not justify my scepticism as to his having seen the problem itself in its true bearings and import, there can be no doubt that the belief of having solved it empirically prevented him from adopting a necessary preliminary to a true solution, viz. that of trying whether the problem could not be presented under a higher and yet more comprehensive formula. Whether

there were not other connections = X between A and B not included in A besides the causal connection. Whether causality or the relation of cause and effect be anything more than a specification or particular application of this higher formula which it shares only in common with other exercises of the judicial power. In short, the assertion of cause and effect is in every instance a synthetic judgment. This is universally admitted, or rather it is not in the power of any man who understands the meaning of the words "analytic" and "synthetic" not to admit it. But are there no other synthetic judgments? The application of the causal connection to the particular phenomena depends beyond doubt on the knowledge given by experience; but it cannot be legitimately concluded from this that the connection itself or that which forms the essence of the notion of cause is likewise derived from experience (given by it, I mean) in contradiction from merely occasioned by it, or called into definite act and distinct consciousness; for this would have been falling into the same confusion with which Mr Hume himself so justly charges Mr Locke's reasoning, or rather the impossible error which Mr Locke exerts himself to confute in his first book in the *Essay on the Human Understanding*. Nor in fact does Mr Hume rest his opinion on any such conclusion; he believed himself to have discovered a sufficient solution in the influence of custom and therefore sought for no other. He did not argue the connection = X is applied by the human mind to the data of experience, therefore it is itself a datum of experience and a judgment *a posteriori*, but the connection X is a synthesis or combination of the repetition of the same impressions and the *nisus* or feeling of the animal life. In other words, the causal connection is the bastard offspring (*progenies hybrida*) of definite impressions from without and indefinite sensation, that is, of outward and inward experience, and altogether therefore experiential or *a posteriori*.

11. On this view it is evident that the sensation being a mere subjective accident of the same necessity and of no greater value than the sensation of faintness in distant objects, or the *nisus* or effort of sight in the attempt to distinguish them, the

experience itself is the sole ground in every instance of the legitimacy or objective truth of the conception. In all reasoning therefore the materials of which or subject-matter are not drawn from experience, the notion of cause and effect is not only inapplicable but without meaning. Hume's premise once granted, the conclusion is inevitable. Nor will I disguise my conviction that it was the obvious consequences of this conclusion that gave it its chief value and interest in the eyes of the Scottish philosopher.[20] The opportunities, I mean, of applying it to the doctrines of religion and of using it as a means of undermining the foundations of our religious convictions or principles, at least those that theologians and metaphysicians had hitherto taken for such, and not of religion only, but the fundamental principles of morality likewise, if more be meant by that term than the dictates of worldly prudence and the necessities and sympathies of custom, and varying therefore as the custom[s] of one age and country differ from those of another. There are few readers who need be informed that this is Mr Hume's own statement of his theory and these are his own deductions, but to be consequent is the *first* requisite, the first and most important requisite, of the reasoner, were it only that with our limited intellects it must often happen that it is a veiw of the consequences that impels us to doubt and re-examine the premises, and this praise with that of as great frankness in the avowal of his conclusions as was compatible with personal safety, and, I am willing to believe, with still more honourable wish to have his purpose understood by those only who were competent to understand his arguments, this praise belongs to David Hume.[21] But the many and important advantages which truth and science have derived from strict consequence even in dangerous error would form a very instructive appendix to a history of philosophy, while the inlaying of infidel premises with pious professions and sentiments, or the conjuring of religious conclusions from Godless premises, is equally injurious to the interests of science and of faith. It tends beyond all causes to stop the progress of the former, and it is sure to sophisticate the latter for a time and finally to be made both the pretext and the instrument of attack and open hostility. However ingeniously the wholesome and nutritious fruits plucked from the tree of revelation and ancient philosophy may be threaded on the barren fig-tree or rather let me say on the poisonous manchineel,[22] they will be more or less injured by the damps and exudations of the supporting branches and sooner or later will fall off, yet leave in the mind of the passer-by a temptation to pluck the native products of the tree that have taken their place. If no connection can be affirmed unless where both *antecedent* and *consequent* are *alike* facts of experience, and no analogical conclusions are valid between subjects of diverse kind (*analogicae ratiocinanti non conceditur* μεταβασις εισαλλο γενος), a spiritual antecedent cannot be presumed from a material phenomenon. For necessary connection is not only exclusively applicable to known, or, by analogy, to possible, objects of the senses; but the supposed necessity which constitutes the whole cogency of the conclusion, the world, that is, the whole aggregate of sensible objects, must have a cause which cannot therefore itself be an object of the sense, is not a necessity of insight, but a necessity of feeling, or rather of blind feeling of necessity, gradually engendered by a repetition of the impressions with which it gradually becomes associated. The same objection applies, and was in fact applied, to the truth of miracles; the testimony on which the truth of the miracle rests in historical, that is, experiential, but here one constituent only of the judgment is the legitimate or possible object of experience. The other half, the miraculous substitute of the antecedent, is not the possible object of human experience and therefore not a legitimate object of human history. Nay, even though the supersensual A were admitted to exist, there would nevertheless result no right of asserting a causal connection between it and the phenomenon B:-for *this*-would be an act of the judgment; but the necessity in the *causal* connection is, according to Mr Hume, no act of the judgment, far rather, it is no act at all, but a mere *affection* of the animal sensibility, a passive *feeling*.[23]

12. Were it not, as it is, of highest importance from the moral interest of the question, it would be indispensable in order to the establishment of [a] logical criterion by which the true nature of the premises may be distinguished that rules (of undoubted legitimacy in forensic reasoning, when what is subjectively true is likewise practically valid) should be prevented from being applied as principles to the determination of objective truth in real science and natural philosophy; the importance of this end, I say, among all the works of modern philosophy, Bacon's *Novum Organum* has the immortal merit of having first fully and worthily set forth. It is indispensable that this last point should be seen with the greatest possible clearness and distinctness. The student must be made to understand that not the relation of cause and effect applied to certain antecedents and consequents in nature in and for itself was the object of Hume's scepticism. What Hume doubted was the *necessity* of the connection between A and any given B not included in A, as a necessity of reason and insight, which connection the metaphysicians hitherto had indeed *exemplified* and of course asserted to exist, in the relation of cause and effect, but which Hume denies *altogether*. He denies, I say, the right of asserting this principle of necessary connection in any case, and that which in the particular case under discussion (namely where A=B represents cause and effect) had been advanced as such, and which he affirms to have been the ground and origin of the belief, this he declares to be a something of a quite different kind, referable to a different source and to be accounted for on an altogether different hypothesis. Mr Hume's argument may be exhibited to the eye in the following simple statement, in which the letter X (as before) stands for the idea of *necessary connection*. There exists *no* X between *any* A and B, where the latter is not included in the former, and that which in the one instance of cause and effect you have mistaken for X is really only = 0, that is, a blind feeling, a delusion engendered by custom. But did Mr Hume deny the cogency, the apodictive necessity, of the mathematics, or did he, like the late ingenious but somewhat

overhasty Dr Beddoes, gravely derive the evidence of the elements of geometry by Euclid from the very same source and place it on the same scale with the elements of chemistry by Lavoisier and [assert] that we have exactly the same certainty and the same kind of certainty in affirming that water is a compound body constituted by the combination of oxygen gas with hydrogen gas in the proportion of twenty-seven to seventy-three, as in the mathematical position that a circle is formed by the circumvolution of a straight line fixed at one end?[24] No, Mr Hume was not disingenuous enough to pretend the former and far too acute a thinker to have been capable of imagining the latter. He neither denied the evidence of mathematics nor doubted the necessary conclusions of common logic. Adopting the opinions first maintained by Sir Kenelm Digby in his treatise of bodies and soul,[25] Hume considered both mathematical and logical reasoning as purely and merely analytical, and the whole mighty pile of science geometrical and numerical as a succession of analytic judgments, or, in the language of Digby and his followers, a series of identical propositions. This being the case, it is easily conceivable that it did not occur to him to enquire whether there were not other judgments standing in the same predicament with that of the causal connection. He received no memento or assistance from his antagonists, and it is no wonder therefore that the discussion dropped without having occasioned any increase of light either for them, himself, or the learned public. Such at least appeared to be the result, and such it would have been, had not the seed, which as it fell unprofitably from the hand of the sower and which wafted and tossed about on the winds of literary rumour, found at length a well-fitted and prepared soil in the mind of a Prussian philosopher who in earliest manhood had already distinguished himself not only as a profound mathematicians by the treatise on the dead and living forces, and as natural philosopher and astronomer by his prophetic system of the heavens[26] (the germ and original idea of Laplace's *Céleste mécanique*,[27] and in which the existence and place of the Georgian *sidus*,[28] of the small extrazodiacal planets, the duplicity of Saturn's ring, etc, were predetermined from the theory, long before either had been discovered by observation), but by the singular dissatisfaction with the existing state of metaphysics, the author declaring himself equally at variance with those who boldly asserted the negative as with those who took for granted the affirmative of the questions, "Is such a science as that of metaphysics possible?" and "Is it already in existence?"[29] Before his acquaintance with the writings of Hume and Berkeley, he appears to have convinced himself that the Epicureans and Sceptics had a great deal more logic on their side than the zeal of the religious party was willing to admit, and that the orthodox had a great deal more truth at the bottom of their opinions than the contemptuous spirit of the Sceptics and matter-of-fact men could bring itself to discover. What Hume had only begun, this philosopher began anew and completed; and what he did the student of judicial logic must now proceed to do.

13. The subject, as we have seen, falls into two questions. Are the mathematical judgments analytic only? For if this should have been a mistake on the part of Hume and his predecessors—if the mathematical reasonings both in the processes of arithmetic and the constructions of geometry be as the ancients, mathematicians, and in fact the whole scientific world till within the last hundred and sixty years had never doubted, should be *bona fide* synthetic judgments, then as their *a priori* character is above all rational doubt, and is fully conceded by Hume himself, there are synthetic judgments *a priori* and other synthetic judgments beside that respecting causality; and this leads to the second question. Are there yet other synthetic judgments not mathematical, but of the same class with that of the causal connection? For should we be able to point out such, then as the synthetic character is common to all, both to the mathematical and to those that fall under the same class with that of cause and effect, it would be incumbent on us to ask whether they are not all alike instances and proofs of synthesis *a priori*. And *this* Mr Hume

himself could scarcely have denied, certainly not consistently with his own admissions. For as the difficulty in any instance consists in the essential character common to all, as expressed in the formula [A]=B by virtue of X, or the necessary connection of one subject with another not included in the former as its constituent predicate; and as this, it has been clearly proved by Mr Hume, is neither derived nor derivable from experience, *then* its existence being nevertheless ascertained, it has a ground independent of experience. But this is what we mean when we say that they are true *a priori*. We have therefore little more to do than to put the student in the way of proving for himself that all mathematical reasoning is truly synthetic or composed of synthetic judgments *a priori*. When he has fully satisfied himself on this point, he will seek to understand how this synthesis is possible, and for this insight we have already prepared in the chapter on transcendental aesthetic, or space and time as the forms *a priori* of the outward and inward sense.[30] Of other synthetic judgments we shall thus have the negative character, viz. that the synthesis is not conditioned by the pre-existing forms of the sense, and may therefore anticipate their positive definition, viz. that this latter class have their condition and ground in the *a priori* forms of the understanding, and with the enumeration and exposition of these forms, together with the rules deducible therefrom, we shall conclude the scientific part of judicial logic or logic as a criterion. The rules and cautions afforded by empirical psychology will form the appendix to this section,[31] distinguished from the rules that are properly scientific, and belong to the science of logic, e.g. the rules of definition, division, method, induction, etc, by the name of maxims. And with these [we shall conclude] the treatise itself, as far as it is a treatise on the causes or legitimate forms of conclusive reasoning and of the criterion of the truth or falsehood of the premises as far as they can be learnt *a priori*, that is, without a previous acquaintance with the particular subjects in question. But neither here can we take leave of the science of logic, in this its most scientific sense, without again calling on the student not to finish his review of what this logic *is* and can effect, without considering what logic is not, cannot effect, or without adverting to the opposite errors, the delusions of superstition on the one hand and the sophisms of a faithless sensuality on the other that have originated from the undue elevation of logic and the understanding as the logical faculty to an equal rank with philosophy and reason, or the undue degradation of the human soul by subjecting all truth to conceptions formed from the senses, or to the notions which the understanding marks, for itself by reflection on its own processes.

Footnotes

1. *An Enquiry Concerning Human Understanding.*

2. See William Mason "Memoirs of His Life and Writings" in *The Poems of Mr. Gray* (York 1775) 384-5.

3. The image is based on one used in Kant's discussion of Hume. *Prolegomena* Einleitung (1783) 7.

4. For *a* similar account of the opposition to Hume, see *P Lects* Lect 6 (1949) 202-3.

5. Kant *C dr V* 788-97 (606-12).

6. See above, p 134 n 2.

7. *A Treatise Concerning the Principles of Human Knowledge* (1710);*Three Dialogues Between Hylas and Philonous* (1713). C must refer specifically to *B Works* II 27-38 and 192-4.

8. For Hume's acknowledgement of Berkeley's precedence, see *Treatise of Human Nature* (1739-40) bk I pt I vii.

9. "[not] to precede, but to precede effectively, not what is concomitant, but what is effectively concomitant." The same quotation is given in part in *SM* (*CC*) 32n and is attributed to Cicero. Cf *De fato* 15.34: " non sic causa intellegi debet ut quod cuique antecedat id ei causa sit, sed quod cuique efficienter antecedent ..." Tr. H. Rackham in Cicero *De ornatore*....(LCL 2 vols 1942) II 231: "cause is not to be understood in such a way as to make what precedes a thin the cause of that thing, but what precedes it effectively, ..." Cf Topica 16.61.

10. "*With* this, therefore *because of* this: or after this, therefore, *because of* this".
11. Kant *C d r V* 792 (609-12).
12. Cf C's account in *BL* ch 5 (1907) 65ff.
13. Cf *BL* ch 5 (1907) I 73. Cf "David Hume Charged by Mr Coleridge with Plagiarism from St. Thomas Aquinas" *Blackwood's Magazine* III (1818)653-7. Cf CN I 973 An.
14. Thomas Brown (1778-1820) *Observations on the Nature and Tendency of the Doctrine of Mr. Hume, Concerning the Relation of Cause and Effect* (Edinburgh 1804). Further comments of Brown are to be found in BM MS Egertion 2801 ff 118-20. His father was a clergyman, and not, as C suggests here, John Brown (1735-88), the founder of the Brunonian system of medicine.
15. OED: " Purse"- "A fragment of live coal starting out of the fire with a report: regarded as a prognostic of good fortune"; "confin"- An oblong piece of the live coal starting out of the fire with a report: regarded as a prognostic of death".
16. Cf *Frost at Midnight* lines 15-16: *PW* (EHC) r 240.
17. *OED*: "winding sheet"- "A mass of solidified drippings of grease clinging to the side of a candle, and regarded in popular superstition as omen of death or calamity".
18. This story has on been identified, although C does refer elsewhere to the limits of her arithmetical skill(*CN* ii 2064).
19. Cf *CL* iv 863.
20. Cf Kant's greater faith in Hume. *C d r V* 733 (597).
21. C expresses himself more forthrighly in *SM* (*CC*)22.
22. C combines two favourite images here—fruit threaded on the barren fig-tree (cf *Friend*-CC ii 314, i 315) and the poisonous manchineel (cf *Lects* 1795 —*CC*—296 and *Friend CC-ii* 261,i 568), in which C persisted in spite of Mr. Boyer's interdict. See *BL* ch 1 (1907)i 5.
23. C is referring here to Hume *An Enquiry Concerning Human Understanding* (1748) vi and x, "Of the Idea of Necessary Connexion" and " Of Miracles".

24. Thomas Beddoes *Observations,* esp 108-10 and 15. in *LS* (*CC*) 173, C probably had this book in mind rather than Dalton. Lavoisier's ratio was 15:85 (*Elements of Chemistr* . . . tr Robert Kerr—Edinburgh 1790-199); the correct oneis 11:89 (J.R. Partington *A history of Chemistry*-1961-70-III 452). CF C's marginal note in Hooker *Works* (1682) (BM copy) 71, where he gives the ratio as 23:77. C was attached to Beddoes and said of his death in 1809 that it took "more hope out of my Life than any former Event except perhaps T. Wedgwood's". *CL* III 174.

25. *Two Treatises: In the One of Which, the Nature of Bodies; In the Other, the Nature of Man's Soule: Is Looked into* . .. (Paris 1644). C borrowed the book from the Carlisle Cathedral library in 1801-2. *CN* I 1004 and n.

26. *Allgemeine Naturgeschichte und Theorie des Hummels*(1755).

27. Laplace *Traité de mecaniqué céleste.* C makes the same assertion in a letter to C. A. Tulk on 12 Jan 1818 (*CL* IV 808). For a full discussion of Kant's relationship to Laplace, see introduction to *Kant's Cosmonogy* . . . ed W. Hastie (Glasgow 1990).

28. The planet Uranus, or *Georgium Sidus,* named in honour of George III by its discoverer, Sir William Herschel (1738-1822), in 1781. It was called "the Georgian" in English almanacs until the midele of the nineteenth century.

29. See above, p 169 n 2.

30. See above, pp 150-73.

31. The appendix is lacking.

Chapter-11

The Philosophy of Logic after Frege

Chapter 11

EXPRESSION, DESIGNATION, AND TRUTH

Few logicians wish to retain all Frege's philosophy of logic,[1] but his terminology of functions and truth-values has perdoctrines even when they profess to have freed themselves from his theory. We must therefore begin this chapter with a discussion of views on meaning and truth.

The peculiarity of Frege's theory of meaning is that he tries to explain the use of all words and other signs by consideration of what is involved in naming. He admits, of course, that verbs,common nouns, adjectives, prepositions, and symbols of various other sorts are not proper names or quasi-names, but he thinks that they are all merely devices for the construction of complex names such as 'the capital of Prussia' and 'the man who discovered the elliptical orbits of the planets'. In working out this line of thought he shows remarkable subtlety, and what he says about sense and reference seems very well adapted to the solution of his puzzle about statements such as 'The morning star is identical with the evening star'. It must be admitted, nevertheless, that there is something very strange in his doctrine that indicative sentences are names or designations for truth-value, and the fact that he comes to this conclusion should make us critical of his initial assumptions.

Frege's doctrine of truth-values is strange and unacceptable because he never succeeds in explaining clearly what these objects are. In one place he says that the truth-value of a sentence (*Satz*) is the circumstance that it is true or false as the case may be. This seems intelligible, but it is quite inconsistent with the suggestion that all true sentences designate one truth-value and all false sentences another. For the circumstance that '5 is a prime number' is true (if we may allow ourselves to speak in this way) is not the same as the circumstance that '2+2=4' is true. In other places he talks simply of the True and the False. This phraseology is intended, no doubt, to suggest that he is dealing with two and only two objects; but what are they? In ordinary usage 'the true' would be taken to mean the same as 'that which is true', but the things that can be true in a primary sense are propositions, or, as Frege would say, thoughts (i.e. what sentences express, as distinct from what they are supposed to designate), and there may be infinitely many of these expressed by different sentences. Are we then to understand that his two truth-values are just the attributes truth and falsity? These are indeed a pair of objects in a large sense of the word 'object', and they can reasonably be called values in a sense which has nothing to do with mathematical talk about substitution for a variable. But it seems absurd to say that every true indicative sentence designates or stands for truth, since sentences are signs of a quite different kind from those which may properly be said to designate truth (e.g. the word 'truth' itself or the phrase 'what Pontius Pilate wished to have defined'). We might perhaps for certain purposes admit the convention of writing :

5 is a prime number = truth

as a substitute for 'It is true that 5 is a prime number', but the possibility of a re-making our language in this way can provide no jusitification for what Frege says. If we took to writing '= truth' after certain indicative sentences and '=falsity' after others, the two expressions would not retain their present meanings but come to be regarded in some other way, e.g. as like the tick and the cross which a schoolmaster uses in marking his pupils' answer to questions.

In his paper *Über Sinn und Bedeutung* Frege tries to make his theory plausible by arguing that it is involved in the distinction which we make between fiction and history. The sentences in an epic poem or a novel have sense, he tells us, but they are not ordinarily classified as true or false, because they are not thought to have reference. The sentences of an historian, on the other hand, are thought to have reference as well as sense. For if we seriously maintain that Odysseus was set ashore at Ithaca while sound asleep, we are prepared to insist that the word 'Odysseus' stands for an object, and this interest of ours in the reference of part of the sentence is intelligible only if we suppose that the sentence as a whole designates something. As in the understanding of any sentence, whether of fiction or of history, the sense of a part is relevant because it helps to determine the sense of the whole, so, it seems, in an inquiry about the truth of an historical statement the reference of a part is relevant because it helps to determine the reference of the whole, namely, its truth-value.

This argument is Frege's best defence, but it does not justify his attempt to distinguish between the sense and the reference of a statement. For if we suppose that an indicative sentence of fiction has precisely the same sense as it would possess in an historical narrative, we must suppose also that it is used to make a true or false statement. Nothing more is required according to Frege's own explanations, since a proposition, or complete thought expressed by an indicative sentence, is always something which must be true or false. There is, of course, an important distinction to be drawn between sentences in fiction and sentences in history, but it is not the case, as Frege assumes, that the former have sense without reference whereas the latter have both sense and reference. The fundamental difference is rather that historians make communications whereas story-tellers only pretend to make communications; and from this it follows that many sentences of fiction are meaningful only in the rather peculiar way in which 'John has the pen of the gardener's wife' is said to be meaningful when it occurs as an example in a grammar book. They are complex signs such as *might* be used for the making of communications in certain circumstances and that is precisely why they *are* used by the story-teller when he pretends for our amusement to be in such circumstances. If anyone misunderstands the situation and thinks that the story-teller is making a genuine communication, he supplies in thought a complete sense for each sentence, and as Frege says, this commonly involves taking certain phrases to be genuine designations; but there is no good reason for saying that it involves treating the sentences of the story-teller as designations of truth-values.

The source of Frege's theory is his assumption that every complete sign must possess both sense and reference, and he was led to this by his preoccupation with names and quasi-names. When for one reason or another we become interested in the study of language and begin to ask questions about meaning, it is perhaps natural that we should look for clues in those situations in which we have enriched language by our own acts, and the most obvious of these is the giving of proper names. Certainly many philosophers before Frege have tried to explain the meaningfulness of words by saying that they stand for things in the way in which the name 'Socrates' stands for Socrates. But the suggestion is unfortunate, because proper names are by no means essential for communication.

Instead of 'Socrats died from drinking hemlock' we might say The snub-nosed philosopher who first asked for definitions of the virtues died from drinking hemlock'. Admittedly the sense of the second remark is not exactly the same as that of the first, since understanding of the second requires knowledge which is not required for understanding of the first; but in many contexts the second could do duty for the first, and there seems to be no imaginable context (other than that of compiling a dictionary of names) in which the purposes served by utterance of the first could not be served equally well by utterance of some paraphrase without a proper name. Nor is this all. In familiar contexts we could eliminate even definite descriptions and words such as 'I', 'you', 'this', 'that', 'here', and 'now', which are all treated by Frege as quasi-names. To do so we should need only a code like that which the post office uses in transmitting greetings telegrams. Corresponding to each frequently repeated sentence of English there would be a single expression without significant parts, and from constant use the latter would acquire the force which now belongs to the former. There are, indeed, examples of this in ordinary communication.When a golfer shouts 'Fore!', those in front take the cry for a warning that he is about to play his ball in their direction. And when a ship's wireless operator sends out the international distress signal, those who pick it up understand without translation that help is required urgently in the place from which the signal comes. No doubt it is impossible that we should conduct all our communication like this, but it is important to realize that the impossibility of the suggestion is connected with the way in which we learn languages, rather than with the way in which we use them when we have learnt them.

In the course of a day each of us has occasion to utter many sentences never heard before in the history of mankind. Thus even a child of ten might say 'I saw a walking doll and an electric law-mower in the shop next to the church where Grandfather dropped the collection plate after the sermon by the archbishop'; and if he did, we should not think that he had performed a great feat. But it is at least very unlikely that the English words of our example were ever put together in just that order until we constructed the example. Now clearly a language which allowed only unitary expressions would be inadequate to our needs, because it would provide no way of dealing with rare situations. Each expression we learnt would be appropriate only to situations of a certain kind, and while we might successfully extend the uses of some of them by analogy and metaphor, we should never be able to acquire a stock large enough for all the purposes now served by common speech. In a highly developed language, therefore, we must have syntax as well as vocabulary, though there is reason to believe that at the very beginning men may have had vocabulary alone. But whether we speak in simple standard phrases or in complex sentences, what we say is always something that could in principle be used on other occasion of the same kind, if there were any such. For thought it is improbable, it is certainly not impossible that at various times and places dozens of children should utter the elaborate sentece we have constructed as an example and each with the same linguistic properity. Nor is the situation very different if we suppose that the language with which we are dealing contains proper names. It may be that in future no one except an actor or a grammarian will ever say 'Socrates is now drinking hemlock', but it is conceivable nevertheless that this sentence should be used to make a sincere and even a true statement.For at some time another Socrates(which means in this context another man called Socrates) may drink hemlock.

A unitary expression is something like a pattern of gesture of a variety of grimace.For saying 'Yes' and nodding the head are just two ways of signifying agreement; and saying 'Well!' with a fallling intonation is an emphatic way of expressing what we sometimes express by raising our eyebrows.But a complex sentence with distinguishable subject and predicate may be regarded in the same way. For saying 'I am tired' is a piece of behaviour which we may use for our purposes in the same way as we sometimes use the dumb-show of closing the eyes and dropping the head. Can we then maintain that in all these cases our sings have both sense and reference? We must certainly distinguish between the general sense of a sign considered as a pattern of behaviour (i.e. what we learn when we learn how to sign is to used) and the various communications which we may make be means of it on different occasions; and we may say correctly that the communications differ because they refer to different circumstances according to the occasion of utterance. But this is not the same as Frege's distinction. For the general sense, of which we talk here is not, like the *Sinn, a* determinate proposition, and the reference of which we speak is not naming or designation. Use of words or phrases with designating function may be involved, as when we say 'Socrates dies from drinking hemlock' or ' The milkman called this morning,; but it is not essential, since reference of the kind we are now considering may be made by the use of signs which have no meaningful parts and it is at least conceivable that all signs should be of that sort. If we wish to use Frege's terminology. We can say only that a particular utterance of a sentences expresses a sense; but for a proper understanding of this we must continue our analysis further.

Economy is the merit which has favoured the survival and development of syntax. Now the first and most obvious measure of economy that we can adopt in the construction of sentences is to use the same vocabulary for expressing statements, questions,commands, and the rest. In a langauge where no expression had any part or aspect that was separately meaningful, there could be no relevant similarity between a qeustion and a statement that answered it, or between a request and a promise to fulfil it. But so far as we know, all human languages of which there is any record contain devices by which sentences containing the same words or word roots may nevertheless be distinguished as indicative, interrogative, imperative, or optative. In Euorpean languages the differences are very often shown by modifications of the special kind of word we call a verb, but even within this linguistic group there are other possibilities. Thus questions are commonly expressed by some adaptation of the indicative form, but this adaptation may be the addition of a particle (*Num venit*?), an inversion of order ('Is he coming?'), or simply a special intonation ('He is coming?).

Sometimes for stylistic or rhetorical reasons the pattern normally appropriated to one kind of communication is used for a communication of a different kind, as when a military order is given by an indicative sentence in the future tense or an emphatic statement is made by means of an interrogative construction. But in every case there is some convention or implicit rule which makes a pattern suitable in its context for the speaker's purpose. And whatever the device of expression may be, it is safe to say that in a complex sentence there is always some feature which has the special function of manifesting the speaker's attitue or interest in speaking. For communication is essentially the deliberate manifestation of an attitude towards a proposition or thinkable state of affairs. The making of a statement is a manifestation of the speaker's belief, the putting of a question a manifestation of the speaker's curiosity or of his wish that the hearer should supply certain information, and so on. Only the commonest kinds of communications have received special names, but among those which are lumped together as exclamations we might, if we chose, distinguish many more varieties. Consider for example, the differences between 'Thank God, that's over!, 'To hell with the Pope!', and 'Smith a bishop! Good heavens!' If we took account of uses of language for purposes other than communication (e.g. for ritual), we should have other distinctions to draw, but we may safely ignore such complications here.

For the logician the chief interst of all this is that it involves a distinction between the manifesting of an attitude and the propounding of a proposition towards which that attitude is manifested. In some of our unitary expressions such as 'Yes', 'Well !', and 'Damn !', there is nothing to indicate the proposition towards which the speaker manifests an attitude, because the utterance of such an expression on a particular occasion is usually enough in itself to show the direction of the speaker's interest. Obviously the opposite case of a unitary expression which does not manifest an attitude cannot occur, since without manifestation of an attitude there would be no communication. But it is conceivable that the development of syntax should have produced purely propositional signs which in association with signs of attitude like Frege's judgement stroke would constitute complete sentences. We might, for example, have expressed statements in the form 'P yes' and questions in the form 'P query' where 'P' itself was neither declarative nor interrogative but simply a sign for propounding a proposition. In fact this has not occurred in any natural language of which we have heard; and so anyone who wishes to discuss a propositional sign in such a language must cite an expression which is also a complete sentence because it includes provision for the manifestation of an attitude. Usually logicians have taken indicative sentences as their examples without thinking of any alternatives. Perhaps they have done so because of some confusion in their minds between logic and epistemology, but there are nevertheless good reasons for the choice.

In the first place, indicative sentences tend to be simpler in construction than any other except imperatives. Secondly, the propositions propounded by statements may be of all sorts, whereas orders or requests always have to do with some possible future action of the hearer.Thirdly, in ordinary speech statements, unlike other communictions, except perhaps questions, are often considered without regard to the attitude of any particular speaker. Presumably the reason is that belief enters into all sorts of complex situations, and many similar statements might conceivably be made by many people in various contexts. The usage is especially common in scientific discussions. But whatever the explanation may be, if anyone asks for the meaning of a statement which is considered in this way, we are content to reply with a phrase of the form 'that so-and-so', although we should consider it necessary to mention the attitude of the speaker if we were trying to give the meaning of an utterance of any other kind. It would perhaps be a little odd to say of any statement that it meant a proposition, but we can certainly say with Frege that statements are often conceived as expressions of thoughts in that sense in which thoughts can be entertained by many people with or without belief.Fourthly, and this is most important, indicative sentences, or rather the forms of words which in certain contexts would be called indicative sentences, may on some occasions be used without assertive force. When we say 'There will be a poor harvest if this weather continues' we do not commit ourselves to the belief that there will be a poor harvest if this weather continues' we do not commit ourselves to the belief that there will be a poor harvest, and so the opening phrase works in this context as a purely propositional sign. Admittedly it is only part of the sign for the proposition which is asserted, but the whole sentence could not do the work of propounding that proposition if this part were not recognizable as a propositional sign in its own right. All this is implicit in the Stoic formulation of inference patterns such as 'If the first then the second; but the first; therefore the second'.

Since it is difficult, if not impossible, to discuss these matters without some specialization of terms, let us agree to say that sentences and clauses like those to which we have just drawn attention are propositional expressions and that they express, propound, or signify propositions. But we must add that while some propositional expressions, such as '2+2=4' and 'Virtue is its own reward', express the same proposition on each occasion of utterance, most of those used in conversation express different propositions on different occasions according to the circumstances of utterance. Now it is obvious that if all our propositional expressions were unitary signs there would be no designations, but it is interesting to notice that these may be lacking also in propositional expressions which have some kind of internal structure. When a lift attendant shouts 'Going up !' the first word of his utterance conveys the idea of motion by his lift in the near future, and the second word supplements this by indicating a direction, but neither designates anything; and it is irrelevant to say that the remark is short for 'My lift is going up', since the attendant omits the first three words of this sentence precisely because they are unnecessary in the context. Why then were designations ever introduced during the syntactical development of language? It seems that the answer is to be found again in considerations of economy. No doubt there might be some way in which a lift attendant could tell a customer without the use of designations that the next lift going down would be found on the opposite side of the passage; but if all our propositional expressions were like workmen's cries, we should need a very great many of them, and some would be used very rarely indeed. There is an obvious advantage in building up sentences as we do from designations and functional signs, since by use of these elements we can cope with an almost unlimited variety of situations in a relatively easy fashion.

In saying this we do not intend to suggest that the subject-predicate pattern which we find in all highly developed languages is a merely arbitrary device. On the contrary, it seems evident that the usefulnes of the device depends on the fact that many, though not all, of the propositions towards which we manifest attitudes are attributive or relational.It is always unsafe to base a metaphysical argument on the pattern of construction used in any particular propositional expression, but if anyone holds seriously that all syntax is a free construction of the human mind, the onus is on him to explain what he means by freedom in this connexion, and in particular to show by examples how the work could have been done in a radically different fashion. The point we wish to make here is quite different, namely that designation should not be taken as a paradigm of all sign-using, since when it occurs it has to be explained as something incidental to the making of communications. To say that 'Socrates' stands for Socrates is only to say that propositional expressions containing the name are appropriate for propounding propositions about Socrates towards which we may wish to manifest various attitudes. That names and quasi-names may be said to possess both sense and reference is a peculiarity of such signs which we must consider in the next section. The basic notion in the theory of meaning is not designation but rather what Frege called expression of a sense.

Once this point has been made clear, it is possible to use some of Frege's results for the formulation of a satisfactory theory of truth. In his account of indirect speech he says that a noun clause such as 'that the planetary orbits are circular' has for its reference the sense of the corresponding sentence 'The planetary orbits are circular'. In other words, by a suitable development of language propositions may be not only expressed but also designated.Naturally the designation of a proposition cannot be a propositional expression according to our technical usage; but it is not even necessary that it should be made form a propositional expression by the prefixing of 'that' or by the introduction of the accusative and infinitive construction as in Latin. For although designations made in this way by adaptation of propositional expressions have a certain priority, phrases like 'Pythagoras' theorem', 'the doctrine of original sin, and 'what Gladstone said in 1883', or even single words like 'materialism' may serve the same purpose. Indeed the variety of signs that may be used for this purpose is limitless, and in order to convince ourselves of the importance of being able to designate propositions we need only reflect how seriously our language would be impoverished if all such signs were lacking. Logic in particular could scarcely be studied without them, since the characteristic words of the logician, such as 'entails', 'inconsistent', 'necessary', and 'possible', are used primarily for making sentences in which the subject terms are designations of propositions. And for the same reason the word 'true' would cease to have that usage which interests philosophers.

In a passage which we quoted earlier Frege says that 'The thought that 5 is a prime number is true' is equivalent to '5 is a prime number', but he fails to see that the principle of this equivalence is a sufficient answer to the philosophical problem about truth. We need the adjective 'true' because we have designations of propositions and require also some way of saying by use of them what could only be said otherwise by means of expressions for the same propositions. If we think of the English word 'that' as a prefix which converts an expression of a proposition into a designation, we may perhaps say that addition of the phrase 'is true' reverses the operation. For when the two occur together they add nothing to what Frege would call the content of the utterance in which they appear, and we are inclined to say that the complex sign 'it is true that' serves only the same rhetorical purpose as the particle 'indeed', i.e. that of indicating a concession or marking the end of a dispute. We must not forget, however, that the word 'true' is often applied to propositions which have not been designated by clauses beginning with 'that' and sometimes even to propositions that could not be so designated by us now. Thus it has been said : 'Whatever a Pope may at any time declare *ex cathedra* concerning faith or morals is true.'Obviously the word 'true' cannot be eliminated from this context by the simple device of formulating expressions for all the papal pronouncements that may ever be made. But it can be eliminated nevertheless by a suitable use of propositional variables, as for example in the paraphrase, 'If a Pope speaking of faith or morals *ex cathedra* declares that p, then p'. And when this is done, it becomes clear that here too the role of the word 'true' is to provide a connexion between propositional designations and propositional expresion. For just as the letter 'p' in the apodosis of our new sentence marks a gap which may be filled by a propositional expression, so the phrase 'that p' in the protasis is a sign which would be converted into a propositional designation by substitution of a propositional expression for the letter 'p'. In formulating the paraphrase we have deliberately used a free, rather than a bound, variable to signify universality, because if we had begun our paraphrase with the quantifier 'for any p' the grammar of the English word 'any' would have suggested that the gaps marked by the letter 'p' were suitable only for designations, and that, of course, is not what we want here.

According to Frege each complete sign expresses a sense and designates something we have called its reference. But we have seen reason to believe that expression and designation are tasks performed by signs of different kinds, and this distinction seems to be important not only for the theory of truth but also for the solution of the difficulties which Frege finds in talking about functions. Just as the sentence 'The Pope is a man' may be said, to express a proposition, so the contributory sign '. . .is a man' may be said to express a propositional function. And though neither of these may properly be said to designate anything, we may, if it suits our convenience, construct signs to designate what they express. Thus 'humanity' and 'being a man' are common English designations for the attribute, or in Frege's terminology, the concept, which we assert of the Pope when we say that he is a man. Frege's troubles are due to the fact that he ignores the need for new signs and tries to use epxressions like 'ξ is a man' for the purpose of designation in spite of their unsuitability for the role. Admittedly he does not often write anything so obviously unsatisfactory as 'the concept, ξ is a man'; but in explanations of his script he often writes 'the concept ϕ (ξ)', and in general discussions he uses such awkward phrases as 'the concept *man*' or 'the concept "man". It is therefore not surprising that he sometimes feels uncomfortable and inclined to complain of the essential inadequacy of language. He assumes wrongly that the designation of a function should be incomplete or unsaturated like its expression, and yet he sees clearly that a sign which is appropriate for use as a predicate cannot also serve properly as a grammatical subject when we wish to talk about the function which it expresses.

In ordinary speech words such as 'humanity' work quite satisfactorily as designations of propositional functions, or attributes, because we are familiar with them and know well how to avoid all danger of confusing them with the corresponding expressions. When logicians suggest, as they sometimes do, that we ought to consider 'humanity' as an abbr-eviation for 'ξ's humanity', they make a mistake. Whereas it is permissible, though undesirable on stylistic grounds, to say 'Humanity is exemplified in the Pope', it is just nonsense to say 'ξ's humanity is exemplified in the Pope'. In a script such as Frege's, however, it is reasonable to expect rules more explicit than those of ordinary language, and if we wish to include designations of propositional functions we should try to show clearly how they are related to expressions. We can do this by adaptation of a device Frege uses in talking of ranges. Just as he writes *a*' (*a is a man*) for 'the class of men', so we may write *a* (*a is a man*) for 'humanity' or 'the character of being a man'. Here it is obvious that the new sign is derived from a functional expression with one gap, but there is not danger of confusion, because the letter inside the bracket is tied to the letter outside and the whole complex sign is obviously a designation. Inverting Frege's membership sign in order to get an expression for having or exemplifying (i.e. what Frege calls falling under a concept), we may then write $\Delta \cup \alpha\phi\ (\alpha)$ as an equivalent in our new notation for $\phi(\Delta)$. We do not suggest these innovations as the best possible symbolism for dealing with the problem, but simply in order to show that Frege's difficulties can be overcome quite easily with means like those he had at his disposal, provided quite easily with means like those he had at his disposal, provided always we recognize a clear distinction between expression and designation. Since $\Delta \cup \alpha\phi\ (\alpha)$ is a propositional expression of fairly complex construction, it naturally includes a functional expression, namely . . . . U - - -, but this should not worry us. For it is no par to four reform to suggeest that propositional expressions can be contructed from designations alone, and so we are untouched by the chief argument with which Frege tries to show the impossibility of talking directly about functions.

There is, however, a quite different consideration which should make us careful about talking of functions in logic. When Frege introduced the word, he thought of a logical function as one whose values were all truth-values. Those considered in primary logic were supposed by him to be from truth-values to truth-values, while those considered in general logic of the first level were supposed to be from objects of any kind to truth-functions and the latter propositional functions by many writers who do not accept Frege's theory of truth-values and perhaps have never examined it seriously. If, however, we come to the conclusion that Frege was wrong in describing an indicative sentence as the name of truth-value, we deny in effect the analogy which led Frege to adopt his functional terminology. Some successors of Frege have tried to think of a function in logic as one from this in the widest possible sense (i.e. in a wider sense that that of Frege's 'object') to propositions, and others use the phrase 'propositional function' as though it were merely a convenient way of referring to a sentence fragment such as ' . . .is wise' or '. . .loves---'. Neither of these explanations would have seemed satisfactory to Frege, and neither is sufficient to justify retention of his terminology. For a function in the proper mathematical sense is a pattern of correlation, not an expression, as the second explanation suggests; and the application of the sign of such a function (e.g.'√') to a designation (e.g. '2') is supposed to produce another designation (e.g. '√2'), not an expression, as the first explanation suggests.

It might therefore be better to abandon Frege's terminology altogether and adopt in its place some way of speaking which does not suggest inappropriate analogies. We might, for example, talk of truth-dependencies instead of truth-functions and of predicates in the logical sense instead of propositional functions or concepts. If we were engaged in the presentation of logic without regard to its history, this is the course we should follow. But in the rest of this work we shall have occasion to notice the writings of many logicians who have used the word 'function' without accepting Frege's theory of truth-values, and for convenience of exposition we shall follow their practice, contenting ourselves with the caution that where the word occurs in our own text it is to be understood as equivalent to one or other of the substitutes proposed above.

In some respects the positive account of truth sketched above is like that of A. Tarski in his paper called 'The Concept of Truth in Formalized Languages'.[2] And we certainly wish to claim for our account, as he does for his, the authority of Aristotle's famous definition of telling the truth as saying of that which is that it is or of that which is not that it is not.[3] But there is a very important difference between our view and that of Tarski. We hold that the adjective 'true' is applicable primarily to propositions, whereas he assumes that it is applicable primarily to sentences. The sentence 'Snow is white' is true, he tells us, if and only if snow is white. Here the sign beginning and ending with quotation marks is to be understood as a name or designation, and the purpose of the whole remark is to show how the necessary and sufficient condition for the truth of the sentence thus *mentioned* can be given by a *use* of that same sentence (or rather of that form of words). In short the main difference between this theory of truth and ours is that. Tarski talks about sentences where we wish to talk about propositions. But, as Tarski himself points out, difficulties arise when an attempt is made to turn his paradigm of explanation into a general definition by use of a variable, i.e. by writing:

For any p, 'p' is a true sentence ij and only if p.

For unless some special convention is made to the contrary effect (and it is very difficult, if no impossible, he says, to do this in a satisfactory manner), the sign which then begins and ends with quotation marks is not, as intended, a sort of functional sign which can be made into a name of a sentence by a suitable substitution for the letter within the quotation marks, but simply a designation of that letter. And he even goes on to argue that the possibility of constructing the paradox of the Liar within ordinary language shows that for this, as distinct from a formalized language of science, there can be no satisfactory definition of truth. This conclusion is so queer that it should make us suspicious of the assumptions from which it is derived; and the source of the trouble seems to be Tarski's unquestioned belief that truth is primarily a property of sentences.

When we are concerned with mathematical formula, (which especially interest Tarski) or with other phrases that resemble his example in not containing token-reflexive words (i.e. words which locate things or events by relation to the circumstances of their own utterance), Tarski's assumption leads to no serious difficulties. For we can certainly talk of the truth of a mathematical formula, and it does not seem absurd to speak of the truth of the general sentence 'Snow is white'. In either case we have to do with a complex sign-type which propounds the same proposition on each occasion of its use, and that is why we can discuss the truth of the sign much as we discuss the truth of the proposition it expresses. But these are special cases. A sentence of the commonest kind may be uttered at different times and in different circumstances to express different propositions, some true and some false. What Jones asserts by saying 'I am hungry' is not the same proposition as what Smith asserts by uttering the words at the same time, nor yet the same as what Jones asserted by uttering the words yesterday. And when we say, as we sometimes do, that a sentence was true at the time of speaking or writing, we obviously mean that it was used then to express a true proposition though it would not be used to that effect now. When he was not immediately interested in putting forward his own theory of truth, Frege was well aware of this feature of language. Writing against psychologism in logic, he says that we may perhaps describe the sentence 'I am hungry' as true for some men and false for others, or true in some circumstances and false in others, but only because it is used to express different propositions on different occasions. 'All determinations of space, time, etc. belong', he says, 'to the proposition (*Gedanke*) whose truth is under consideration : being true is itself spaceless and timeless.'[4]

In order to escape from these difficulties those who are inclined to agree with Tarski may perhaps say that the sentences to which they ascribe truth in the basic or primary sense are token utterances, that is to say passing events of speech. These are certainly not what Tarski himself had in mind when he wrote his paper, since they cannot be designated by designations of the kinds he discusses, namely quotation-mark names and structural-descriptive names built up by use of such devices as spelling. But we do sometimes use the word 'sentence' to refer to a thing of this sort, as when for example, we shay that a speaker paused for breath in the middle of his first sentence; and if we ascribe truth to such a thing, we sall at least have no difficulty about its possibly becoming false later on. It is clear, however, that when a token sentence is supposed capable of truth, the condition for its truth cannot be given by Tarski's device of saying 'if and only if' and then repeating the sentence under consideration. For a token sentence is not a form of words but a passing event and so cannot be *used* in this way any more than it can be *mentioned* in any of the ways in which Tarski mentions the sentences that interest him. Nor do we in fact talk commonly of the truth of token utterances. When they are considered in this connexion, it is usually as expressions for propositions.

It is one of Tarski's main contentions that the paradox of the Liar is due to an inconsistency whereby ordinary language allows for the application of its own words 'true' and 'false' to its own sentences. And he seems to be right in thinking that *semantical* considerations (as he calls arguments of the kind produced in his paper) require a distinction of language levels. For there is obviously a good sense in which the possibility of constructing the sentence '"Snow is white" is true' presupposes the possibility of constructing the sentence 'Snow is white'; and this reflection may be used to explain why the Liar's curious utterance fails to express any proposition at all. But it is a gratuitous paradox (in another sense of that word) to say that ordinary language is inconsistent because it claims universality or omnicompetence. Ordinary language is not a closed system, but whatever we make it in our talking; and if semantic considerations show the need for a distinction of language levels, the distinction will be made within ordinary language. For although natural languages such as English and French are in a certain sense alternatives to each other and to technical symbolism, ordinary language as Tarski discusses it is not an alternative to some extraordinary language which has been or may be devised by logicians for all the legitimate purposes now served by ordinary language. Rather, it is the matrix within which all other systems of communication are developed, and so not to be criticized like the unsuccessful production of a professional rival.

The anxiety of many logicians to insist that truth is an

affair of sentences rather than of propositions is due to a phobia of abstract entities, and this in turn seems to arise from two sources. The first, which has been noticeable among philosophers ever since Plato aroused opposition by his talk of a supersensible world, is an obsessive desire to be economical in thought. The second, which belongs to more recent history, is a violent reaction against all attempts to talk about the structure of the world. When such a phobia has been diagnosed, the patient should be encouraged, and even urged, to carry out his programme of elimination systematically instead of merely making oracular pronouncements. If he can be induced to persevere for a sufficiently long time, he may in this way be brought to realize that it is impossible for him to say all he wants to say without speaking of qualities, relations, beliefs, hypotheses, conclusions, and the rest. The cure will be complete when he is ready to admit that, although Plato and his followers fell into the absurdity of talking about the supersensible as if it were something that might be observed by a kind of super-sense, this is a very poor reason for holding that all attempts to designate supersensible objects are in some way improper. For if we are to talk at all about our use of language, we must allow ourselves to say that a sentence or a predicate phrase expresses something. And in order to say what it is that such a sign express we require not another expression but a designation, since, in any true expository statement of the form '. . .expresses---' the signs which fill the two blanks must both be designations, the first for an expression and the second for what that expression expresses. It is foolish therefore to deny ourselves this facility merely because it has sometimes been abused.

It is unlikely, however, that the programme of confining attention to sentences would ever have been widely adopted by logicians but for the fact that we have words which in some contexts mean the same as 'sentence' and in others the same as 'proposition'. In our examination of Bolzano's work we saw that the German word *Satz* is sometimes a grammatical term equivalent to 'sentence' or 'clause' but at other times indicates a law, theorem, principle, or proposition, i.e. something which can be expressed variously in different languages and described as true or false. In English the word 'sentence' is more narrowly specialized than *Satz* and not normally regarded as a proper subject for the adjectives 'true' and 'false'. But our word 'statement' is almost as versatile as *Satz* within a somewhat different range. For it can mean either an indicative sentence or the act of stating something; and apart from all these usages it can occur in the closely knit phrase 'make a statement', where it is not to be paraphrased separately. Those who find it plausible to ascribe truth to sentences seem to be influenced by the fact that 'indicative sentence' is linked as it is with 'statement' and through 'statement' with 'proposition'.

Sometimes, no doubt, mention of propositions arouses misgivings because writers such as Bolzano have assigned them to a queer limbo between language and reality. But it is mistake to suppose that use of the word 'proposition' need commit us to any unacceptable novelty. As they are commonly used in modern times, the words 'sentence' and 'proposition' serve for the making of two different classifications among actual and possible events of speech. Each such event is an utterance of a sentence, that is to say the production of an instance of a certain form of words which might in principle have other instances. For it is impossible to speak without speaking in some language, i.e. using repeatable signs.But we have seen that the several utterance of one type sentence may express different propositions according to the circumstances of their occurrence; and it is obvious also that a single proposition may be expressed by utterances of many different type sentences, since there is not just one language in which we must say all that we have to say. When grammarians use the word 'sentence' (as they commonly do) for a form of words, they wish to refer to the common features of utterances that resemble each other almost completely in sound or some other perceptible character but may differ considerably as vehicles of communication. An example is the sentence 'I have the pen of the gardener's wife' which generations of schoolboys have tried to translate into French without bothering to ask themselves 'What pen?' or 'What gardener?' When, on the other hand, logicians use the word 'proposition', they wish to refer to the common features of utterances that do substantially the same work of communication, except in respect of attitudes, though they may differ completely in sound or other perceptual character. Anyone who is frightened by what Bolzano says may, if he wishes, ascribe truth and falsity to the determinate propositional signs we here call utterances. But if he takes this line, he must, like Leibniz, recognize that truth cannot be an affair solely of actual utterances, since it makes sense to talk of the discovery of previously unformulated truths. And with the concession of truth to possible utterances, including those of non-human minds, he allows all that is required in the modern view of propositions. In short, there is not more dangerous abstraction involved in logicians' talk of propositions than in gammarians' talk of sentences, though the latter sometimes seems more readily acceptable because the notion of resemblance in perceptual character is easier to grasp than that of resemblance in function. As we shall see in a later section of this chapter, there are some peculiar problems about the way in which references to propositions may occur in discourse, but for the solution of these it is not necessary to go beyond the account of propositions we have sketched here.

THE THEORY OF DESCRIPTIONS AND THE VARIETY OF DESIGNATIONS

Frege introduced his distinction between sense and reference by consideration of the statement 'The morning star is identical with the evening star', and we have seen that it is well adapted to provide a solution for the question that worried him in this context. For while the two phrases 'the morning star' and 'the evening star' are designations of the same object, they obviously have different senses. But how is this admission to be reconciled with our attempt to show that expressions and designations are signs of radically diferent kinds? The answer is that these designations, like many others, are derivatie from expressions and may therefore be said to have sense in a derivative way. When we use the phrase 'the morning star' as a subject in a sentence, we do not thereby express the proposition that there is one and only one star frequently visible in the morning, but our use of the phrase presupposes acceptance of that proposition. In the language of everyday life a sentence containing the phrase 'the morning star' is said to imply that there is one and only one star frequently visible in the morning. This is not a usage of 'implies' much discussed in treatises of logic, but it is interesting and rather complicated. In one way implication of this kind seems to be less than expression. For if a man who has used a phrase implying a certain proposition goes on to formulate that proposition, we think that he has added something. In another way, however, implication of this kind is more than mere expression. For a man may express a proposition without manifesting or purporting to manifest belief in it; but if he uses a pharse which implies that proposition, he is understood to have committed himself, even though the sentence in which the phrase occurs is not indicative. Thus if a man invites a new acquiantance to visit him and say 'Please bring your wife', he does not assert the proposition that the acquaintance is married, but he certainly lets it be understood that he believes that proposition. To designate anything is to mark it down or single it out for attention; and so when a speaker uses a definite description in the singular as though he were trying to designate something, it is natural that he believes in the existence of one and only one thing answering to the description, since otherwise his procedure would be pointless. When a man is unsure of the truth of this existential proposition, he can qualifiy his remarks in an appropriate way. When, for example, he is uncertain whether a new acquaintace is married, he may say 'If you are married, please bring your wife'. In this context the description does not seem to single out for attention a determinate thing which might perhaps have been described in some other way. For the condtional clause has the effect of cancelling the commitment which would otherwise be conveyed by use of the definite description. In view of what many logicians have said it is perhaps worth noticing also that a definite description may occur in the plural, i.e. with an implication of the existence of *more than one* thing answering to it. We say,for example, 'The original apostles were all Jews'.

Frege was well aware that in ordinary language the use of a definite description as subject in a singular statement presupposed acceptance of a proposition not explicitly asserted, and he saw that if the description failed to designate anything the statement as a whole could not be said to be true or false. But he thought it important to insist on the application of the principle of excluded middle to all well-formed formulae of his own script, and he therefore undertook, as we have seen, to provide a reference of some sort for every definite description in his system, while admitting that sometimes the reference would be quite independent of the normal intention of a person using the description. Later logicians have tried to cope with the difficulty in other ways.

Whitehead and Russell proceed in *Principia Mathematica* as though the proposition which is ordinarily said to be implied by the use of a description were stated explicitly in the sentence containing the description. According to their view 'The King of France is bald' is equivalent to $(\exists c)\{(x)[K(x) \equiv x = c]. B(c)\}$, or 'There is a thing, say *c*, such that (i) a thing is King of France if and only if it is identical with *c*, and (ii) *c* is bald', which certainly expresses a false proposition if either there is no King of France or there are more than one[5]. But in order to maintain their view consistently they find it necessary to distinguish between primary and secondary occurrence of a description. Thus if anyone says 'The King of France is not bald' meaning $(\exists c)\{(x)[K(x) \equiv x{=}c].{\sim}B(c)\}$, the description has primary occurrence, whereas if he uses the same form of words meaning $\sim(\exists c)\{(x)[K(x) \equiv x{=}c].\ B(c)\}$, the description has secondary occurrence. It will be seen that in the first case the speaker is supposed to be committed to the existential implication of his description while in the latter case the whole sentence may express a true proposition even though there is not single King of France. In their own symbolism the distinction is made clear by a device something like the use of a quantifier to show the scope of a generalization. Thus our example of primary occurrence would be rendered by the formula $[(\; x)K(x)]\{\sim B(\iota x)\ K(x)]\}$ and our example of secondary occurrrence by the formula $\sim [(\iota x)K(x)]\{\sim B(\; x)K(x)]\}$.Here repetition of the description as a prefix to a bracketed expression is taken to indicate that the implication of the description belongs only to the bracketed expression. There is, however, a convention that for simplicity the prefix may be omitted when its scope would be the smallest bracketed expression in which the description occurs as a term.

Hilbert and Bernays, on the other hand, dispose of the difficulty by refusing to admit any definite description as a term until the proposition which it implies has already been proved.[6] From this ruling it follows that an arrangement of signs which is not admissible as a formula at one stage of development may nevertheless become admissible at another when more theorems have been demonstrated.

What are we to say of these three suggestions? Considered as rival proposals for legislation whereby the principle of excluded middle may be preserved in relation to formulae of the artificial language of mathematical logic, they are all alike respectable, but each has its peculiar advantages and disadvantages. Frege's scheme gives most liberty to the user of descriptions and is the easiest of the three to operate; but it is also the most arbitrary in its departure from ordinary usage. The scheme of Whitehead and Russell avoids extravagance and yet allows wide liberty to any user of descriptions who wishes to make everything explicit; but it does so only at the expense of a considerable complication of symbolism. The scheme of Hilbert and Bernays is very simple to operate and also very natural in the sense that it corresponds closely to the usage of natural langauges; but it restricts the liberty of a user of descriptions, and it makes the notion of a well-formed formula relative to the degree of development of the system, which may be regarded by some as a defect. For our own part, we prefer the third suggestion, but we think it would be a mistake to talk as though either of the other two were wrong in the context of mathematical logic.

Unfortunately discussion of the technical merits of these proposals has often been confused by philosophers with debates on other questions. This is due to the fact that Russell presented his proposal as a contribution to philosophical analysis. He maintained in the first place that what he said about definite descriptions in his mathematical logic was also a correct account of the way in which definite descriptions were used in ordinary language, and secondly that there was a distinction between descriptions and logically proper names corresponding to the distinction between two kinds of knowledge which he called knowledge by description and knowledge by acquaintance. We have already seen that the first of these contentions is mistaken, and we need say no more about it, except that Russell was led into error by his very reasonable desire to find an escape from the doctrine of Bolzano and Meinong, according to which the phrase 'the present King of France', being significant, must stand for something, though not necessarily for an existent.[7] But the second raises an interesting problem which we must notice here.

According to Russell a *logically proper name* is one used to designate an object of which the speaker is directly aware at the time of speaking, e.g. something which he sees in a basic and unanalysable sense of the word 'see', and it designates what it does without saying or implying anything about it. Ordinary proper names do not satisfy these strict standards. Thus 'Homer' is to be understood as equivalent to 'the author of the *Iliad*' or something like that, and is really a description. We can sensibly say 'Homer did not exist', if 'A' is a logically proper name. Russell admits, indeed, that it is difficult to find anything in ordinary speech which is a logically proper name, but he thinks the words 'this' and 'that', used with reference to sense data, may perhaps be cited as examples.[8] There is a good deal of dubious epistemology here which need not concern us, but it is interesting to notice that all three accounts of definite descriptions within mathematical logic seem to presuppose the possibility of designations which are not descriptions. For a definite description is constructed by use of a functional expression and it fulfils the normal intention of the user only if there is something satirfying the function. But if all designations are descriptions, justification of the use of a description seems to involve an infinite regress. For a proof that something is the one and only so-and-so will presumably involve reference to the thing by means of another designation. As might be expected, this argument to show that there must be designations which are not descriptions is most impressive when presented in connexion with Russell's account of descriptions. For according to him every statement in which a definite description has primary occurrence is an abbreviation for a complex existential statement, and every existential statement is constructed by application of a quantifier to a functional expression derived from a statement of simpler pattern by omission of one of its constituents. But Frege before him and Hilbert and Bernays after him have also talked as though there must be elementary statements of the subject-predicate pattern in which the subject is not a definite description but a proper name, attached in some more direct way to what it designates. To Hilbert and Bernays the point is of no great importance, because they are content to treat statements like '2+2=4' as elementary for their purposes. But it should have worried Frege more than it did, because he maintained that every designation has a sense which suggests at least that they are all descriptions.

In a footnote to his article *Über Sinn und Bedeutung* Frege writes :

'In the case of an actual proper name such as "Aristotle" opinion as to the sense may differ. It might for instance, be taken to be the following: the pupil of Plato and teacher of Alexander the Great Anyone who does this will attach another meaning to the sentence "Aristotle was born in Stagira" than will a man who takes as the sense of the name: the teacher of Alexander the Great who was born in Stagira. So long as the reference remains the same,, suc variations of sense may be tolerated, although they are to be avoided in the theoretical structure of a demonstrative science and ought not to occur in a perfect language.[9]

This is unsatisfactory, because it confuses the sense of the name with what it suggests to this or that hearer and so obscures the peculiar character of ordinary proper names. A man who had learnt the word 'Aristotle' from a classical dictionary but remembered nothing of the article there except that Aristotle was born in Stagira would not for this reason regard the statement 'Aristotle was born in Stagira as a pointless remark like 'The man born in Stagira was born in Stagira'. On the other hand, he would certainly agree that it was useless to say 'Aristotle is called Aristotle'. The moral of this is obvious. An ordinary proper name works like a definite description which has for its implication or presupposition the existence of something called by that name in the circle of the speaker and the hearer. Some, such as the personal name 'Tommy', imply in addition that the thing so called is of a certain kind, e.g. a young male human being. And when necessary the selective power of any proper name may be reinforced by additional words, as in 'your Tommy', 'Jones minor', 'the London in Ontario'. Proper names, like descriptions, may admittedly be used sometimes without an implication of existence, i.e. when they are forced to commit suicide. But the fact that it seems slightly paradoxical to say 'Homer never existed' shows clearly that the normal use of a proper name presupposes the existence of something called by the name. Thus the words 'New College' became a proper name when they were first used by the inhabitants of Oxford as though they were equivalent to the phrase 'the college to which people here commonly refer when they say "New College"'.

To say, as Russell does, that ordinary proper names are a kind of definite descriptions may be confusing, but it is clear that ordinary proper names and definite descriptions raise the same problems, since their use implies, but does not guarantee, the existence of things of which they are designations. Is it then reasonable to look for what Russell calls logically proper names? According to his explanation, if 'A' is a logically proper name, it is not merely pointless, but senseless, to say 'A exists', because, although 'A' must designate something, it must do so without implying possession of any character by the thing. This seems to be an impossible requirement. For designation is essentially the selection of something for attention by means of a sign, and a sign which is to serve this purpose must have some implication, though this need be no more than the notion that there is something which it designates for a certain group of persons. When, however, Russell says that a word cannot be a logically proper name unless it designates something of which the speaker is immediately aware, he introduces another requirement of a very different sort. For this pronouncement suggests that what he wants is not a designation without any existential implication but rather a designation whose implication is guaranteed true. Now the theory of knowledge which he presents in this connexion may be wrong, and it must be admitted in any case that the knowledge which he ascribes to the speaker cannot furnish any guarantee to the hearer, but it is very interesting to note that there is at least one designation for the hearer as well as for the speaker. This is the word 'I'.

Not all token reflexive pronouns have this peculiar property. When a timid person thinks mistakenly that there is someone under his bed and summons up courage to say 'You had better come out', his token 'you' fails to designate anything, though he utters it sincerely. And when in the story of *The*

Emperor's New Clothes a courtier is represented as saying 'This is fine stuff' though he cannot see any cloth in the hands of the rascally tailors, it is made clear that the word 'this' can be used for purposes of deception in such a way that it designates nothing. But neither false belief nor bad faith (as distinct from dramatic convention) can lead to a use of 'I' in which it fails to designate something. And that, of course, is why Augustine and Descartes were especially interested in the sentence 'I exist'. Whereas 'You do not exist' and 'This does not exist' are merely self-stultifying remarks, 'I do not exist' is self-refuting. For here the denial of existence is incompatible not only with the existential proposition implied by the use of the subject term, but also with the fact that the remark has been made. It would be a mistake, however, to suppose that the word 'I' enjoys a unique privilege among signs used for reference. Although the adverbs 'here' and 'now' can scarcely be called designations, their task is to help in the selection of objects for attention, and they cannot fail to do their part satisfactorily. If a man purports to speak of something that happened in Lyonnesse in the reign of King Arthur, he may believe mistakenly that there is a place called Lyonnesse and that there was once a king called Arthur, or he may conceivably intend to mislead others into such beliefs; but no use of the words 'here' and 'now' can be imporoper in either of these ways. The reason is obvious: 'here' and 'now', like 'I', presuppose in use no more than what must be the case because there is an utterance. In a language with well-developed syntax they appear as three signs among others used for the purpose of reference, but they are peculiar in adding nothing to what is implicit already in a unitary expression. When a man shouts 'Help', he gives us to understand quite adequately by this single word that he the speaker wants help at the place and at the time of his speaking.

In the last resort all reference to particular things or events in space and time consists in the location of them by relation to the act of speech. For just as a proper name like

'Socrates' singles a thing out for attention as that which is called by the name in the circle to which speaker and hearer belong, so a description like 'the milkman' does its work by supplying enough detail to identify an object *in the context of speech*. And even more fundamental than either of these is the use of tenses or temporal particles to mark the time of an event by relation to the time of speaking. In an artificial language where the rules of usage of a symbol take on account of its context of utterance it is impossible to express any singular propositions about matter of fact, and so a script like Frege's can be no more than a supplement to a natural language, extremely useful for precise discussion of the relations of generalities in mathematics and natural science, but inadequate by itself for the ordinary purposes of life and also for metaphysical analysis. In fact the only designations ever used in mathematical logic by Frege and his successors are symbols for abstract entities such as universals, classes, and numbers. Like all designations, these do their work only because they have implications in the sense explained above, but their implications are of a sort that no one could reasonably deny, and so they usually pass unnoticed. Thus anyone who speaks of humanity, or of being a man, assumes quite naturally that there is something which all men have or would have in common. This presupposition of the usage has never been called into question except by persons who have an obsessive fear of metaphysics, and their caution is obviously misplaced, since the things to which a general term is applied must at the very least have in common the feature of being things to which the term is applied. Similarly anyone who uses the numeral '2' as a designation in sentences such as '2 is the smallest prime number' thinks that it stands for an object because he assumes that there is something common to all sets that have two members. In this case it is not so easy to explain the connexion of the noun with the adjective from which it has been derived in historical times, but it is clear at least that no one can attribute any meaning to a statement about a natural number without recognizing the possibility of using the corresponding numeral in the counting of objects of any kind.

The upshot of our discussion may be summarized as follows. The activity of designation is not the paradigm of all sign-using, but something incidental to the expression of propositions in languages which have reached the syntactical level of development. A sign called a designation may be said to have a sense, not because it is itself an expression of anything (for it is not), but because its use presupposes acceptance of an existential proposition. If it is singular, it implies the existence of just one thing of a certain kind; if it is plural, it implies the existence of more than one thing of that kind. A designation of the sort for which Russell coined the technical term 'definite description' is a phrase derived in fairly obvious fashion form a functional expression which could be used in a formulation of the existential proposition it implies. An ordinary proper name, say 'Socrates', in equivalent in use to a description of the form 'the thing called Socrates', though it would be a mistake to treat it as an abbreviation for such a description, since it is presupposed by the phrase 'called Socrates' and is therefore obviously more primitive. Similarly token-reflexive words like 'you' and 'this' are equivalent in use to descriptions such as 'the person I am now addressing' and 'the thing to which I am now attending'. If the proposition implied by a designation is false, the designation fails to designate anything. But there is one designation, 'I', which cannot fail to designate something whenever it is used by a speaker in accordance with its grammatical conventions. It has this peculiarity because it serves only to make explicit something which is implicit already in any unitary expression. For a proper understanding of the role which designations of particular things and events play at the syntactical level of discourse, it is desirable indeed to remember at all times that complex sentences work as wholes in the same way as unitary expressions and may therefore express different propositions in different contexts. Designations which are supposed to stand for abstract entities raise special problems, but they too involve implications of existence, though this fact may be over looked until the implications are debated by philosophers.

PROBLEMS OF INTENSIONALITY

In modal logic we talk of propositions, ascribing to them attributes such as possibility and relations such as strict implication. It is therefore necessary that our symbolism should provide in some way for the designation, as well as for the expression, of propositions. Lewis and most other writers on the subject avoid the introduction of any special new symbolism by assuming tacitly that whenever a propositional expression occurs in a place appropriate for a designation of a proposition it shall be read as though it were preceded by some prefix such as 'the proposition that . . .' Thus $\Diamond P$ is taken as an abbreviation for *It is possible* that -*P* and $P \rightarrow Q$ as an abbreviation for *The proposition that- P strictly implies the proposition that-Q*. In the last chapter we introduced the sign as a prefix for converting the expression of a proposition into a designation, but stipulated that it could be omitted when it might conveniently be supposed to have been absorbed by a special modal sign such as that of Lewis,. Obviously there is nothing to be gained from printing it in contexts where omission leads to no misunderstanding, though it may be useful on occasions as a reminder of the fact that the statements we make in modal logic are about propositions and have designations of propositions for their grammatical subjects and objects. The construction with which we have to deal here is like that of indirect speech. As Frege noticed in his article *Uber Sinn und Bedeutung,* a clause beginning with 'that' has for reference that which would be the sense of the words if they appeared without 'that'.

Since the effect of the sign § is to convert expressions of propositions into designations of the same, it may be used also in the symbolism of logic to construct designations of propositional functions in a fashion that evades Frege's difficulties. That is to say, we may write §*xFx* when we wish to refer to the sense of the functionalk sign *Fx* and similarly §*xyG*(*x*,*y*) when we wish to refer to the sense of *G*(*x*, *y*). Here a letter or letters must be inserted after to bind the variable or variables in the functional expression which follows, and § can no longer be read as though it were an abbreviation for 'the proposition that'. But just as *P* can be taken as short for 'that which is true if *P*', so the more complex sign §*xFx* can be taken as short for 'that which is true of *x* if *Fx*'. And it is an advantage to have a symbolism which brings together propositions and propositional functions. For talk about them gives rise to similar problems. In philosophical discussions of logic they are often grouped together as intensions by way of contrast with truth-values (regarded as objects), classes, and individuals, which are all called extensions. The terminology of 'intension' and 'extension' was originally introduced, as we have seen, for discussion of general terms, but the modern usage has arisen by a natural development and may be accepted as a conveinent way of discussing related topics. Sometimes it is said also that a definite description such as 'the King of France' has an intension, namely an individual concept such as being the sole king of France.[10] Whether or not we like this terminology, we can agree that a description of the form (ιx) *Fx* must have a sense, and when there is occasion to talk directly of that sense we may, if we wish, designate it by a complex sign of the form §[*(fx' y) (Fy⊃ y =x)*]. In all three permissible cases the presenting of § to an expression (delimited if necessary by brackets) makes a designation for the sense of that which follows, and so the prefix may perhaps be called an intensional abstractor.

A language as a whole may be said to be intensional if it allows for the designation of intensions where such designation is essential i.e. not eliminable by deflationary translation like that from *it a true that-P* to *P*. Obviously all the natural languages of avilised peoples qualify for this title. And so also does Lewis's symbolism, since it is a tacit convention of his script that a sign occurring as the grammatical subject of the predicate ◊ or as the subject or the object of the verb → shall be taken to be a designation of what is ordinarily expresses: we noticed earlier that there is a similar convention in ordinary English about clauses which follow the verb 'say' but are not introduced by 'that'. It is possible, however, to conceive languages in which intensions can be expressed but never designated: these are said to be extensional. The terminology is a little confusing, because those who are familiar with the history of the words naturally start by thinking of an intension as something expressed and an extension as something designated; but if we are to make use of the words in this context, we must free ourselves from that association and think of an extension as being either an individual, a class, or a truth-value and of an intension as being either an individual concept (if this rather queer phrase may be allowed), a propositional function, or a proposition. It is possible, as we have seen, to have a rudimentary language in which propositions can be expressed but nothing at all designated. According to the definition given above, such a language would be extensional. If it were enriched by functional expressions and designations of individuals and classes, it would still remain extensional: But if designations of propositions, propositional functions, and individual concepts were added, it would become intensional. In short, the difference is one in respect of the types of entities which languages admit as subjects of discourse, and an intensional language is essentially more complicated than an extensional, since it allows both expression and designation of that for which an extensional language more complicated than an extensional, since it allows both expression and designation of that for which an extensional language would allow only expression.

In his article *Über Sinn und Bedeutung* Frege recognized clearly the possibility of taking propositions as subjects of discourse, but in his *Begriffsschrift* and again in his *Grundgesetze der Arithmetik* he made no provision for this or any other feature of intensional language. Presumably the reason, for this omission was that he saw no need of intensional language for the presentation of mathematics. In the first edition of *Principia Mathematica* Whitehead and Russell follow the same course. While recognizing the possibility of intensional statements such as 'Socrates believed that his soul was immortal', they confine their discussion for the most part to the characteristics of extensional statements. But there appears in the *Begriffsschrift* and again in *Principia Mathematica* a logical principle.

$$x = y \supset (fx \supset fy)$$

which seems at first sight to be inconsistent with the admission of intensional statements. It is in effect the converse of Leibniz's principle of the identity of indiscernibles, 'Eadem sunt quorum unum potest substitui alteri salva veritate', and it may perhaps be called the principle of the indiscernibility of identicals.[11] So far as we know, it has not been questioned even by those philosophers who find Leibniz's assertion unplausible, yet it seems to have extraordinary consequences. Let us suppose, for example, that we substitute '12' for x, 'the sum of the third and fourth prime numbers' for y, and 'the Pope knows that the number of the apostles is . . .' for f. Then we get a true statement for $x = y$ and another true statement for fx, but two applications of the *modus ponens* yield the conclusion 'The Pope knows that the number of the apostles is the sum of the third and fourth prime numbers', which, to say the least, is very doubtful. By similar arguments we can prove paradoxes in the theory of modality, as for example that any true statement of identity is necessarily true. For the morning star is identical with the evening star and the morning star satisfies the function expressed by the words 'it is necessary that the morning star is identical with . . .'. Therefore, it seems, the evening star must also satisfy the function, i.e. it is necessary that the morning star is identical with the evening star.

How are we to deal with this awkward situation? In his *Tractatus Logico-Philosophicus* (5.54) Wittgenstein asserts that one propositional sign can occur in another only as an argument of a truth-function. As it stands, this statement is clearly false, since the propositional sign 'it will rain tomorrow' does not appear as an argument of a truth-function in the sentence 'Brown thinks that it will rain tomorrow'. But it may perhaps be taken as an epigrammatic way of saying that every utterance made in an intensional language can be translated without loss into an extensional language. The Thesis of Extensionally, as it is now called, was adopted by Russell in the introduction to the second edition of *Principia Mathematica,* published in 1925, and defended at length by Carnap in his *Logical Syntax of Language,*[12] first published in 1934.

Complex signs of the kind we construct with our intensional abstractor can be celiminated very easily from some contexts where they occur together with expressions specially designed for reversing the work of the abstractor. Thus the sentence §*P is true* can be replaced by *P* and §*yFy is true of X* by *FX*. But these are special cases. In general Carnap relies on a method of reduction in which designations of intensions are replaced by designations of expressions while predicates which are appropriate to intentions are replaced by corresponding predicates appropriate to expressions. Thus 'Brown thinks that it will rain tomorrow' is reduced on his principles to 'Brown says to himself with a feeling of conviction "It will rain tomorrow"', 'It is necessary that 7+5 = 12' to 'The statement '7+5 = 12' is analytic', 'Plato wrote a book about justice' to 'Plato wrote a book containing the word "justice" or some equivalent', and so forth. When a sentence or phrase occurs in the translation within quotation marks, it is to be understood as forming part of a designation for itself, and must therefore not be construed as a grammatical constituent of the main sentence. In particular it must not be supposed that a word or phrase which occurs as part of such a sentence within quotation marks may be replaced at will by another which happens to have the same reference. For the conventions of quotation allow us to use ' "7+5 = =12" as a designation for the sentence

'7+5 = 12'. but they certainly do not allow us to use ' "7+5 = the number of the apostles" ' as a designation for the sentence '7+5 = 12'. From this consideration, it seems, we can immediately obtain a solution for our puzzles. When, for example, we realize that the statement. 'It is necessary that the morning star is identical with the morning star' means the same as "The sentence "The morning star is identical with the morning star" is analytic', we can see that it is not about the morning star but about a certain set of words, and that there is no function expressed by the jargon phrase 'It is necessary that the morning star is identical with *x*' any more than there is by the words 'The sentence "The morning star is identical with *x*" is analytic'.

Objections may be raised to some of the reductions by which Carnap illustrates his thesis. We may doubt, for example, whether all thinking is speaking to oneself. But the thesis is undoubtedly very plausible. When we first hear of the paradoxes of intensionality, we feel inclined to say that being necessarily identical with the morning star is not a real attribute of idependently existing objects, such as we had in mind when we first read Frege's existing objects, such as we had in mind when we first read Frege's principle of the indiscernibility of identicals, but rather something connected with human language; and thesis of extensionality gives precision to this idea. If we reject thc thesis, our reason should not be merely dissatisfaction with some of Carnap's illustrations, but rather an objection of principle to his way of dealing with intensional statements; and it is therefore best to take for critical examination a simple case of indirect speech, that is to say, a case in which it seems most plausible to say that the use of intensional language is only a substitute for a report of words actually uttered.

Let us consider, then, the statement 'Cavemen told their children that fire hurts'. This is easily understood, but no intelligent person who hears it supposes that cavemen said to their children the English words 'Fire hurts', or indeed any other words of any known language. If it is insisted that the statement must really be about the sounds which the cavemen uttered, the best reduction we can offer is 'Cavemen said to their children some phrase which meant in their language the same as "Fire hurts" now means in English'. This must be true if the original is true, and conversely if this is true the original must be true. It should be noticed, however, that the remark attributed to the cavemen is specified here by its equivalence in meaning to an English sentence. If we follow this method, we avoid an obvious return to intensional language such as would be involved in saying 'Cavemen said to their children some phrase which meant in their language that fire hurts'. And we do not even commit ourselves to any view about meaning which could conceivably be thought dangerous. For we say only that the phrase used by cavemen meant the same in their language as a certain English sentence means now, and it may be that the notion of having the same meaning can be explained satisfactorily without what is sometimes called abusively the reification or hypostatization of meaning. But the reduction we offer is nevertheless unsatisfactory because it introduces a reference to the English language which was not in the original.[13]

How can we avoid this unwanted reference without returning to the use of a 'that' clause? Only by allowing ourselves that looser use of direct speech which is common in translations. When a fundamentalist reads in his bible 'God said : Let there be light', he may possibly believe that God uttered certain words of Hebrew; but unless he is very silly, he does not assume that God said anything in English. So too if we produce the statement Cavemen said to their children "Fire hurts"', persons of intelligence will not understand us to imply that cavemen spoke English, and anyone who takes the trouble to translate our remarks into French will translate the words inside the quotation marks as well as the rest. But this device of quasi-quotation is itself a variety of intensional language. For in this context ' "Fire hurts" ' does not occur as a designation of the English sounds corresponding to the marks

'Fire hurts', but rather as an equivalent of the phrase 'that fire hurts'. Sometimes indeed the two devices approach so closely in spoken English that it is pointless to ask which has been used. If a small child who has been cautioned by a foreigner against playing with matches asks his mother 'What does he say?', the mother's reply may be represented in print equally well by 'He says "Fire hurts" 'or by 'He says fire hurts'. Nor is this surprising; for there can be little doubt that in all languages the main devices for designating intensions have evolved from quasi-quotation of words or phrases sufficient to express those intentsions.

Carnap, who has been that most vigorous proponent of the thesis of extensionality, does not claim that it is a necessary truth, and the considerations which we have just put forward suggest that its plausibility is due to an important but little discussed ambiguity in our use of inverted commas. Although Carnap professes to replace intensional statements by statements that refer only to symbols, he cannot in fact make his translations seem acceptable except by allowing each symbol he mentions to retain its linguistic status. In short his quotation marks do not, as he thinks, indicate mention as distinct from use, but rather a special use which is founded on mention and amounts in effect to designation of the sense which the symbol would express if it occurred without quotation marks. It is possible, nevertheless, to learn something from the extensionalist attempt to deal with the paradoxes of intensionality. For an intensional abstractor works in some ways like inverted commas.

In any propositional expression which contains a designation of any kind the sense of the whole depends on the sense of the designation as well as on the sense of the other signs occurring in the expression, but in the simple cases which are called extensional the truth-value of the proposition expressed by the whole does not depend on the sense of the designation as distinct from its reference. Thus the proposition that the morning star goes round the sun in distinguishable from the proposition that the evening star goes round the sun, but they have the same truth-value, because the morning star is identical with the evening star. This is the purport of the principle of the indiscernibility of identicals. On the other hand, in the more complicated cases which are called intensional the truth-value of the whole may well depend on the sense of some designation contained within a propositional designation which itself forms part of the whole. Thus it is true that it is necessary that the morning star is the morning star, but not true that it is necessary that the morning star is the evening star. In general, whatever the letters *F, G,* and *H* may signify, the truth-value of the proposition expressed by $F\,\{\S G[(\iota x)Hx]\}$ depends on the reference of $\S G[(\iota x)Hx]$, and this depends on the sense of $\S G[(\iota x)Hx]$, and this in turn depends on the sense of $(\iota x)\,Hx$, so that from the equation.

$$(\iota x)Hx = (\iota y)\mathrm{F}y,$$

which guarantees only identity of reference, we cannot safely conclude

$$F\{\S G[(\iota x)Hx]\} \equiv F\{\S G[(\iota y)\mathrm{F}y]\}$$

In such a case the intensional abstractor, which directs attention to the sense of the sign falling within its scope, serves also as a reminder against reliance on the principle of the indiscernibility of identicals to justify substitution within that scope.

Our task would be greatly simplified if we could go on to say that no expression of the form $F(\S Gy)$ ever expresses a propositional function. For then we should have an almost exact parallel between the rules for the use our intensional abstractor and those for the use of quotation marks: the principle of the indiscernibility of identicals could be accepted without qualification or restriction, and there would be no puzzles about quantifiers operating across intensional abstractors to bind variables within the scope of such abstractors, because there would be no meaningful expressions with quantifiers in that position. But the fact of ordinary usage are against this sweeping suggestion. In English the sentence 'There was he thing he said he liked' is clearly distinguishable in meaning from 'He said there was one thing he liked' and there can be no doubt that the first has the form $(\exists y)F(\S Gy)$. Being thought stupid by Lenin, being suspected of opportunism by Trotsky, being feared as a rival by Stalin— these are all intensional functions (or predicates), and anyone who reads through a newspaper with an interest in the question at issue can easily find expressions for many more. In this connexion it is important, of course, to distinguish between $F(\S Gy)$ and $F(Gy)$. Whereas the former expresses an intensional function which may have as a value the proposition expressed by $F(GZ)$, the latt-er expresses an intensional proposition about the function designated by $\S yGy$; and it is precisely in order to preserve this distinction that the argument in the latter must be bound by another y inserted immediately after the §.

Our troubles arise from the fact that there are intensional functions and that some of them cannot be satisfied by an object as such but only by an object considered as falling under a certain description. Thus Ocdipus wished to kill the haughty stranger who ordered him to give way on the narrow road from Delphi to Phocis, but he did wish to kill his father, although the haughty stranger was in fact his father. If anyone says that functions like this have a special status in logic because their expressions occur only in second-order discourse (i.e. discourse that presupposes a simpler use of symbols in the sense of being about what they express, though not about them directly), we can agree very readily; but there seems no good reason for denying that they are functions, and once that point is conceded, it becomes clear that the only way out of our perplexities is to qualify the principle of the indiscernibility of identicals by making it apply only to extensional (i.e non-intensional) functions.

To insist on the principle of the indiscernibility of identicals is to say in effect that for the context of our assertion we recognize none but extensional functions. To qualify it in the way just suggested is to admit that if Fx expresses an intensional function we cannot argue *formally* from the two premisses Fx and $X=Y$ *to the conclusion* Fy. Sometimes no doubt the nature of an intensional context shows clearly enough that one name or description can be substituted for another *salva veritale*, but it is a mistake to hope for rules of substitution valid in all such contexts. Let us suppose, for example, that there is no doubt of the truth of the statement 'St Thomas Aquinas said that the Philosopher's doctrine of the soul was correct'. May we repeat it with 'Aristotle' substituted for 'the Philosopher'? Surely. For even if St. Thomas wrote the Latin word *Philosophus* rather than *Aristotels* in the passage which we profess to report, our substitution is well within the bounds of the license permitted by custom to a user of indirect speech. It may be argued, indeed, that for many readers our new version will be preferable to the original, as being less open to misunderstanding. May we, then, if we wish, substitute the Stagirite' for 'the Philospher' ? It is impossible to give a simple answer. In the eighteenth century there would probably have been no harm in the change, because almost every reader would have recognized the phrase as a modern description of Aristotle, introduced for reasons of literary fashion, and therefor been under no temptation to suppose that St. Thomas identified Aristotle by reference to his birthplace. In the twentieth century some readers would recognize the eighteenth-century mannerism, but others might conceivably be misled into thinking that St. Thomas mentioned Stagira, and others again who did not know the Aristotle was born at Stagira might even suppose that St. Thomas had in mind another person. There can be no formal rules of substitution valid for intensional contexts, because the notions of saying, believing, knowing, wishing, intending, etc., which we often express by means of intensional language are not formal notions. There are indeed conventions to be observed in contexts of various kinds (for without conventions of some sort there could be no communication such as we have in fact), but it would be misleading to speak of these subjects of study for logic. Logic, as we consider it in this book, is concerned with the forms of propositions as distinct from their subject-matter, and the only part of the theory of intensional statements which can properly be called formal is pure modal logic. It is not surprising therefore that this has aroused most interst among logicians.

In a true modal statement, either of the form $\Box\S G[(\iota x)Hx]$ or of the form $\Diamond\, G[(\iota x)Hx]$, substitution of $(\iota y)\, Fy$ for $(x)Hx$ may lead to falsity, or even to absurdity, if it cannot be authorized by anything more than a contingent assertion.

$$(\iota x)Hx = (\iota y)\ Fy.$$

Thus it would be ridiculous to argue form the modal premises

$$\Diamond\ \S(12 < 13)$$

and the historical truth

$$12 = \textit{the number of the apostles}$$

to the modal conclusion

$$\Box\ \S(\textit{the number of the apostles} < 13).$$

Nor is it sufficient to say, as in **Theophrastus'** theory of modal syllogisms, that the conclusion must agree in modality with the weaker premiss. For it is equally ridiculous to argue form the modal premiss.

$$\Diamond\S{\sim}(\textit{the number of the apostles} < 13)$$

and the historical truth

$$\textit{The number of the apostles} = 12$$

to the modal conclusion

$$\Diamond\S{\sim}(12 < 13).$$

On the other hand, substitution can be made in all such contexts *salva veritate* when the designation which is to be substituted has *necessarily* the same reference as that which it is to replace, e.g. when '7+5' is to be put for '12'. This is not to say that the result of substitution will then be an expression with exactly the same sense as the original, but simply that the change will make no difference to the truth-value of the whole. Two designations which have necessarily the same reference may nevertheless be different in sense, and so capable of making a difference in sense between two otherwise similar expressions in which they occur, but they must be so related that either can replace the other in a modal context without falsification. In order to understand why this is so let us consider once more the way in which designations occur in modal contexts.

If the proposition expressed by $\Box\S G[(\iota x)Hx]$ is true, the reason must be either that the propositional function expressed by Gy holds for all possible arguments or that it is entailed by the sense of the designation $(\iota x)Hx$. For an example of the first situation we may take the statement 'It is necessary that the last Stuart queen should be either dead or not dead'. Since everything must be either dead or not dead, we may replace 'the last Stuart queen' here by any other designation of the same general type without affecting the truth-value of the whole. For an example of the second situation we may take the statement 'It is necessary that the last Stuart queen was woman'. Here the sense of the designation is all-important. If we wrote instead 'the last Stuart monarch', we should still succeed in referring to Queen Anne, but our new staement would still swucceed in referring to Quee Anne, case, however, the existential presupposition of the designation used by the speaker is no part of what he declares to be necessary. He believes presumably that there was a last Stuart queen, but not that *this* is necessary, and he can if he wishes make the point clear either by adding the words 'if indeed there was such a queen 'or by recasting the whole statement in the form 'The last Stuart queen would necessarily be a woman'. For these new ways of speaking leave the substance of the modal assertion unaltered while cancelling the commitment ordinarily implied by use of a designation. In logical symbolism we can produce the same effect by introducing $H'x$ as an abbreviation for $Hx(y)\ [Hy \supset y = x]$, i.e. with the sense of *x is the only H thing,* and then writing $\Box\S(x)[H'x\ Gx]$ in place of $\Box\S G[(\iota x)Hx]$.

Modal assertions from which designations have been eliminated in this way may be said to be in reduced form. If the propositional function expressed by *Gx* is truistic, □§(*x*)[*H'x Gx*] must be true, whatever *Hx* may signify, and so the f`irst of the two cases we distinguished above may be subsumed under the second.

In this argument we have assumed, of course, that any designation which appears in a modal context may be treated as a definite description or as an abbreviation for such, e.g. that 'Queen Anne' may be treated as an abbreviation for 'the Queen called "Anne," and '12' as an abbreviation for 'the number common to all sets which are equivalent in Cantor's sense to the set of numerals {"1", "2", "3", . . ., "12"}'. This procedure is forced on us by the need for attending in such contexts to the sense of our designations. In extensional contexts, for which the principle of the indiscernibility of identicals holds without restriction, proper names may be used without much thought of their sense, so that substitution of 'Napoleon' for 'Bonaparte' or *vice versa* seems sometimes to be no more than a matter of style. But the situation is very different in modal contexts. For it is said to be necessary that Napoleon is identical with Napoleon but merely contingent that Napoleon is identical with Bonaparte; and in order to understand this we must, as Frege argued, pay attention to differences of sense, i.e. we must think of the two names as though they were abbreviations for descriptions. It is certainly not necessary that there existed a person called 'Napoleon'; but it is necessary that the sole person called 'Napoleon', if there is any such, should be identical with the sole person called 'Napoleon'.[14]

Returning now to the problem of substitution in modal contexts, let us suppose that we have for a datum

$$\Box\S[(\iota x)Hx = (\iota y)\ \mathrm{F}y].$$

From this there follows in accordance with ordinary rules for the use of definite descriptions the formula §H'[(ιx)Fx], and by the procedure explained above this in turn can be reduced to $\Box\S(x)[\mathrm{F}'x\ H'x]$. But the statement

$$\Box\S G(\iota x)Hx]$$

can be reduced to $\Box\S(x)[Hx\ \iota Gx]$, and so it is easy to see that with the supposition of necessary identity set out above it must entail the consequence $\Box\S(\mathrm{F}x)[x \supset Gx]$, which itself is the reduced form of

$$\Box\S G[(\iota x)\ \mathrm{F}x].$$

By a similar argument it can be shown that necessary identity of reference in two designations is a sufficient condition for the replacement of either by the other *salva veritate* in a statement of possibility.

When we turn to consider the possibility of using quantifiers to operate across modal signs and therefore across intensional abstractors, it is natural to suppose that the relations between formulae which combine modal signs in various ways with quantifiers must be governed by rules like those for the relations between formulae which combine modal signs in various ways with signs of conjunction or disjunction. Now the latter are generally agreed and can be set out in the following diagram, where for brevity and case of comparison we have introduced the convention of omitting from each formula the intensional abstractor which would follow in an unabbreviated version immediately after the modal sign:

Obviously, therefore, analogy requires that the former should be as indicated in the corresponding diagram where universal quantification takes the place of conjunction and existential quantification the place of disjunction :

Formulae of the inner ring are those which raise no problem because their quantifiers occur within the scope of their modal signs, while those of the outer ring are the debatable formulae which have quantifiers operating across modal signs. The unnumbered arrows represent entailments guaranteed by generally accepted principles of logic, while those to which numbers have been assigned represent entailments suggested by the analogy mentioned above.[15] It will be noticed that entailments of the latter group are the only links between formulae of the two rings, and that they are not all mutually independent. By substitution and contraposition (3) can be derived from (1) and (4) from (2), or vice versa. If these relations are all accepted, the square and the diamond prefixes of modal logic may be said to behave like new universal and existential quantifiers respectively. This again is what analogy would lead us to expect. For when we say that a proposition is necessary, we mean that it would be true in all conceivable worlds, and when we say that a proposition is possible, we mean that it would be true in some conceivable world.

Admittedly it is not easy to find examples which make all the numbered relations intuitively plausible. But it may perhaps be argued that the reason for this is the same as the reason for the difficulties some logicians feel about the reduction principles of modal logic. In natural languages modal words undoubtedly occur sometimes after quantifiers; but wherever they occur, they are nearly always used in elliptic fashion, i.e.

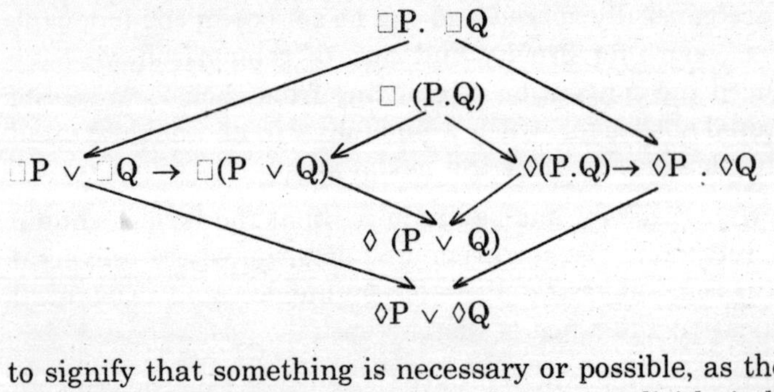

to signify that something is necessary or possible, as the case may be, in relation to something else not explicitly indicated but easily identified by the hearer. In the technical symbolism, of modal logic, on the other hand, everything is supposed to be made explicit. If, then, we try to render the sense of the technical symbolism in ordinary speech, we may find ourselves in difficulties because the words we use suggest supplementation

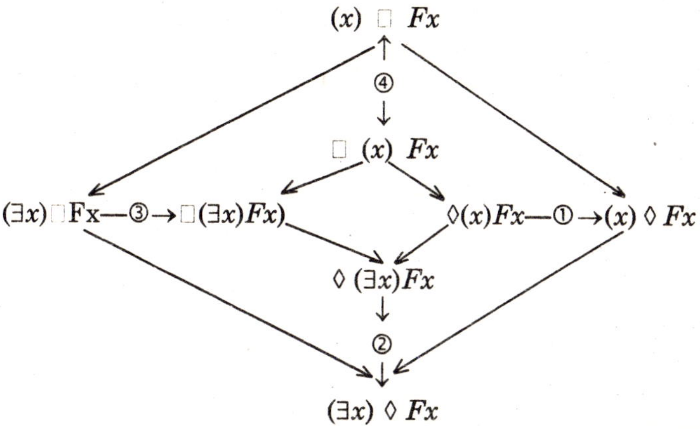

where no supplementation is needed. Let us suppose, for example, that $(\exists x)\ \Diamond Fx$ is taken to mean 'There is something which may be on fire' and $\Diamond(\exists x)\ Fx$ to mean 'There may be something on fire'. Immediately we come on the difficulty that the two English sentences are certainly not equivalent. For the first can be used to state that something is inflammable, and the second to say that our information does not rule out the existence of a fire. But if these assertions were properly translated back into the symbolism of modal logic, the results would be much more complicated than the two formulae linked in our scheme by the relation (2). In modal logic the diamond signifies only self-consistency and according to this strict interpretation the two formulae just mentioned seem to be logically equivalent, at least for the non-empty universe which logicians commonly assume. Unfortunately no logician who adopts the strict interpretation has offered examples which make the relations numbered (I) and (3) seem thoroughly satisfactory.

None of the systems of moal logic considered by C.I. Lewis contains any provision for the operation of quantifiers across modal signs, and the development we have sketched in the last few paragraphs has not been accepted by all logicians. Those who object to it argue either that the innovation is useless or that it is senseless. Thus according to G.H. von Wright it is an unnecessary complication, because everything that can be expressed in this way can be expressed more simply otherwise.[16] He bases his case on the assumption that all attributes of things can be divided into two groups, the formal, whose presence in the things that have them and absence in the things that do not have them is necessary, and the material, whose presence in the things that have them and absence in the things that do not have them is merely contingent. Thus arithmetical attributes are supposed to belong to the first group, and colours to the second. From this assumption (which he calls the Principle of Predication) it seems to follow that, to anyone who can tell whether an attribute is formal or material, quantifiers operating across modal signs are useless. For if Fx expresses a formal attribute, $(\exists x)\Box Fx$ and $(\exists x)\Diamond Fx$ are both equivalent to $(\exists x)Fx$; and if Fx expresses a material attribute, the first is obviously absurd while the second is a truism.

Von Wright admits that there are apparent exceptions to his principle; but it is open to a general objection which he does not notice. Whether an attribute belongs necessarily to a subject which has it does not always depend solely on the nature of the attribute. Being less than 13 is an arithmetical attribute, and we may, if we like, say that it belongs necessarily to the number 12; but it is false that the number of the apostles is necessarily less than I3 , although the number of the apostles is undoubtedly I2. It looks as though von Wright may have been misled here by the dubious distinction between modalities *de dicto* and modalities *de re* which he takes over from medieval writers. If the phrase *de re* is supposed to exclude dependence of the modality on the sense as distinct from the reference of the subject term, then paradoxically the only true modal statements *de re* are those in which the subject term can be replaced *salva veritate* by any other designation for a thing of the same category, i.e. statements like 'Queen Anne is necessarily dead or not dead', where the subject term contributes nothing of importance and the truth of the whole depends on the truistic character of the expression 'dead or not dead'.

W.V. Quine's objection to quantificaiton across modal signs is more radical; for the says not merely that it is useless, but also that it is meaningless, and he even suggests that we should do well to abandon the whole theory of modality together with the talk of propositions and attributes which it seems to require. His arguments may be summarized freely as follows, with the help of an example we have used already. Those who allow the use of modal words and phrases think that $(12 < 13)$ expresses a true proposition. If we accept this, we shall presumably admit also that the phrase $(x < 13)$ expresses a function satisfied by the number 12, and then we can scarcely refuse to allow the formation of the existential sentence $(\exists x)$ $(x < 13)$. But how are we to understand this novelty? It cannot be just the assertion of the existence of a number possessing a certain property; for if there were such a number, anyone who put forward the assertion might properly be asked to justify it by stating explicitly which number had the property, and it would not matter for this purpose whether he replied by saying '12' or 'the number of the apostles', since these designations have the same reference. On the other hand, it is useless to suggest, as some logicians have done, that the variable x may take as its values intensions of some sort. For if we admit intensions as possible values of our variables, we must abandon the principle of the indiscernibility of identicals, and then, because we have no clear criterion of identity, we shall be unable to say what we want to say about extensions:

'Intensional and extensional ontologies are like oil and water. Admission of attributes and propositions, along with free use of quantification and other basic idioms, rules out individuals and classes. Both sorts of entities can be accommodated in the same logic only with the help of restrictions, such as Church's, which serve to keep them from mixing and this is very nearly a matter of two separate logics with a universe of each.'[17]

It cannot, we think, be the proper business of a philosopher to ban the mention of propositions and attributes or to say that we must drop the words 'possible' and 'necessary' from our logical vocabulary. There may perhaps be metaphysical puzzles about the status of propositions something like those that have been raised about the nature of political societies; but just as it would be wrong to protest against the extravagances of Hegel by saying 'There are not states' so it is a mistake to counter the queer assertions of Bolzano and Meinong by saying 'There are no propositions'. If, as Quine has shown, there is something wrong with the common attempts of logicians to make quantifiers operate across modal signs, we must look for the source of the trouble in the details of their symbolization rather than in any general fault of all talk about propositions and modalities. When we appraoch the problem in this way, we find in fact that it can be solved without much difficulty.

Construction of a formula such as $(\exists x)$ Fx or $(x)\Diamond Fx$ presupposes that we know already what is meant by formulae like $F\gamma$ and $\Diamond F\gamma$. Let us consider the first case in some detail. We have seen already that a designation occurring with a modal context can always be eliminated. If the designation is not a definite description but a proper name (e.g. 'Napoleon'), we first of all replace it by a definite description with the same sense (e.g. 'the person called "Napoleon" '). Next we extract from our description, say $(\iota x)Gx$, the predicate $G'x$ which means *x is the sole G thing*. And finally for $F[(\iota x)Gx]$ we write $(x)[G'x \supset Fx]$, or (x) $[G'x \supset Fx]$, which is just another way of asserting together in the terminology of necessity all the propositions expressible by entailment formulae of the form $G'Z/FZ$. Now when we meet the formula $(\exists x)$ Fx, we do not know what is the relevant description of the thing or things which are said to be necessarily instances of the character expressed by Fx, but there are only two possibilities to be considered. $(\exists x)$ Fx may mean *There is something which under any description is necessarily F*, or it may mean *There is something which under some description is necessarily F.* If the first interpretation (*de re*) is that intended, $(\exists x)$ Fx cannot express a true proposition unless Fx is a truistic predicate and therefore entailed by any conceivable description. But this is as much as to say that the disputed formula is equivalent to is $(x)Fx$. If, on the other hand, the second interpretation is that intended, $(\exists x)$ Fx cannot express a true propositin unless there is something which among its permissible descriptions has one entailing the predicate Fx. But this is as much as to say that the disputed formula is equivalent to $(\exists x)Fx$. Therefore $(\exists x)\Box Fx$ cannot on either interpretation represent a new kind of proposition. By a similar argument it can be shown that, if $(x)\Diamond Fx$ has any meaqning at alll, it must be equivalent either to (x)Fx or to $\Diamond(\exists x)Fx$, and so here too it appears that there is no need to admit the operation of quantifiers across modal signs. We might indeed have avoided all this debate by retaining throughout the relational account of modality which we introduced in the last chapter; but in that case we should be have overlooked the interesting development of language whereby it is possible to construct statements of the forms $F[(\iota x)Gx]$ and $\Diamond F[(\iota x)Gx]$, and we should hae been unable to give a plausible history of recent discussion about intensionality.

IDENTITY, FUNCTIONS, AND CLASSES

In his *Begriffsschrift* and again in his *Grundgesetze der Arithmetik* Frege takes identity as a basic notion for which it is necessary to formulate special axioms. In *Principia Mathematica* (*13.01), on the other hand, Whitehead and Russell avoid the need for special axioms of identity by introducing $X = \gamma$ as an abbreviation for (f) $[f\,!\,X \supset f\,!\gamma]$. The sign ! which they use here after the letter f is intended to show that the functions under consideration are all *predicate* in a technical sense of that word. This restriction is required by Russell's Ramified Theory of Types, as we shall see in the next chapter, but the authors go on to point out that it involves on real loss of generality, since the Principle of Reducibility, which they introduce to modify the rigour of the Ramified Theory of Types, allows us to work with the definition as though it treated of all functions without qualification. Sometimes the distinction between predicative functions and others is said to be one of *order,* but this way of speaking is not the same as that usage in which discourse that requires intensional language may be said to be of higher order than discourse expressible in purely extensional language, and it is not sufficient to dispose of the difficulty connected with intensional language. If we admit the existence of intensional functions while using the definition just as it stands, we find ourselves committed to the curious conclusion that there can be no identity unknown to rational men. The morning star, it seems, cannot be identical with the evening star because there is at least one function, namely being known by all rational men to be identical with the morning star, which is satisfied by the former but not by the latter. For this reason what has been said above in reference to Frege's treatment of the topic in *Principa Mathematica.* That is to say, the definition of identity given by Whitehead and Russell must be qualified in such a way that it refers only to extensional functions. Is there then any good reason for preferring one treatment to the other?

In Frege's system, as in *Principia Mathematica*, the theory of identity is supposed to be part of logic, but it is not quite clear why it is included, and a hostile critic might object that Frege has given us no general account of logic by which we can judge whether he has remained faithful to his programme at this point. When, however, the notion of identity is introduced by means of a definition, it seems evident at first sight that the theory must be part of logic. For now the signs of identity occur only as a device for the abbreviation of propositions which could be stated with signs that are all admittedly logial. But this apparent advantage can be gained only by use of the quantifier (f) in the definition. It is true that according to his own explanations Frege's formula

$$x = y \supset (fx \supset fy)$$

should be treated as an abbreviation for

$$(f)[x = y \supset (fx \supset fy)].$$

But we have seen that the logician is entitled to use free variables of a special style for the expression of the universality which belongs to his own utterances. Taking advantage of this we can write

$$X = \gamma \supset (FX \supset F\gamma)$$

in place of Frege's own formula, not indeed as a simple substitute, but rather as the expression of truistic schema. In the system of *Principia Mathematica,* on the other hand, the use of *bound* functional variable is essential for the definition of identity. For while Whitehead and Russell wish us to understand that an expression of the form $X = \gamma$ may be regarded as an abbreviation for an expression of the form $(f)[f\,!X \supset f\,!\,\gamma]$, they certainly do not wish to suggest that any expression of the form $X = \gamma$ may be replaced wherever it occurs by an expression of the form $F!X \supset F!\gamma$ or vice versa. Now application of quantifiers to functional variables marks the transition to a calculus much more complicated than the simple or restricted calculus of propositional functions which we have considered so far in this chapter. If we think that this new calculus should be accounted part of logic, then we may say that Whitehead and Russell have reduced the theory of identity to logic, provided always that they can find some satisfactory way of qualifying their definition so that it deals only with nonintensional functions. But if for any reason we wish to talk of identity without raising for ourselves immediately all the difficulties of the new calculus, then we must return to Frege's course and present the theory of identity as a less comprehensive calculus in which two special axioms are added to the axioms and rules of the restricted functional calculus. One reason for doing this is precisely the fact that the theory of identity is closely bound up with the distinction of intensional and extensional language. Frege's distinction between *Sinn* and *Bedeutung* was first suggested to him by reflection on statements such as 'The morning star is identical with the evening star', and it may be the importance of this distinction in his thought which led him to introduce identity as a basic notion.

When he wrote his *Begriffsschrift*, Frege saw no need to make special provision for the enlarged calculus of functions in which quantifiers are applied to functional variables. But when he recast his system of logic for the purposes of his *Grundgesetze,* he added a new axiom of quantification which can be rendered in modern symbolism by the formula

$$(f)g_x(fx) \supset g_x(hx).$$

This means in effect that what holds for all functions of the first level with one argument holds for any of them. As in Frege's own script, the small letter written as subscript of the functional letter *g* is supposed to show that any argument suitable for the succeeding bracket must be a function of the first level with one argument. It is a kind of binding prefix, though not a quantifier. Obviously the new axiom is very similar in character to the axiom of quantification for individual variables, namely,

$$(x)fx \supset fy.$$

But in Frege's system it is the only explicit authority for the application of quantifiers to fuctional variables, and is therefore by no means superfluous. Without this momentous innvoation Frege could not even have made it seem plausible that arithmetic is reducible to logic. If he had thought it necessary to apply quantifiers to functional variables of the second and higher levels, he might perhaps have enunciated a separate axiom of quantification for each successive level. But we have seen that he felt ill at ease with formulae which involved functional variables of higher levels and that he tried to simplify his task by talking instead about classes and classes of classes.

It was probably the cumbrousness of his own notation that made Frege dislike formulae with bound functional variables. And this in turn was due to the contrast which he thought it necessary to make between functions and objects. But whatever we may think about Frege's general views about functions, we must admit that there is something new and strange in the use of bound functional variables. This becomes evident when we try to find a literal translation for the formulae in which they occur.

Although it is not easy to find strict equivalents in ordinary language for formulae with bound individual variables, that difficulty can usually be overcome by judicious use of 'thing' and various pronouns. Thus $(\exists x)[Fx.Gx]$ may be rendered as though it were an abbreviation of the near-English sentence *There is something such that it F's and it G's.* But when quantifiers are applied to functional variables, the grammar of the symbolism departs so far from that ordinary language that it is no longer possible to give a literal, or word-for-sign, translation of the formulae. How, for example, are we to read $(\exists f)[fX.f\gamma]$? When logicians construct a formula of this kind, they sometimes try to render it orally by the very-far-English sentence *There is some f such that X f's and γ f's.* Such mixed jargon is obviously inelegant, but apart from that it is unsatisfactory because it fails to make clear the role of *f*. In the body of the formula the letter is taken properly enough to mark a gap that could be filled by a functional expression such as a varb, but in the prefix it is treated as though it were what mediaeval logicians called a general term of second intention, equivalent perhaps to 'function'. Having heard first the phrase 'there is some', we naturally expect to hear next a common noun, but later on we find that the letter which has been made to do duty as a noun must also take the place of a verb. Similar difficulties arise when quantifiers are applied to propositional variables. In each case the source of the trouble is the fact that, although English has words like 'somehow' and 'however', it contains no construction corresponding exactly to the use of a quantifier with a variable *expression* of the grammatical status of a verb or complete clause. If we want to say in natural language what is said in the symbolism of logic by the formula $(\exists f)$ $[fX.f\gamma]$, we can produce nothing nearer than

There is some predicate satisfied by 'X and also by γ. This is indeed fairly close, but it is not a word-for-sign rendering of the logical symbols unless indeed we alter our conventions for the use of the latter, first by taking *f* in the body of the formula as a gap sign which marks a place of a *designation* of a function and then by taking the ordering of the signs in any complex ex-pression of the form *FX* to mean that *FX* is satisfied by *X*.

Frege did not think it possible to talk about a function without grammatical impropriety, and for that reason he could not treat functional variables as signs which marked gaps to be filled by complete designations. In his view a function was essentially something incomplete, and he thought it inevitable that this peculiarity should be reflected in the form of the special axiom or axioms of quantification used for the enlarged calculus of functions. If we distinguish carefully between expression and designation, we can talk about functions without falling into Frege's perplexities, but the new interpretation of logical symbolism suggested in the last paragraph will not save us from the need for a special rule or axiom when we begin to apply quantifiers to functional variables. In the restricted calculus of functions we have rules for reasoning with expressions of the forms $(x)Fx$ and $(\exists x)Fx$, where Fx is supposed to be an abbreviation for any functional expression containing *x;* but if we adopt the convention that *FX* is short of *F is satisfied by X,* our rules will not longer enable us to deal with formulae of such patterns as $(x)[Gx \supset Hx]$ and they will certainly not suffice to explain the application of quantifiers to variables in the position of *F*. There is nevertheless something unsatisfactory in the introduction of separate rules of quantification for different kind of variables, and it seems desirable therefore to consider whether any simplification can be achieved by use of new symbolism.

One way out of the difficulty is to let *FX* retain the sense it received from Frege but introduce a new functional constant η with the meaning of 'satisfies'. Since the new symbol is a kind of transitive verb, the signs which occur on the two sides of it in a simple formula must both be designations, and the meaning requires that the second at least should be designation of a function. Thus as a variant for FX we have $X\eta\gamma$, where γ is short for $\S xFx$. Sometimes indeed the first sign used η with may designate an ordered sequence of two or more things while the second designates a predicate which can be satisfied if at all only by such a sequence. This will happen whenever a relational proposition is transcribed into the new notation. Instead of $G(X,\gamma)$ we then have $\langle X,\gamma\rangle\ \eta Z$, where Z is short for $\S xyG(x, y)$. In yet other formulae both signs which go with η may be designations of functions, i.e. when a function itself is said to exemplify some character. If, however, either or both of the designations which occur with η in a simple formula is replaced by a variable, we get an expression which can serve as a matrix for general statements. Thus matrices of the forms $x\eta\gamma$ and $X\eta y$ will be equally open to quantification in accordance with the ordinary rules of quantification theory, and we may write for example $(\exists z)[X\eta z.\ \gamma\eta z]$ to express the proposition that there is some predicate which the things called X and γ both satisfy. Furthermore, apart form the simplification which it allows in the expression of general propositions about functions, the new notation has the great merit of making clear that the theory sometimes called the enlarged calculus of propositional functions is in effect the theory of satisfaction. It would be foolish of course, to suggest that should be taken as the sole functional expression of our language and used in the formulation of all propositions without exception. For when we wish to ascribe a definite attribute to a thing called X there is obviously nothing to be gained from writing $x\eta\S\ yFy$ rather than FX; and in any case the possibility of designating a function always presupposes the possibility of expressing it. But it is an important fact that the enlarged calculus in which we talk of functions with complete generality can be presented as a system with one new sign not reducible to those of ordinary quantification theory. For this is as much as those of ordinary quantification theory. For this is as much as to say that it is the theory of the notion expressed by the sign.

When he discussed philosophical problems in German, Frege frequently spoke of a thing's falling under a concept, but for reasons which we have already examined he felt dissatisfied with such language and therefore never tried to develop a calculus of satisfaction such as we have just suggested. On the other hand, the calculus of class-membership by which he tried to evade the difficulties of his own notation for applying quantifiers to functional variables is very similar in structure. For just as FX may be rendered by $X\eta\S yFy$, so too it may be rendered by $X\varepsilon yFy$, where ε is an abbreviation for 'is a member of'. And just as one thing's being related to another in a certain way can be regarded as the satisfaction of a relational predicate by an ordered couple, so too it can be regarded as the membership of that same ordered couple in a class of ordered couples Indeed the only important difference between the two calculi is the condition of identity for their distinctive types of entity. When he introduced a notation for classes in his *Grundgesetze,* Frege laid down an axiom (V) which can be rendered in modern symbolism by the formula

$$(xFx = yGy) \equiv (z)[Fz \equiv Gz].$$

This is as much as to say that for classes we have

$$(X = Y) \equiv (w)[\omega\varepsilon X \equiv \omega\varepsilon Y].$$

The corresponding proposition does not hold for predicates or concepts, and it would not even be correct to say for them

$$(X = Y) \equiv (w)[w\eta X \equiv w\eta Y].$$

For while it follows from the identity of two predicates that they must necessarily be satisfied by the same things, the converse is not true. All equilateral triangles are necessarily equiangular triangles, and vice versa, but the meaning of 'equilateral triangle' is not the same as the meaning of 'equiangular triangle'.

Historically it is of some interest that the development of mathematical logic, which began with the attempts of Leibniz to formulate a calculus *de continentibus et contentis*, should reach its culmination in the work of Frege, Whithehead, and Russell with a theory of class-membership. But we must not attach too much importance to a similarity in name. Leibniz did not distinguish clearly between the relation of a member to a class and the relation of a class to a super-class of which it is a part, but most of what he had to say was appropriate only to the second relation. Certainly Boole's algebra of classes, which we regard as a realization of Leibniz's project, is a theory of the interrelations of classes whose members, if they have any, are all drawn from a common domain of individuals called the universe of discourse. In effect this calculus is a fragment of the restricted calculus of propositional functions. Frege's calculus, on the other hand, is concerned not only with relations of inclusion, exclusion, and overlap, between classes of the same level, but also with the membership of one class in another. In short it is Cantor's theory of sets presented as derivative from the enlarged calculus of propositional functions. Even if he had not been worried by the application of quantifiers to functional variables, Frege would probably have wished to talk about classes for the same reason as led Cantor to talk of sets. For the carrying out of his programme it is necessary to show (*a*) that arithmetic can be elaborated within the theory of sets and (*b*) that the theory of sets can properly be described as part of logic. Whether or not these points can be established will be considered in the following chapters. Here we need only consider what is involved in talking of classes or sets rather than of functions.

Although Frege regarded statements about classes as substitutes in certain contexts for statements about functions, he did not think it possible that classes and functions should be the same. According to his explanations statements about classes can be substituted for statements about functions only when these latter statements are such as would hold true for all functions materially equivalent to those under consideration. This view was shared by Whitehead and Russell when they wrote the first edition of *Principia Mathematica.* But in the new introduction which he wrote for the second edition of that work Russell declared that he no longer found any need to distinguish between classes and functions because he thought that all functions were extensional, i.e. accepted every assertion of the form

$$(x)[Fx \equiv Gx] \supset [H(Fx) \equiv H(Gx)],$$

where in accordance with his convention Fx and Gx are designations of functions.[18] If he means by this that there is no provision in his symbolism for expressing intensional functions, then what he says is no doubt correct, but it is not very important. If, however, he means that all functions of functions expressible in any symbolism whatever are extensional, his pronouncement is of great philosophical interest but highly controversial, to say the least. This is in fact the context in which the debate about intensionality started and from which the rather puzzling modern use of 'intensional' and 'extensional' is derived.

In the past many logicians have talked of classes because they hoped in this way to avoid difficulties about universals. They have supposed, for example, that a class of material things might be admitted as an entity even by the most hard-headed, because it could itself be regarded as a composite material things even if its members were not all collected together in one place like the stones of a heap. But Russell and his followers are under no illusions on this score. Quine, for example, points out that the class of states of the U.S.A. is not the same as the class of counties of the U.S.A., although the territory comprised in the states is the same as the territory comprised in the counties.[19] If there is a danger in talking of abstractions, we shall not escape from it by using the class notation, since classes are themselves abstractions. Nor shall we by this means avoid the need to use functional expressions other than at some level in our language. For every designation of a class is either a sign of the form xFx or one whose meaning and reference are determined by recourse to a sign or signs of this mind. Sometimes, indeed a class may be indicated by enumeration of its members, i.e. by construction of a class sign of the form $x(x{=}V\ x{=}Z\ V...)$, but it is evident that they cannot all be indicated in this way. For if they were, all true statements of class membership would be tautologous. In modern times logicians who prefer to talk of classes rather than of functions do so for the purpose of evading the problems of int-ensionality, and sometimes they even say that the classes of which they speak *are universals.*

In this connexion it is interesting to notice that logicians who agree in showing a preference for the class notation may nevertheless disagree much as philosophers of the past disagreed about universals. According to Quine realism, conceptualism, and nominalism are all to be found in the works of modern writers on the foundations of mathematics.[20] By 'realism' he means apparently a willingness to assume the existence of classes and classes of classes whenever our symbolism suggests the possibility of such assumptions, by 'conceptualism' a policy of admitting the existence of classes only when we are in a position to establish their constitution, and by 'nominalism' an attempt to dispense with any assumption of the existence of classes. In practice the three attitudes are supposed to show themselves in greater or less willingness to apply quantifiers to class variables. It is doubtful whether this use of the old labels can serve any good purpose, especially if (as often happens) realism is mistakenly identified with Platonism. But the fact that Quine and some others feel an inclination to talk in this way shows very clearly that they do not think it possible to dispose of all problems about universals mearely by adopting a class notation. And here, of course, they are right.

When in a so-called higher-order functional calculus quantifiers are applied to variables which mark places for functional signs, the essential novelty of the resulting system may be overlooked because no new symbol has been introduced. On the other hand, if we present the system explicity as a theory of exmplification or membership, we may perhaps overlook the fact that different sorts of basic entities are now assumed as possible values for the variables of our underlying general logic or quantification theory. In this connexion Hao Wang has written :

'The contrast between one-sorted and many-sorted quantification theories is more basic than that between first-order and higher-order predicate calculi. While higher-order predicate calculi and theories formulated therein all are many-sorted systems, there are many-sorted theories such as geometry dealing with points, lines, and planes which are not formulated in higher-order predicate calculi. While many-sorted quantification theories treat all predicates on an equal basis, higher-order predicate calculi reserve a special pedestal for the membership relation. Indeed, an n-th order predicate calculus is nothing but an n-sorted theory which contains a single axiom (the axiom of comprehension) asserting that every meaningful formula of the system defines a set.'[21]

A theory is many-sorted if it has variables of different kinds, each restricted to a different range of objects as possible values. Differences of kind among variables may be indicated typographically, but this is not essential; for it can be shown sufficiently by context. If in a version of plane geometry we see the phrase *x lies on y*, we know that the letter x marks a place for designations of points and the letter y a place for designations of lines. Nevertheless, if the theory is really many-sorted, it must be assumed that the rules of quantification are repeated for each separate kind of variable. They will, of course, be precisely the same in form for each kind; but the requirement that they should be repeated is irksome, and it is natural to ask whether we cannot do all we want to do with a one-sorted general logic in which rules of quantification are formulated once only.

The answer seems to be that we can transcribe every many-sorted theory into a standard one-sorted idiom if we allow our variables to take as their range of values the sum of all the categories of the theory under consideration and then re-introduce the distinction of categories by means of a number of categorial predicates e.g. 'is a natural number', 'is a point', 'is a line') with which we can formulate conditions for the theorems of the system. Thus instead of saying :

$$x(y+z) = xy+xz,$$

where it is to be understood that the variables have for their range of values only the category of natural numbers, we say:

If x, y, z are natural numbers, $x(y+z) = xy+xz.$

This standardization (as it is sometimes called) is a procedure we follow without hesitation in ordinary speech, and it seems unexceptionable. It is interesting also to notice that in many cases at least the transcription of a many-sorted theory into a standard one-sorted idiom can be carried through without the addition of any new categorial predicates. In these cases the distinction of categories can be made by the formulation of category conditions with the symbols already available.[22]

Among many-sorted theories that which deals with membership, i.e. the theory of sets, has a special importance, as mathematicians recognize when they use the little 'elementary' for those branches of their study which do not presuppose it. But it is by no means obvious that this is the only many-sorted theory required mean obvious that this is for the completion of science. Sometimes Russell and other philosophers who draw inspiration form his work have talked as though there can be only one basic category of individuals and apart from that various categories of sets. Conceivably their thesis may be correct. It is at least an interesting piece of philosophical speculation which may some day suggest a detailed programme for the unification of science. But we fall into error if we think that it is guaranteed by considerations of logic. In different contexts entities of different categories may be considered as individuals, and so the letters which logicians sometimes call individual variables mark gaps that may be filled with any names or designations which complete their formulae in significant fashion. If metaphysics is concerned, as Aristotle thought, with the nature of basic entities, its questions cannot be answered from considerations of formal logic, not because this latter study is independent of the structure of the world, but rather because it is concerned with patterns which may recur at different levels.

NECESSITY AND LANGUAGE

Although Frege had much to say about he principles of syntax and always thought of himself as the designer of a new language which would be especially suitable for scientific purposes, he did not, like many of his predecessors, regard logic as an *ars sermocinalis,* and he certainly did not hold the view of Hobbes and Berkeley that logical necessity is imposed by human rules for the use of words. On the contrary, when he said that arithmetic could be reduced to logic, he insisted that he did not mean to treat it either as a branch of psychology or as a branch of philology. For him logic was the most general of all sciences about reality, the *doctrina formarum* of which Leibniz had written, and only connected with grammar because it treated of the basic patterns which every natural language must be able to express. This was also the doctrine of Whitehead and Russell when they wrote *Principia Mathematica.* But in more recent times the conventionalist theory of a necessity has been adopted by many philosophers, and logic is even treated by some as though it were identical with semantics, i.e. with the study of those linguistic rules or customs which give words their significance. The change seems to date from the publication of the *Tractatus Logico-Philosophicus* by Ludwig Wittgenstein in 1921, though it is almost certain that Wittgenstein did not at first intend anything of the kind.

In the years before 1914, when he was studying in Cambridge with Russell, Wittgenstein remarked that truths of logic could not be satisfactorily defined as all those expressible in a certain vocabulary but might be distinguished from others by a special character which he called tautology, meaning by this not repetitiousness but rather vacuity. Russell referred to this suggestion as follows in a work which he wrote while serving a sentence of impriosonment for his pacifist activities:

'We may take the axiom of infinity as an example of a proposition which, though it can be enunciated in logical terms, cannot be asserted by logic to be true. All the propositions of logic have a characteristic which used to be expressed by saying that they were analytic, or that their contradictories were self-contradictory. This mode of statement, however, is not satisfactory. The law of contradiction is merely one among logical proposition; it has no special pre-eminence; and the proof that the contradictory of some proposition is self-contradictory is likely to require other principles of deduction beside the law of contradiction. Nevertheless, the characteristic of logical propositions that we are in search of is the one which was felt, and intended to be defined, by those who said that it consisted in deducibility from the law of contradiction. This characteristic, which for the moment we may call tautology, obviously does not belong to the assertion that the number of individuals in the universe is *n*, whatever number *n* may be. . . .Logical propositions are such as can be known *a priori*, without study of the actual world. . . . This is a characteristic, not of logical propositions in themselves, but of the way in which we know them. It has, however, a bearing upon the question what their nature may be, since there are some kinds of propositions which it would be very difficult to suppose we could know without experience. It is clear that the definition of "logic" also must be sought by trying to give a new definition of the old notion of "analytic" propositions. Although we can no longer be satisfied to define logical propositions are those that follow from the law of contradiction, we can and must still admit that they are wholly different class of propositions from those that we come to know empirically. They all have the characteristic which, a moment ago, we agreed to call "tautology". This combined with the fact that they can be expressed wholly in terms of variables and logical constants (a logical constant being something which remains constant in a proposition when *all* its constituents are changed)—will give the definition of logic or pure mathematics. For the moment I do not know how to define tautology. (The importance of "tautology" for a definition of mathematics was pointed out to me by my former pupil Ludwig Wittgenstein, who was working on the problem. I do not know whether he has solved it, or even whether he is alive or dead.)"[23]

Although he maintained that the truths of logic were in a certain sense vacuous, Wittgenstein did not think that they were unimportant, and at this stage in his development he was far from believing that they were arbitrary creations of mankind. In one of the more connected passages of his *Tractatus* he wrote :

'Logical sentences (*Sätze*) describe the scaffolding of the world, or rather they present it. They "treat" of nothing. The presuppose that names they reference and that atomic sentences (*Elementarsätze*) have sense. And this is their connexion with the world. It is clear that it must show something about the world that certain combinations of symbols—which essentially have a definite character—are tautologies. Herein lies the decisive point. We said that in the symbols which we use something is arbitrary, something not. In logic only the latter expresses: but this means that in logic it is not *we* who express, by means of signs, what we want, but in logic the nature of the essentially necessary of signs, what we want, itself asserts. That is to say, if we know the logical syntax of any sign language, then all the these (*Sätze*) of logic are alredy given.'[24]

The tautological character of logical assertions was supposed to be made clear by the truth-table method of exposition, and it was though to be a matter of no great importance that the truth-conditions of universal and existential assertions could not be presented in tables of finite complexity. The emphasis which Wittgenstein placed on his definitions of truth-functions by truth-tables was due, of course, to his conviction that logic did not deal with any special class of things or relations in the world but solely with the nature of what we might perhaps call logical complexity. In one place he writes :

'A Truth-operation is the way in which a truth-function arises form atomic sentences . . . Every sentence is the result of truth-opeations on atomic sentences. . . All truth-functions are results of the successive applications of a finite number of truth-operations to atomic sentences. Here it becomes clear that there are no such things as "logical objects" or "logical constants" (in the sense of Frege and Russell).'[25]

But Wittgenstein was not content to say that logical truths were tautologies.He maintained also that the tautologies of logic were the only necessary truths and the whole realm of *a priori* knowledge:

'From the existence or non-existence of one state of affairs (*Sachverhalt,* i.e. possible atomic fact) we cannot infer the existence or non-existence of another. States of affairs are independent one of another.'[26]

Logical research means the investigation of *all regularity.* And outside logic all is accident. . .A necessity for one thing to happen because another has happened does not exist. There is only *logical* necessity. At the basis of the whole modern view of the world lies the illusion that the so-called laws of nature are the explanations of natural phenomena."[27]

The result is something like the philosophy of Hume, and it is not surprising than in the dozen years after the publication of the *Tractatus* the Logical Positivists of the Vienna circle led by Moritz Schlick tried to combine Wittgenstein's account of logic with the Humean tradition they had inherited from Ernst Mach. But there is an important difference between the two philosophical systems. Whereas Hume tried to recommend his conclusions by psychological analysis, Wittgenstein confined himself for the most part to oracular pronouncements without any supporting arguments except such as could be derived from consideration of the symbolism of *Principia Mathematica.* The explanation seems to be that he simply assumed without question the sufficiency of this symbolism as the syntactical apparatus for an ideal language. We have noticed already that he refused to recognize the possibility of an irreducibly intensional language which allows for the designation of propositions in contexts such as 'Jones believes that the earth is flat'. When he talks of logic as a set of tautologies and refuses to allow any importance to rules of inference such as Frege, Whitehead, and Russell had thought it necessary to add to their primitive propositions,[28] his reason seems to be that rules of inference which allow us to pass from one formula of *Principia Mathematica* to another cannot themselves be formulated within the special symbolism of that work. The way in which a language provides for what he sometimes calls 'the logic of the world'[29] can, he thinks, be shown in a language but never stated. This thesis must be untrue, if it is supposed to apply to all natural languages. For, as Wittgenstein himself admits at the end of the *Tractatus,* its truth would involve the senselessness of the pronouncement in which it as asserted.[30] But it is certainly correct that the special symbolism of *Principia Mathematica* does not allow for the translation of all the English letterpress of that work.

Although Wittgenstein thought that the world consisted of independent atomic facts which could be pictured by atomic sentences (in that metaphorical sense of 'picture' in which the *fact* that the word 'out' appears after a man's name on a board at the foot of a staircase may perhaps be said to picture the *fact* that he is out of his room on that staircase at that time),[31] he never gave any examples or explained what kind of facts he had in mind. Some of his followers, wishing to connect his work with that of Hume for the reason given above, jumped to the conclusion that atomic facts must be about sense-date and sensibilia. This was also the assumption of Russell in his lectures of 1918 on *The Philosophy of Logical Atomism*[32] and in a number of later works. But Wittgenstein did not commit himself to such a view, thinking apparently that the question was one to be settled empirically and therefore in some way below the dignity of his work :

'It is clear that we have a concept of the atomic sentence apart from its special logical form. Where, however, we can builld symbols according to system, there this system is the logically important thing and not the single symbols. . . .If we know on purely logical grounds that there must be atomic sentence, then this must be known by everyone who understands sentences in their unanalysed form . . . . It is the *application* of logic which decides what atomic sentences there are. What lies in its application logic cannot anticipate. . . . If I cannot indicate atomic sentences *a priori*, then it must lead to obvious nonsense to try to indicate them.'[33]

Clearly at this stage in his development Wittgenstein made a sharp distinction between the syntax and the vocabulary of science, thinking of the former as known *a priori* in a study of logic such as *Principia Mathematica* and of the latter as learnt only in connexion with particular experiences. He was right, no doubt, to try to defend the formal purity of logic, but there is something very strange in his refusal to consider more carefully the problem of its application. And it is this refusal which leads to his curious doctrine that there is no necessity outside of logic.

Like Frege, Wittgenstein introduces negation with a truth-functional definition, i.e. by saying that ~ P is true if and only if P is false, and sometimes he seems to think it is sufficient to say that P is false if the state of affairs which it pictures is not realized.[34] But in one place he says :

'The negating statement (*der verneinende Satz*) determines a logical place *other* than determined by the negated statement. The negating statement determines a logical place with the help of the logical place of the negated statement, by describing it as lying one side this later.[35]

Taken seriously, this implies that the posibility of using a negative particle significantly depends on the objective incompatibility of various thinkable states of affairs. For the otherness or exclusive of which Wittgenstein speaks here is presupposed by the construction of negative statements and must therefore be a relation independent of our use of a negative sign, though elsewhere he assumes that there can be no such incompatibility. Perhaps it was his loose use of the word 'logical' that blinded Wittgenstein to this inconsistency in his system. When he says that there is no necessity except that of logic, he seems to mean by 'logic' the theory of our use of sign; but when he talks of the logic of the world and speaks in particular of positions in logical space, he seems to mean something which might more properly be called metaphysics. If there is, as his words suggest, a system of alternatives within which we select items for affirmation or denial whenever we utter statements of contingent fact, the structure of that system must certainly embody all the principles of impossibility and necessity that can ever be formulated, but the study of the system will not be the restricted formal science which Frege called logic.

Apparently Wittgenstein was sometimes worried by misgivings about his doctrine of logical necessity. Towards the end of his *Tractatus* he wrote at unusual length :

'As there is only a *logical* necessity, so there is only a *logical* impossibility. For two colours, e.g., to be at one place in the visual field is impossible, that is, logically impossible, since it is excluded by the logical structure of colour. Let us consider how this contradiction presents itself in physics. Somewhat as follows : that a particle cannot at the same time have two velocities, i.e. that it cannot at the same time be in two places, i.e. that particles in different places at the same time cannot be identical. (It is clear that the logical product of two atomic sentences can neither be a tautology nor a contradiction. The assertion that a point in the visual field has two different colours at the same time is a contradiction.)'[36]

Critics soon noticed the insufficiency of this attempt to exhibits incompatibility of colours as a case of logical (i.e. formal) contradiction, and in 1929 Wittgenstein himself wrote with reference to this example : 'Atomic propositions, though they cannot contradict, may exclude one another.'[37] This admission is fatal to the doctrine of the earlier work, but Wittgenstein was still so much under the influence of his own loose usage that he tried to present this change as a reform of *logic* rather than as an abandonment of his thesis that there is no impossibility outside logic.

It is evident on reflection that no statement can ascribe a character to a thing unless it thereby excludes some other character. Even Spinoza, who thought that there was only one substance, God or Nature, and might therefore be inclined to blur the outlines of things, said that all determination is negation;[38] and it may be that no philosopher has ever tried to talk of a specification compatible with every other specification. But many philosophers have written as though they thought that contrary opposition of predicates was something instituted by human beings without consideration of the nature of things. Thus P. F. Strawson has said : 'It is . . . . our own activity of making language through using it, our determination of the limits of the application of words, that makes inconsistency possible.'[39] It is true, of course, that the inconsistency of words is established by human customs in the use of words; but our determination of the limits of the application of a general word is not selection of all the particular things to which we shall thereafter apply it. Rather it is selection of the specific varieties of character that may be exhibited by things to which we shall apply the word, and these specific varieties must be inconsistent in a non-linguistic sense. When definition is conceived as the fixing of boundaries (and that is the original sense of the word), the space within which it operates must be supposed to have for its points not individuals but perfectly specific universals which are mutually exclusive.

Although Wittgenstein presented formal logic in his *Tractatus* with an unnatural and misleading disregard for its application, he maintained there what might be called an absolutist view of logical truths. That is to say, he talked as though there was, and could be, only one system of logic, namely a simplified version of that presented in *Principia Mathematica*. But among some who might called his followers the emphasis he had placed on the importance of symbolic conventions soon led to sympathetic consideration of the possibility of alternative logics such as those suggested by Post, Lukasiewicz, and Heyting. Thus we find Carnap writing in 1934:

'*In logic there are no morals.* Everyone is at liberty to build up his own logic, i.e. his own form of language, as he wishes. All that is required of him is that, if he wishes to discuss it, he must state his methods clearly, and give syntactical rules instead of philosophical arguments. The tolerant attitude here suggested is, as far as special mathematical calculi are concerned, the attitude which is tacitly shared by the majority of mathematicians.'[40]

In asmuch as it has encouraged to investigation of alternative formal systems and so helped to throw light on the structure of the generally accepted systems of two-valued formal logic, this conventionalist attitude has had good effects. For those who think of logic as an uninterpreted calculus it is indeed the proper attitude to adopt. But if logic is supposed to be connected, as Carnap implies, with language, i.e. if its formulae are to be interpreted as laws about negation, conjunction, universality, and the rest, conventionalism is a poor philosophy of logic, since it presupposes another view which it professes to reject. When, as Carnap urges, we set out explicitly a sequence of syntactical rules or conventions, we must use some language to formulate them, and reliance on this language inevitably carries with it acceptance of some logical principles which are not established by convention alone. Thus in order to express any rules for our new symbolism we must use some device for expressing conditional dependence. With these we naturally take for granted the appropriate logical principles; and when we have finished, we do not call our new system logic in the ordinary sense unless it reproduces some of the principles we already assume.[41] In reply to Carnap's remark that there are no morals in logic we may therefore say (i) that logic in the proper sense consists essentially of restrictive laws about the possible combinations of propositions, and (ii) that such laws cannot be introduced by conventions made without knowledge of logical restrictions, any more than moral laws can be introduced by conventions made without knowledge of moral obligations. The conventionalist theory of logic is indeed strangely like the social contract theory of justice which Plato puts into the mouth of Glaucon in the second book of his *Republic*.

In the period of forty years after the first publication of his *Tractatus* Wittgenstein's views about logic became widely known and very influential among philosophers of a positivist or antimetaphysical cast. During the process of popularization the master's doctrine was inevitably modified in various respects, partly through the efforts of admires to systematize his oracular utterances and partly through the spread of reports about his later oral teaching, but a good deal also through the simplifying zeal of persons who were more interested in attacking metaphysics than in elucidating the theory of deduction. What has emerged is a new version of Hobbesian conventionalism in which not only the arithmetical theorems discussed by Ferge but all truths ascertainable *a priori* are said to be analytic or logically necessary and therefore merely tautologies true by definition, that is to say, uninformative by-products of human activity in the making of rules for the use of symbols. Sometimes, however, those who declare that statement of necessary truth tell us nothing about the world go on to remark that tautological formulae may be used to give instruction about linguistic rules, as when, for example, a grownup says to a child 'An oculist is an eye-doctor', meaning thereby to teach the child the use of the comparatively rare English word 'oculist'. And so it is often maintained that an utterance of a tautological formula is informative if, and only if, it is taken as short for a remark about a language, namely for a remark to the effect that the rules of the language in which it is formulated are such as to make it tautological.

Any philosophical simplification which attains such wide popularity as this doctrine has achieved must contain some important truth, that is to say, some truth which requires emphasis at the time; and is easy to see what the truth is in this case. Anything we come to know *a priori* is a second-order truth about the relations of propositions or a truism derivative from such a truth, and in either case it is learnt by reflection on the meanings of words or other symbols. An animal such as a dog may perhaps be said to know a contingent fact such as that there are two sheep in a field, but it seems absurd to say that a dog can know even a very simple truth of arithmetic such as the proposition that 2+2=4; and the reason can scarcely be that all non-human animals lack the special kind of intuition which according to Kant enables us to learn arithmetical truths. Many misleaing accounts of *a priori* knowledge have been inspired by Plato's notion of contemplation (θεωρια) as a kind of intellectual gazing in which the soul may read off facts about super-sensible objects; and if we are to free ourselves from the influence of these, it is no doubt important that we should realize the connexion of *a priori* knowledge with the use of symbols. But the simplfying conventionalism of the twentieth century has produced other results which are by no means improvements in our intellectual apparatus. In particular it has led to the blurring of two valuable distinctions.

First, those who adopt this view assume that the terms 'analytic' *a priori*, and 'necessary', taken respectively from logic, therefore knowledge, and metaphysics, are coextensive. No doubt a proposition which is analytically true can be known *a prior* and every proposition which can be known *a priori* is necessary. But it is by no means obvious that the converse relations holding analytic is understood in the sense of Frege, there may well be truths known *a priori* which are not analytic because they do not follow from laws of formal logic even when explicit definitions are this admitted as new transformation rules. An example which we has often been discussed is the proposition that nothing can be both red and green all over at the same time. Another is the proposition that the relation of temporal precedence is transitory but irreflexive. Furthermore, if we can ever be sure that certain perceptible characters and relations provide a model satisfying the postulates of an abstract geometry, this too must be a part of knowledge *a priori* but not analytic. It is not possible to say in the same way that there are necessary truths (i. e. truths without alternatives) which we cannot know a priori; for products of an example would clearly involve a claim to *a priori* knowedge But it is at least conceivable that there are such. We commonly admit that there are truths of mathematics which no one in fact knows, and it does not seem absurd to suggest that there may be necessary truths about unperceived qualities or relations which no human being can ever know because (as Locke might say) none has the requiste ideas.

The situation is even worse when, as sometimes happens, the three terms 'analytic', *a priori*, and 'nacessary' are assumed to be not only conextensive but also synonymous, so that any one of them may serve as contradictory to any of the three corresponding terms 'synthetic', 'empirical' and 'contingent'. For an example we may take A. J. Ayer's *definition* of anylytic and synthetic *priori* positions (i.e. in his usage, statements): 'A proposition is analytic when its validity depends only on the definitions of the symbol it contains, and synthetic when its validity is determined by the facts of experience.'[42] Obviously such confusion makes Kantanotion of synthetic *a priori* truths seem completely absurd, though this notion has been accepted in recent times by mathematicians as great as Frege, Poincaré, Brouwer, and Hilbert. It has in fact has been suggested that the phrase 'synthetic *a priori*' is no better than a mystifying substitute for 'contingent necessary'.[43] But that is not all. At the same time Frege's thesis that truths of arithmethematic are analytic becomes indistinguishable from the triviality that such truths are known *a priori*. And even the positivist assertion that all *a priori* truths are analytic becomes a simple and therefore pointless tautology. Since, however, positivists do not all behave as though their main doctrine were a simple tautology, it seems that in this context some of them must commit a mistake like that which has been called in ethics the naturalistic fallacy namely the mistake of equating in thier theory words which are ordinarily used to perform different tasks and then going on to use the words as though they had not been equated.

Secondly, modern conventionalism confuses logical and linguistic rules in a way that leads to serious misunderstanding. We have seen an example of such confusion already in a quotation from Carnap, but we must now investigate the tendency a little farther. When philosopher say that necessary truths are all established by linguistic convention they seem to have at the back of their minds the notion that (as Wittgenstein said) the world consists of facts which are all independent and contingent and that what men call necessary truths are no more than shadows or projections of the rules they themselves have adopted for speaking and writing. So powerful is the influence of this simplified picture that conventionalists sometimes regret the prevailing use of the one word 'truth' for talk of contingent and necessary truths. In their view it would be better to keep the two notions clearly apart by talking instead of facts and conventions. If it is objected that there is something paradoxical in the equation of 'necessary' and 'conventional', they reply that in application to a truth the word 'necessary' expresses no more than the speaker's resolution to stand by a certain form of words in all circumstances. There are, they say, no alternatives to a necessary truth *within the speaker's language,* but only because he himself has limited his language in that way. Since they also maintain that (as Wittgenstein said) necessity is all logical necessity, they are naturally led on to say that logical statements about linguistic statements of a certain kind, namely statements about linguistic inconsistency (or relations definable by reference to this) which can be translated in full from one language to another.[44] The provision about translation is put in to meet the objection that logic is not commonly supposed to be concerned with any particular language. According to P. F. Strawson :

'The important thing is to see that when you draw the boundaries of the applicability or words in one language and then connect the words of that language with those of another by translation rules, there is no need to draw the boundaries again for the second language. They are already drawn. This is why (or partly why) logical statements framed as one language are not just about that language.'[45]

If this means that logical rules are rules for all possible languages, it amounts in effect to an admission that they are not conventional and therefore not linguistic in any ordinary sense of that word but rather requirements to be satisfied in the making of what we ordinarily call linguistic rules. Sometimes, however, philosopher of this persuasion talk of the logic of ordinary language and even of the logical behaviour' of particular English words, as though they were engaged in some sort of *a priori* philology. It has been stated, for example, *as a point of logic* that attention is a polymorphous concept because the English word 'attend' may coverd many different activities. No doubt the English word 'attend' has many different uses, but if logic is an *a priori* science it cannot claim this discovery, since the existence of the various uses is an historical accident. In German, as it happens, there is no single word with the same range of application as 'attend', though German is not a notably poorer language than English.

We have seen already that inconsistency of general words presupposes incompatibility of characters. From this it follows immediately that necessity cannot be merely a product of linguistic rules and customs. It is, of course, an historical accident that the sounds 'red', 'yellow', 'green', and 'blue' are used as they are in communication by speakers of the English language, and a truism that any language in which we can find exact renderings for the four English words must contain sounds subject to rules like those holding in English for 'red', 'yellow', 'green', and 'blue'. But it is neither an historical accident nor a truism (at least in the pejorative sense of that word) that there is a range of distinct hues which can be divided as we divide it by use of our colour words. Anyone who accepts conventionalism ignores this and thereby commits himself in practice to the view that general words are merely names with multiple denotations. John Stuart Mill recognized this mistake in the work of Hobbes and devised his theory of connotation to remedy it; but, as often happend in the history of philosophy, the error has reappeared in a new guise. Instead of saying 'The world consists of individuals: universals belong to language' modern conventionalists say 'The world consists of facts : necessities belong to language.'

If our argument is correct, the earlier heresy is implicit in the later. But apart from this, it is interesting to notice that the later heresy can be refused directly by a consideration like that which is generally admitted to be fatal to the earlier. Just as individuals are essentially correlative to universals and therefore inconceivable by themselves, so facts which are contingent in the sense of belonging to ranges of possible alternatives are essentially correlative to laws of necessity or impossibility and therefore inconceivable without the latter. The argument assumes a notion of possibility which is ignored by conventionalists, but even within their own assumptions it can be argued that, if convention makes necessary propositions necessary, convention must also make contingent propositions contingent, that is to say, non-necessary. Here the consequent is unacceptable to conventionalists—unless indeed they take it to be a version of the trivially true thesis that convention determines what forms of words shall express contingent propositions, in which case they must interpret the antecedent in an equally harmless fashion. For if it is not merely trivial, the consequent must mean that the facts of which the world consists are neither necessary nor contingent in themselves. We shall see later that some philosopher have defended such a view, but they do not call themselves conventionalists and they have been attacked by those who accept the title.

Wittgenstein's ideas have had more influence among philosophers than among mathematical logicians. Thus Tarski wrote in 1936: 'The concept of *tautology* (i.e. of a statement which "says nothing about reality")... to me personally seems rather vague ... but has been of fundamental importance for the philosophical discussions of L. Wittgenstein and the whole Vienna circle.'[46] At this time it had recently been shown by Godel (in a proof which we shall have occasion to notice later) that the ordinary notion of consequence does not coincide with that of formal derivability. With this new discovery in mind Tarski wrote :

'In every deductive theory (apart from certain theories of a particularly elementary nature), however much we supplement the ordinary rules of inference by new purely structural rules, it is possible to construct sentences which follow, in the usual sense, from the theorems of this theory, but which nevertheless cannot be proved in this theory on the basis of the accepted rules of inference. In order to obtain the proper concept of consequence, which is close in essentials to the common concept, we must resort to quite different methods and apply quite different conceptual apparatus in defining it.'[47]

The method which he then proposed was in essentials that of Bolzano, though at the time of his first publication on the subject he knew nothing of this part of Bolzano's work.

Tarski himself has summarized his account of the consequence relation as follows :

'Let *L* be any class of sentences. We replace all extra-logical constants which occur in the sentences belonging to *L* by corresponding variables, like constant being replaced by like variables, and unlike by unlike. In this way we obtain a class *L'* of sentential functions. An arbitrary sequence of objects which satisfies every sentential function of the class *L'* will be called a *model* or *realization of the class L of sentences* (in just this sense one usually speaks of models of an axiom system of a deductive theory). If in particular the class *L* consists of a single sentence *X*, we shall also call the model of the class *L* the *models of the sentence X.* In terms of these concepts we can define the concept of logical consequence as folllows :

The sentence X follows logically *from the sentences of the class K if, and only if, every model of the class K is also a model of the sentence X.*'[48]

Later he adds:

'We can agree to call a class of sentences *contradictory* if it possesses no model. Analogously a class of sentences can be called *analytical* if every sequence of objects is a model of it. Both of these concepts can be related not only to classes of sentences but also to single sentences . . . We can also show . . . that those and only those sentences are analytical which follow from every class of sentences (in particular from the empty class) and only those contradictory from which every sentence follows.'[49]

As Tarski himself insists, his essay is an attempt to work out clearly the implications of the old doctrine that the relation of logical consequence holds between statements in virtue of their forms. But his development of the doctrine has some curious features which deserve notice.

In the first place Tarski's explanation of logical consequence is given by reference to logical form as expressed by logical constants, and takes no account of the role which definitions have commonly been thought to have in this connexion. Thus according to him 'Socrates was a male' may be said to be a consequence of the pair of sentences 'Socrates was a father' and 'Every father is a male' but not of the first sentence alone; and the second sentence of the pair, namely. 'Every father is a male', which Kant would certainly have described as a 'analytic' does not qualify for that title in Tarski classification, because the pattern 'Every—is . . .' is not satisfied by every pair of objects. Apparently the reason for this strange result is that Tarski has tried to carry through his analysis without reference to transformation rules and therefore can only take notice of definitions when they are presented in the form of true universal statements.

Secondly, although Tarski thinks of the relation of consequence as one holding between sentences and therefore tries to explain it by reference to forms of sentences (which he calls sentential functions), his account is not entirely syntactical, i.e. concerned solely with the relations of signs to each other, but involves the notion of satisfaction. According to the terminology of his essay 'The Concept of Truth', which we noticed in an earlier section, this is a fundamental concept of semantics, that is to say, of the science in which we consider the relations of signs to things and things to signs. We say that John and Peter satisfy the condition '*x* and *y* are brothers' if and only if John and Peter are in fact brothers. Now from this it follows that Tarski's definition of logical consequence involves reference to what is the case in the world. Thus to consider only the simplest possible example, in his theory the peculiarity of an analytic sentence (which follows from any class of sentences) is that all specimens of its form are in fact true statements. No doubt every analytic sentence has this characteristic , but philosophers may be surprised that it should be treated as the defining characteristic rather than as a consequential property.

Thirdly, although Tarski makes the notion of logical form central in his account of consequence, he, like Bolzano before him, finds himself unable to define it precisely, and therefore concludes :

'Underlying our whole construction is the division of terms of the language discussed into logical and extra-logical. This division is certainly not arbitrary. . . . If, for example, we were to include among the extra-logical signs the implication sign, or the universal quantifier, then our definition of the concept of consequence would lead to results which obviously contradict ordinary usage. On the other hand, no objective grounds are known to me which permit us to draw a sharp boundary between the two groups of terms. It seems to be possible to include among logical terms some which are usually regarded by logicians as extra-logical without running into consequences which stand in sharp contrast to ordinary usage. In the extreme case we could regard all terms of the language as logical. The concept of *formal* consequence would the coincide with that of *material* consequence.[50]

We may add that in this extreme case the concept of the analytic would concide with that of the true.

Perhaps our three difficulties are interconnected. So long as we have no worry about the recognition of logical signs, Tarski's condition for the holding of the consequence relation seems to be suficient, inasmuch as it does not obviously admit anything which would not ordinarily be called a case of logical consequence. But even at this stage in our reflection it does not seem to be necessary, since it excludes those cases of consequence which depend on connexion by definitions. If, however, as we commonly think, a definition is a stipulation that certain expressions shall be understood to be consequences of certain other expressions, the defect is not surprising. For in order to define the relation of consequence in such a way as to provide for connexions by definition it would be necessary to say among other things that a sentence was a consequence of a certain other sentence if there was a stipulation or rule of language to the effect that any sentence of a form exemplified by the one was to be accounted a consequence of a corresponding sentence of a form exemplified by the other. Such a provision would be no more circular than a legal provision that for the purposes of a certain act of parliament any establishment is a shop which belongs to a class of establishments in respect of which the competent minister has issued a certificate to the effect that they are to be treated as shops. But it would be very different from Tarski's account of consequence, since this latter is concerned solely with satisfaction of sentential functions by objects. When next we go on to consider Tarski's doubts about the possibility of drawing a clear line between logical and extra-logical signs and the conclusions which he says would follow from admission of the impossibility of drawing such a line, we see that the source of all the strangeness in his account of consequence is his assumption that the holding of the relation depends only on the truth of a universal proposition. For just as many philosophers who profess to follow Hume have said that the necessity with which an effect follows its cause is no more than the inclusion of this particular sequence in a constant natural association, so he says that the necessity with which a consequence follows in the logical sense from premisses is not more than the inclusion of this particular sequence in a universal fact about the satisfaction of certain sentential functions. If following his own suggestions, we enlarge the range of sentential functions under consideration by including among the constant factors of our sentences not only the traditional logical constants but all unrestricted general terms such as 'man', 'iron' 'fire', & c., we find that Tarski's definition of consequence covers not only logical consequence but also all consequence in virtue of natural laws. In short, the definition amounts to a generalization of the constancy theory of natural necessity. But the result can give no pleasure to followers of Hume, since it involves rejection of their view that there is a difference of kind between logical and natural necessity.

In defence of Tarski's definition it may perhaps be argued that for a sentential function such as *If p then not-not-p* we can know *a priori* that it is satisfied by every sequence of objects, whereas for a sentential function such as *if x has taken arsenic x will die* we can only conjecture universal satisfaction on empirical grounds. This is true, but there is nothing in Tarski's account of the matter to explain the difference, and he does not allude to it himself. Nor is it appropriate that a distinction of kinds of consequence should be made to depend on a distinction between cases in which we can and cases in which we cannot gain knowledge *a priori*. On the contrary, the epistemological distinction should be explained by an account of the differences of the cases; and it is just this which is lacking so far.

We have seen that conventionalism involves nominalism and that, if it is taken seriously, it can be made to yield the thesis that the world consists of facts which are not in themselves either necessary or contingent. We have seen also that Tarski's account of consequence excludes the possibility of one sentence's following from another by virtue of an explicit definition, and that his attempt to define the relation of consequence by reference to universality ends with a blurring of the distinction between the laws of logic and the laws of nature. To most logicians these results appear undesirable, and we have assumed that they are not desired by the authors of the theories under consideration. But there is at least one philosopher, W.V. Quine, who accepts them all.

His views can be summarized best in his own words :

'My present suggestion is that it is nonsense, and the root of much nonsense, to speak of a linguistic component and a factual component in the truth of any individual statement. Taken collectively, science has its double dependence upon language and experience; but this duality is not significantly traceable into the statements of science taken one by one..... The totality of our so-called knowledge or beliefs, from the most casual matters of geography and history to the profoundest laws of atomic physics or even of pure mathematics and logic, is a man-made fabric which impinges on experience only along the edges. Or, to change the figure, total science is like a field of force whose boundary conditions are experience. A conflict with experience at the periphery occasions readjustments in the interior of the field .... But the total field is so underdetermined by its boundary conditions, experience, that there is much latitude of choice as to what statements to re-evaluate in the light of any single contrary experience . . . . Any statement can be held true come what may, if we make drastic enough adjustments elsewhere in the system. Even a statement very close to the periphery can be held true in the face of recalcitrant experience by pleading hallucination or by amending certain statements of the kind called logical laws. Conversely, by the same token, no statement is immune to revision. Revision even of the logical law of the excluded middle has been proposed as a means of simplifying quantum mechanics; and what difference is their in principle between such a shift and the shift whereby Kepler superseded Ptolemy, or Einstein Newton, or Darwin Aristotle? . . . Ontological questions, under this view, are on a par with questions of natural science. Consider the question whether to countenance classes as entities. This, as I have argued elsewhere, is the question whether to quantify with respect to variables which take classes as values. Now Carnap has maitained that this is a question not of matters of fact but of choosing a convenient language form, a convenient conceptual scheme of framework for science. With this I agree, but only on the proviso that the same be conceded regarding scientific hypotheses generally. Carnap has recognized that he is able to preserve a double standard for ontological questions and scientific hypotheses only by assuming an absolute distinction between the analytic and the synthetic: and I need not say again that this is a distinction which I reject.'[51]

This is an agreeably bold attempt to present a unified account of the scientific enterprise, and especially impressive at a time when many professional philosophers talk as though an interest in synoptic philosophy were a form of mental illness. But, like the Absolute Idealists whose ways of thinking he has adapted to empiricism, Quine is too tolerant of paradoxes and too contemptuous of common sense. As we noticed in an earlier section, he rejects not only the whole theory of modality but also the notions of propositions, attributes, and relations. With these go even the notion of meaning, because it is traditionally connect with talk of analytic statements. To him the clearance seems no sacrifice, but rather a removal of dangerous rubbish. To many others, however, it seems like the act of captain who in fear of running his ship around tries to lighten it by throwing the compass overboard. No doubt Quine a right to be dissatisfied with the suggestion that a statement may be made true by linguistic rules alone. For there is something absurd in talk of making truths. Dr. Zamenhof invented the rules for a language in which it is possible to construct infinitely many new sentences such as *Ciu patro estas viro,* but, unless they have been corrupted by bad philosophy, even the fondest admire of his work do, not claim that he made infinitely many new truths. It is a mistake, however, to suppose that because no statement is made true by linguistic rules alone, every statement must be related to experience in the same way. To assume this is to accept the basic thesis of conventionalism, that the world consists of facts without necessities. If we are candid in our consideration of the evidence, we must concede that the assertion that 2+2 = 4 differs not only in degree but in kind from the assertion that Everest is higher than Mont Blanc. Geography and pure mathematics are indeed both parts of one great fabric elaborated by mankind, but they are not parts of the same sort.

The strongest point in favour of Quine's thesis is that many statements of unrestricted universality seem to hover in our theory of knowledge between empirical and *a priori* status. It was discovered empirically in comparatively recent times that iron can be magnetized; and yet, if a modern physical scientist were asked whether he could conceive the possibility of abandoning this generalization, he might feel puzzled and reply that he was half-inclined to treat is as something beyond empirical question. Many cases of this kind have been discussed by F. Waismann, who has suggested independently a view of science something like that of Quine,[52] and some of his most interesting examples are from common pre-scientific talk. Is the statement 'We see with our eyes' an empirical generalization, or is it a truth discoverable by reflection on the meanings of the words 'see' and 'eye'? We cannot answer such a question without deciding what custom has hitherto left undecided. For the most part we use general words satisfactorily by following analogies, much as judges settle cases under the common law; but when one of us is called upon to give a decision about the applicability of a word in an unfamiliar situation, then, like a judge who has no precedent to guide him, he must in effect legislate. Philosophers, with their tidy minds, have often refused to recognize these facts and discussed natural languages as though these were systems of rules and definitions rather than sets of customs. But for beings such as we are it is essential that our languages should grow as they do. It is not a defect of English that we have not decided whether the word 'eye' means properly on organ of vision or an object of a certain shape and chemical composition which may conceivably have nothing to do with vision. So long as we find only facts such as we have met, we can describe them adequately without making a choice between these alternatives. Our word 'eye' is certainly not meaningless, but its meaning is not as fully determined as it could be, and so there is a possibility for further legislation if this should be required or suggested by the development of science. A similar example of the complexity of ordinary usage is the statement 'Kittens are the offspring of cats'. We hold that we can recognize kittens without any difficulty by their appearance alone, and yet we feel inclined to say that being the offspring of a cat is involved in the meaning of the word 'kitten'. If anything turned up which looked exactly like a kitten but was demonstrably not the offspring of a cat, there would be need for a decision which no one has hitherto found necessary.

A curious instance of additional specification of meaning during the past few centuries may be noticed by any modern reader who studies carefully the argument by which St. Thomas Aquinas tries to prove the thesis that after the resurrection there will be no use of foods (*quod in resurgentibus non erit usus ciborum*).[53] First the saint says that with the end of the life of corruption there will not longer be any need for food to replace material lost in the course of corruption. Next he makes the point that food will be unnecessary after the resurrection for purposes of growth, since everyone will rise in the right size (*in debita quantitate*). And then, moved perhaps by consideration of his own figure, he goes on to remark that it would be a denial of the good ordering of God to suppose that eating will take place after the resurrection. For a man who eats wihout losing anything by corruption will grow to an immoderate size (*perveniet ad immoderatam quantitatem*). Indeed, if after the resurrection a man continues to eat through the whole of his unending life, we must suppose that he will grow to infinity (*oportet dicere quod corpus hominis resurgentis in infinitum augeatur*). But that, he says, is impossible. Now here we have an argument which is conducted up to a certain point with scientific rigour. But when we consider it seriously in the context of modern science, the saint's thesis seems absurd. For, if it is sensible to talk about a resurrected body as he does, it must be sensible also to inquire what happens during the voluntary movements of this body. Obviously there must be contraction of muscles. But this involves oxidation of carbo-hydrates and a consequent wastage of muscular tissue, unless the loss is made good by food, which St. Thomas refuses to allow. More generally, a resurrected body as described by St. Thomas would be a *perpetuum mobile* functioning contrary to the laws of thermodynamics. To this it may perhaps be replied boldly that resurrected bodies are not subject to the laws of nature which men have found applicable to corruptible bodies. But at this point it becomes clear to most of us that we no longer think of these laws of nature as purely empirical generalizations which might be abandoned without abandonment of the notion of an organic body. In our science, and therefore in the more highly evolved levels of our language, they are now linked by the theory of metabolism; and if anyone says there might be a living organism without metabolic processes, we feel inclined to say that he is putting words together in a meaningless fashion.

The Humean account of natural laws, which was until recently the orthodoxy of empiricists, arose from an imagist theory of meaning. Hume remarked quite rightly that it was always possible to imagine the contradictory of any supposed law of nature, and concluded from this that no such law could be a law of objective necessity. Later exponents of his doctrine, who think of meaning as determined always by initial conventions, point to the fact that the negation of a supposed law of nature is never a formal self-contradiction or reducible to such without assumption of the law itself. Neither argument proves what is required of it. It is true, of course, that we can imagine in the strict sense of that word (i.e. picture in the mind's eye) men living on and on without food. But this is irrelevant, since the question at issue is not about our powers of imagination. It is true also that before the development of physiology there was no obvious linguistic defect in the sentence 'A man will live for ever without food', and that even now, if we choose for a time to concentrate attention on the contexts in which we originally learnt the constituent words, we can give a sense of some sort to the remark. But this too is irrelevant, since a remark may be said to have sense merely because it is not excluded by any well-recognized rule of usage.

At any time the meanings of the words we use are fixed by two factors, namely (i) their relations to perceptible features of certain situations which evoke their use and (ii) their relations to each other within the fabric of our language. Philosophers in the empiricist tradition have sometimes given their attention exclusively to relations of the first kind, but there are many words which have no such relations, and for all words (e.g. even colour words) relations of the second kind are at least equally important. Even before the development of science our language is a complex structure which touches experience only at certain places, but with the development of science the internal ties become more and more complex, and there appear new words such as 'electron' and 'gene' which are far removed from experience yet not necessarily far removed from all reality. The purpose of this tightening of the internal structure of a language is to make it fit the world more closely. So long as we can freely make sentences such as 'A man will live for ever without eating' there is an undesirable looseness in the linguistic garment we have made for the world, and so, like good tailors, we must take in the slack. Such deliberate adjustment, which has been attempted only within the last few centuries, is the method of empirical science, and the recognition of its peculiarity should remove the serious misunderstandings which have arisen about necessity and language.

Quine goes much too far when he tries to abolish the distinction of contingent and necessary truths. On the one hand, statements of history and geography always remain contingent because it would be pointless to exclude alternatives by linguistic legislation; and on the other hand, statements such as 'Nothing is both red and green all over at the same time' are necessarily true from the beginning, because they are guaranted by the rules we follow from the beginning in distinguishing colours. But it is not always easy to determine the status of the propositions of unrestricted universality which we formulate in the empirical sciences. So long as we are prepared to allow that one of these may be refuted, we cannot claim to know its necessity *a priori.* If ever we accept one without reservation, then in so doing we claim such *a priori* knowledge. But here we must be prepared to distinguish cases according to the degree of insight involved. If we simply decide to regard iron as magnetic by definition, we exclude the possibility fever using the word 'iron' for any non-magnetic metal, but we do not thereby increase our understanding of connexions in the physical world. And if we introduce this further specification of the meaning of the word 'iron' only in order to distinguish iron from some other metal with which it would otherwise be confused, we even make the statement 'Iron is magnetic' useless for purposes of inference. If, on the other hand, when able to recognize iron satisfactorily without testing it for this property, we succeed in deducing this property from a theory of the constitution of iron which not only covers a number of other generalizations about iron but is itself part of a much wider theory about matter in general, we think rightly that we have gained a great increase of understanding. In either case, however, we may be able to say that our unrestricted generalization is transformed by a development of language into a truism guaranteed by an assumed principle of necessary connexion. Logic, as we have tried to present it in our section on modal logic, is the theory of such necessary connexion—not the theory of all the several connexions that hold between various universals, but the theory of that kind of connexion in general, and that is why it must occupy a unique position in our account of science.

Quine recognizes that logic has a special place among the sciences, but insists that it too is subject to revision :

'Re-evaluation of some statements entails re-evaluation of others, because of their logical interconnexions—the logical laws being in turn simply certain further statements of the system, certain further elements of the field. Having re-evaluated one statement we must re-evaluate some others, which may be statements logically connected with the first or may be statemetns of logical connexions themselves.[54]

This is an unfortunate piece of equalitarianism. For principles without which it is impossible to conceive any system such as he describes have a clear title to separate consideration. Being presupposed in the very concept of a system, they at least are absolutely *a priori,* whatever may be said of the contents of any particular system at any time.

For a correct account of science it is essential to admit that, in a division between the world and those features of language which are man-made, necessary connexions belong to the world no less than contingent facts. Unfortunately the influence of the conventionalist theory of necessity which has been derived from Wittgenstein's work is so strong that even K. R. Popper (who is not a general receptive to influences form that quarter) has written :

'I regard, unlike Keneale, "necessary" as a mere word, as a label for distinguishing the universality of laws from "accidental" universality. Of course any other label would do as well, for there is not much connection here with logical necessity. I largely agree with the spirit of Wittgenstein's paraphrase of Hume: "A necessity for one thing to happen because another has happened does not exist. There is only logical necessity."'[55]

Elsewhere, however, he has written :

'A statement may be said to be naturally or physically necessary if, and only, if, it is deducible from a statement function which is satisfied in all worlds that differ from our world, if at all, only with respect to initial conditions ?[56]

This seems to mean that a natural law holds for all *possible* worlds that contain instances of the same' attributes and relations as are exemplified in the actual world and of these only. But Popper compares his definition with Tarski's definition of analytic truth, failing to notice that when we speak of truth in all possible worlds with the same recurring features we introduce something radically new, namely just what the defender of objective necessity wishes. No necessity, whether logical or natural, can be reduced, as Popper seems to think, to bare universality, since it is conceivable that even proposition of unrestricted universality should be true contingently. But there can be no objection to a definition of necessity as truth in all possible worlds, since the peculiarity of the concept to be defined is preserved here by the modal word 'possible'. Clearly the universality with which something holds even for worlds distinct from the actual world cannot be merely contingent.

What we propose, however, is not that the notion of necessity should be defined in this way, but rather that the more convenient notion of involution should be recognized as a fundamental concept in the description of nature and even in the explanation of the working of ordinary language. If the notion has indeed this role, the theory of it must occupy a privileged place among the sciences. In the two remaining chapters of this book we shall have occasion to consider again the relation of this theory to the studies called mathematical, and the reult of the discussion should be a clearer understanding of its importance.

Footnoes

1. The most faithful follower is A. Church, who has defended Frege's views in various places, e.g. in 'The Need for Abstract Entities in Semantic Analysis' *Proceedings of the American Academy of Arts and Sciences,* lxxx (1951), pp 100-12, and in the introduction to the first volume of his *Introduction to Mathematical Logic.*

2. First published in Polish in *Travaux de la Societe des scie-nces et des lettres de Varsoie,* Class III, Math-Phys., xxxiv (1933); German translation in *Studia Philosophica,* i (1936), pp. 261-405; English translation in *Logic, Semantics, Metamathematics,* pp. 152-278.

3 *Metaphysica,* pp. 7 (101 l[b] 125)

4 *Gg.,* vol. i, pp. xvi-xvii.

5 *Principia Mathematica,* I, *14

6 *Grundlagen der Mathematik,* i,§ 8.

7. B. Russell, 'On Denoting', *Mind,* N.S. xiv (1905), pp. 479-93; reprinted in *Logic and Knowledge,* pp. 41-56.

8. *Principia Mathematica* i, pp. 174-5; 'The Philosophy of Logical Atomism', *The Monist,* xxviii (1918), pp. 495-527, reprinted in *Logic and Knowledge* (see especially p. 201).

9. *Uber Sinn and Bedeutung,* p. 27.

10. R. Carnap, *Meaning and Necessity,* pp. 41, 180-1.

11. This title was suggested by W. V. Quine in his book *From a Logical Point of View,* p. 139.

12. §§ 67-71, 74-81.

13. Cf. A. Church, 'On Carnap's Analysis of Statement of Ass-ertion and Belief', *Analysis,* x (1950), pp. 97-99.

14. In *Principia Mathematica*, *14. 28, Whitehead and Russell say in effect that $(\iota x)Hx = (\iota x)Hx$ is true if and only if $(\exists x)H'x$ is true. This restriction on substitution in the formula $x = x$ is required by their account of formulae containing definite descriptions. In ordinary English the problem of existential implication is treated in the way indicated above.

15. The four numbered principles may be found in R. Carnap's *Meaning and Necessity* (1947), p. 186 Cf. also Ruth Barcan, 'A Functional Calculus of First Order Based on Strict Implication', *The Journal of Symbolic Logic*, xi (1946), pp-I-16.

16. *An Essay on Modal Logic*, p. 27.

17. *From a Logical Point of View*, p. 157. The work of Church to which Quine refers is 'A Formulation of the Logic of Sense and Denotation' contributed to *Structure, Method, and Meaning: Essays in Honor of Henry M. Sheffer*, 1951.

18. *Principia Mathematica*, 2nd ed., vol. i, p. xxxix.

19. *Mathematical Logic*,§ 22.

20. *From a Logical Point of View*, pp. 127-9.

21. 'On Denumerable Bases of Formal System', *Mathematical Interpretation of Formal Systems* by Th. Skolem and others, (1955), p. 76. The term 'many-sorted' was introduced by A. Schmidt, Uber deduktive Theorien mit mehreren Sorten von Grunddingen; *Mathematische Annalen*, cxv (1938), pp. 485-506.

22. Hao Wang, 'Logic of Many-sorted Theories', *Journal of Symbolic Logic*, xvii (1952), pp. 105-16.

23. *Introduction to Mathematical Philosophy* (1919),pp.202-5.

24. *Tractatus Logico-Philosophicus*, 6.124. Here and in later quotations we have departed occasionally from the English translation of Ogden and Ramsey.

25. Ibid. 5.3-5.4

26. Ibid. 6.3-6.371.

27. Ibid. 2.061-2.062.

28. Ibid. 5.132 and 6.126

29. Ibid. 6.22.

30. Ibid. 6.54.

31. *Tractatus Logico-Philosophicus,* 1, 2.1, 2.14.

32. *Logic and Knowledge,* ed. R. C. March, pp. 178-281.

33. *Tractatus,* 5.555-5.5571.

34. Ibid. 2.06, 4.1.

35. Ibid. 4.0641.

36. Ibid. 6.375-6.3751.

37. 'Some remarks on Logical Form', *Aristolelian Society,Supplementary Volume,* ix (1929), pp. 162-71, esp.p. 168.

38. *Ep.* 50.

39. *Introduction to Logical Theory,* p. 9.

40. *The Logical Syntax of Language* (English translation, 1937), 17.

41. This argument against conventionalism is presented with cogent detail by W. V. Quine in his essay, 'Truth by Convention, contributed in 1936 to *Philosophical Essays for A.N. Whitehead* and reprinted in *Readings in Philosophical Analysis* (ed. Feigl and Sellars), 1949, pp. 250-73.

42. Language, Truth, and Logic (1936), p. 103.

43. P.F. Strawson, *Introduction to Logical Theory*, p. 263.

44. P.F. Strawson, *Introduction to Logical Theory*, p.11.

45. Ibid, p.12.

46. 'On the Concept of Logical Consequence' first published in Polish in *Przeglad Filozoficzny*, xxxix (1936), pp. 58 68, reprinted in English in *Logic, Semantics, Metamathematics* (1956), pp.409-20 esp. pp.419-20.

47. Ibid., pp. 412-13 .

48. Ibid., pp, 416-17 .

49. Ibid., pp.417-18 .

50. *Logic, Semantics, Metamathematics* (1956), pp.418-19.

51. 'Two Dogmas of Empiricism' originally published in The *Philosophical Review* (1951), reprinted with modifications in *From a Logical Point of View*, pp.20-46,esp. 42-43 and

45-46.

52. 'Analytic-Synthetic',*Analysis*, x (1949), pp. 25-40 ; xi (1950-1), pp. 25-38, 49-6r 115-24; Xii(1953), pp. 73-89.

53. *Summa contra Gentiles*, iv.83.

54. *From a Logical Point of View*, p. 42.

55. *The Logic of Scientific Discovery* (1959), p-438.

56. Ibid., p. 433.